The Anglican Church Role in the Process of Reconciliation in Rwanda

Reverend Henry Settimba

Copyright © Henry Settimba 2009

All rights reserved. No part of this publication may be reproduced, stored in a retrieval system or transmitted in any form or by any means, electronic, mechanical, audio, visual or otherwise, without prior written permission of the copyright owner. Nor can it be circulated in any form of binding or cover other than that in which it is published and without similar conditions including this condition being imposed on the subsequent purchaser.

ISBN 978-1-905399-46-8

Cover Design by Duncan Bamford
http://www.insightillustration.co.uk

Edited by Jan Andersen
http://www.creativecopywriter.org

PERFECT PUBLISHERS LTD
23 Maitland Avenue
Cambridge
CB4 1TA
England
http://www.perfectpublishers.co.uk

CONTENTS

Chapter	Title	Page
	Preface	vii
	Acknowledgements	ix
	Glossary of Kinyarwanda/French	xiii
Chapter 1	Introduction	1
1.0	Background to the Study	1
1.1	The Structure of the Study	3
1.2	Research Objective	8
1.3	The Hypotheses	10
1.4	Methodology of Data Collection	11
1.5	Primary Sources	11
1.6	Research Questionnaires	11
1.7	Interviews	12
1.8	Observations	15
1.9	Secondary Sources	16
1.10	Analysis	17
1.11	Codifying Data	18
1.12	Issues of Confidentiality and Ethics	20
1.13	Significance of the Study	22
1.14	Organisation of the Thesis	23
1.15	The Study Area	25
Chapter 2	The Belgian Ethnicity Debate (analysis of interviews)	29
2.0	Introduction	29
2.1	Pre-Belgian Identity of Rwanda	31
2.2	Creating a New Identity in Rwanda	38
2.3	The Root of Conflict	63
	Conclusion	68

Chapter 3	A Paradigmatic Change of Structure and Relationships in Rwanda	71
3.0	Introduction	71
3.1	The Grand Narrative Theory	77
3.2	A Critical Analysis of the Belgian Administrative Social Structure	90
3.3	The Lack of Ethnics in Social Structure of Belgian Rule	92
	Conclusion	102
Part 1	**Genocide and its Aftermath: Analysis of Interviews and Literature**	105
Chapter 4	Interpretation of Genocide	105
4.0	Introduction	105
4.1	Different Interpretations of Genocide	109
4.2	Witness to the Killings	129
4.3	The State of Security After Genocide	150
4.4	Infiltrators' Loss of Local Support	159
	Conclusion	160
Chapter 5	Challenges Facing the Anglican Church in Rwanda	163
5.0	Introduction	163
5.1	Église Épiscopale au Rwanda (EER)	165
5.2	Église Épiscopale au Rwanda - New Leadership	176
5.3	The New Leadership and the Composition of Anglican Church Congregations	183
5.4	Pastoral Ministry	185
5.5	A Silent and Compromised Anglican Church	188

5.6	Survivors felt Neglected by the Anglican Church	198
	Conclusion	201
Part II	**The Historical and Theological Analysis**	203
Chapter 6	**The nature of division in the post-genocide Anglican Church**	203
6.0	Introduction	203
6.1	The Revival Heritage	205
6.2	The Strains of Conversion	225
6.3	Deepening the Christian Faith in the Anglican Church	248
6.4	Contextual Theology	254
	Conclusion	267
Chapter 7	**The Anglican Church and Reconciliation**	271
7.0.	Introduction	271
7.1	The Anglican Church's Commitment to Reconciliation	273
7.2	Methods and Initiatives of Reconciliation	283
7.3	The Anglican Church Palaver Mode of Reconciliation	304
7.4	Lessons From Other Reconciliation Groups	313
7.5	Theological Bases for Reconciliation	315
7.6	Incarnation Theology for Reconciliation	327
7.7	The Difficulties with Reconciliation	329
	Conclusion	331
Chapter 8	**Conclusion**	335
8.0	A Review of the Study	335
8.1	The Poverty Trap	336

8.2	A Lesson for the Anglican Church in Rwanda	342
8.3	The Crucial Challenge for the Anglican Church in Rwanda	346
	Bibliography	351
Appendix I	**Questionnaires**	373
Appendix II	**A Questionnaire for Interviews**	373
Appendix III	**Comments for Interviews**	375
Appendix 1V	**Rwandan Documentary**	375

Preface

The purpose of the thesis is to investigate the source of the Rwandan conflict that ended in genocide and the role of the Anglican Church in the process of reconciliation, to contribute to local interpretation of the conflict and to raise practical and theoretical questions about the Belgian era. It is therefore necessary to have a background of the political events and the Christian teaching before the genocide, in order to discover how fundamentally diverse influences led the Anglican Church leadership in the Rwandan conflict. This will be done through a triangulation analysis to tease out relative structural variables, such as Belgian ideology and social political theories. The central purpose of this is to examine the reliability, replication and validity of claims that the conflict was based on the so-called natural hatred between Hutu and Tutsi and explore in more detail the historical and sociological perspectives that surround the conflict. The first chapter describes the methodologies employed to investigate the source of the conflict seeing through the eyes of the people being studied.

This was done in order to compare local claims with different sources and to argue for the role of the Anglican Church in the reconciliation process. The second chapter analyses the historical background of the roots of the conflict. The third chapter seeks to examine the theories behind the historical development of the economic structure and the changes in human relations that might have made genocide possible. The fourth chapter is devoted to analysis of the interviews as well as different interpretations of the causes of conflict before the genocide. The fifth chapter assesses the recovery of the Rwandan Anglican Church and describes the challenges and the tasks facing the Anglican Church in Rwanda. Chapter Six examines the missionary methods of conversion, the nature of teaching given to converts, the religious aspects of changes and the impact on social structures. Chapter Seven examines various models of theoretical interpretation along with the theological imperatives of Anglican Church involvement in the reconciliation process and, finally, Chapter Eight is an overview of the thesis.

Acknowledgements

This study was completed with the direct and indirect assistance from various institutions and people. I wish to express my sincere gratitude to all of my supervisors; firstly to the Revd Professor Leslie Francis and Dr Robert Pope at the University of Bangor. I am also grateful to my supervisors, Dr Tina Beattie, Professor Liam Gearon and to the Director of Studies Dr Lynn Thomas at Roehampton University for their academic support. About their coolness and competence, I cannot say enough. Enormous thanks are due also to Hackney Parochial Charities, for their financial support and in particular to the Revd Canon William Hurdman for his exceptional kindness to me, which went far beyond the call of duty. This study also relied heavily upon fieldwork carried out in Rwanda and several institutions have been very helpful in the completion of this study. In this regard, I am grateful to the assistant Rector and academic staff of Butare National University of Rwanda who gave their time and invaluable access to the library and its resources.

I would also like to thank the Anglican Archbishop of Rwanda, the Most Right Revd Emmanuel Kolini and Freda Kolini who provided an invaluable link with Rwanda and who gave me great support in times of sadness and difficulty. I wish to thank all respondents for the exemplary way in which they treated my request for information and responded to many thought provoking questions. By far the greatest expression of gratitude, respect and sympathy is reserved for the families who were prepared to share their experiences with me during the course of this study in explicit and harrowing detail. It is to these people that I dedicate this study. While I have never been in a position to offer any direct assistance in their struggle and their suffering, I remain optimistic that the findings of this study, if acted upon, can in the long term bring about positive, beneficial change.

I wish also to acknowledge the valuable help and advice I received from the staff of the Church Missionary Society and the General Secretary of the Mid-Africa Mission, Waterloo. I would like to express my deepest appreciation to the Revd Richard Murigande of the Refugee Department, World Council of Churches, Geneva. Canon Dr Francis Ndyabahika and Revd Professor John Rutiba of the Department of Philosophy and Religious Studies at Makerere University, Kampala, Uganda also deserve special thanks.

I wish to thank my former colleagues in H.M Prison Holloway Chaplaincy, namely the Revd Phillip Derbyshire, Revd Dr John Pridmore, Revd Jonathan Wikes and Revd Dr Jenny King. Also, I wish to thank the Diocesan Bishop of London and, at that time, Area Bishop of Stepney, the Right Revd Dr John Sentamu and in particular the Right Revd Lord Richard Chartres whose last ditch effort enabled me to undertake this study.

Special thanks go to my family and to Mr Robert Smith who provided constant encouragement and support during the various stages of this study. I would like to express my gratitude to Dr Amanda Robinson at the University of Bangor who computerised the questionnaires to ensure that the estimates were as reasonable as possible.

I also wish to take this opportunity to extend my thanks to Professor John Eade for providing me with information about work translated into English about the genocide in Rwanda from Anna-Maria Brandstetter at the Institute for Ethnology and Africa Studies, Germany; from the Research Office at (Roehampton University), especially Professor Trevor Dean and Professor Neil Taylor for the financial help received through their recommendation.

Thank you also to Mrs Kristen Pilbrow, the Research Administrator, for her supportive endeavours.

I am quite sure that all of this support has played a great part in the completion of this study and I will always be grateful for it.

List of Abbreviations

AIDS:	Acquired Immune Deficiency Syndrome
ATR:	African Traditional belief
CDR:	Committee for the Defence of the Republic
CID:	Criminal Investigation Department
CMS:	Church Missionary Society
DP:	Democratic Party
DRC:	Democratic Republic of Congo
FRONASA:	Front for National Salvation
HIV:	Human Immune Deficiency Virus
ICRC:	International Committee of the Red Cross
MU:	Mothers' Union
MRND	National Republic Movement for Democracy and Development
NRA:	National Awareness Army
NGO:	Non Governmental Organisation
PWRDF:	Primate's World Relief and Development Fund
RANU:	Rwandan Alliance for National Unity
REACH:	Reconciliation, Evangelism and Christian Healing Association
RRWF:	Rwandese Refugees Welfare Foundation
RPF:	Rwandese Patriotic Front
RTCM:	Radio Télévision Libre des Mille Collines
RLMC:	Radio Libre Collines
RPA:	Rwandese Patriotic Army
UN:	United Nations

UNHCR:	United Nations High Commission for Refugees
UNHRFOR:	United Nations Human Rights Field Operation for Rwanda
UNAR:	Rwandese African National Union
UPC:	Uganda People's Congress
USA:	United States of America
UNAMIR:	United Nations Peacekeeping Force in Rwanda
UNHCR:	United Nations High Commission for Refugees
UNHRFOR:	United Nations Human Rights Field Operation for Rwanda

REFUGEE: This term has been used by the Rwandan government to mean those who fled their homes in search of sanctuary, even though they are not considered as refugees under international criteria, since they did not cross any national borders.

Rwandan Names: Each family member usually has his or her own individual surname as well as first name. Hence siblings can have different names and having a common surname is not a sign of being related, but of coincidence.

Local Administration: Rwanda is divided and subdivided into administrative units known as prefectures, sous-prefectures, communes, sectors and cellules, the cellule being the smallest. The prefect is the highest local government official, with sous-prefects and bourgmestres. Councillors are responsible for the smaller units.

Glossary of Kinyarwanda/French Terms

ABAHUTU:	Hutu
ABATUTSI:	Tutsi
ABATWA:	Twa
IBUKA	Remember (an organisation of genocide Survivors)
ITORERO:	Recruits or a selected few set apart
INTERAHAMWE:	Those who attack together (militia group)
IMPUNZAMUGAMBI:	Those who have the same goal (another militia group)
INYENZI:	A term of abuse for the RPF meaning 'cockroach'
INKOTANYI:	RPF Soldier of the Rwandan Patriotic Army
FAR:	Rwandese Armed Forces
GACACA	Traditional conflict resolution (Gacaca courts)
RYANGOMBE:	The eternal God
PARMEHUTU:	Party for Liberation of the Hutu
TWESEHAMWE:	Let's all together
NYOGOSENGE:	Aunt
UBUHAKE:	Employment arrangement (slavery) in modern days
UBURETWA:	Traditional economic system
UBUMWE:	Togetherness or Unity

The Map of Rwanda

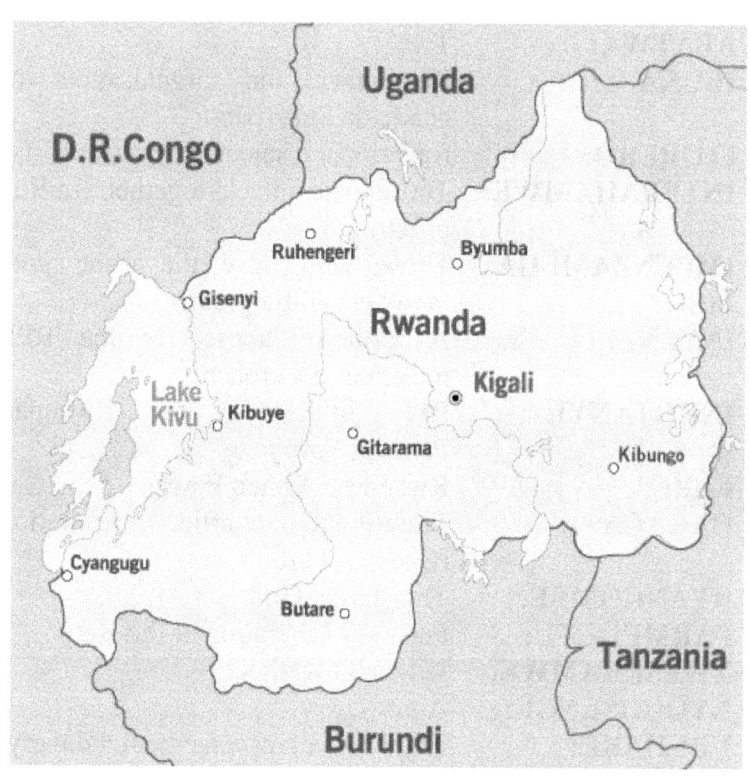

[1] www.safarimasters.com/abtrwanda.htm

Chapter One

Introduction

1.0 Background to the Study

At the beginning of 1994, Rwanda was embroiled in a tragic civil war. On the night of 6 April 1994, an aircraft carrying President Habyarimana of Rwanda and President Cyprien Ntaryamira of Burundi crashed, killing all of the passengers. Shortly afterwards, members of the Presidential Guard, the National Gendarmerie and militia units known as 'Interahamwe' began to execute people known or suspected of supporting a broad-based transitional government that was to include members of the RPF.[1]

By early July, humanitarian agencies based inside and outside Rwanda estimated that one million people, most of them members of the Tutsi minority, had been killed in a countrywide massacre. Evidence gathered by Amnesty International, the UN and others also suggested that over two million Rwandans had fled Rwanda; most of them to the Democratic Republic of Congo, Tanzania, Kenya, Malawi, Uganda and Gabon.[2]

In the aftermath of the genocide there were several isolated incidents reported as a result of the mass repatriation of refugees to Rwanda that developed into a full-blown, organised insurgency in May and June 1997. The situation of Interahamwe and refugees forced into exile in countries that were too close, especially the Democratic Republic of Congo, had a particularly significant effect on the crisis situation in Rwanda. Due to the fact that the

---

[1] Amnesty International, Index: AFR 47/17/94, p.11.
[2] The figure quoted in connection with the refugee population by United Nations High Commission for Refugees (UNHCR) July 1994.

forces that had implemented the genocide were defeated, many of the refugees were veteran fighters who had survived military defeats by the RPF. The conflict, however, continued, killing civilians and dramatically increasing, with armed insurgency going on throughout the country, offering the greatest challenge to the RPF in restoring peace and stability. This conflict further led to the deaths of thousands of civilians, prisoners, insurgents and RPF soldiers. A number of foreign nationals were also killed.

The country was effectively a war zone with losses on both sides.[3] According to local residents interviewed and reports from humanitarian organisations, the most vulnerable were genocide survivors and Tutsi refugees in camps. The attackers soon become known as 'infiltrators' consisting of ex-FAR and Interahamwe 'refugees' who used the language of Hutu extremism as a rallying cry.[4] They sustained a campaign to destabilise Rwanda throughout their exile in camps in the Democratic Republic of Congo. Similarly, the refugees who had returned from the Democratic Republic of Congo, were fed a constant diet of anti-RPF fervour in the camps, making it easier for Hutu refugee returnees to sympathise with the ambitions of the infiltrators, or to be directly involved. They quickly gained considerable support for their campaign of violence among local residents, whose attacks were to recapture power for the former regime. This took place on an almost daily basis.[5]

The purpose of this study is, firstly, to trace and examine the diverse influences leading to the political crisis, including the relationship between Hutu and Tutsi, secondly, to examine the role that the Anglican Church

---

[3] Cf. African Rights, Rwanda, The Insurgents in the Northwest, September 1998, p.1.
[4] African Rights, Rwanda: Death, Despair and Defiance, pp.1-45.
[5] Ibid.

played in the process of reconciliation and, thirdly, to examine the challenges ahead for both the Anglican Church and politicians in Rwanda today.

Since Christian teaching is that 'in Christ we are one' and assuming it is the mission of the Anglican Church in Rwanda to reconcile people to Christ, this mission then legitimises the role of the Anglican Church in the reconciliation process. This is my central concern: that the Anglican Church cannot be left out as one of the impinging factors in play. This is a focus of the thesis; Christian teaching will be argued as having had an impact on the socio-cultural construction of Rwandan relations, which in turn has had a direct influence on the development of human relations. In Rwanda there is also a general belief that the Anglican Church has much to offer. Those interviewed felt that if the Church would take the right approach to the process of reconciliation, it would succeed in the task of guiding people through the emphasis on 'Love thy neighbour'. This study will therefore involve analysis of an ethnic conflict that seems to have been encouraged in Rwanda by Belgian rule and that has plagued the Rwandan people ever since.

1.1 The Structure of the Study

The study opens with a general introduction; this includes the statement of the problem, research objectives and hypotheses, methodologies of study and the relevance of the role of the Anglican Church in the process of reconciliation in Rwanda. The study will try to make the case for examining the conflict by looking at some of the arguments that advocate the Anglican Church's role in the process of reconciliation. The study is organised into eight chapters. Each chapter has a similar format. The issues examined and analysed in the chapter are introduced and then an overview of the whole subject under discussion is given and the main findings presented. As a consequence of this structure, findings are supported by a set of tables used in each chapter as evidence of local responses to a survey of the Anglican Church in Rwanda. Each set of tables provides statistical figures of the feelings and attitudes of respondents in general. Age group of respondents: 27% for 18-24, 31% for 25-34, 19% for 35-44, 21% for 45+, while 2% refused to answer. In relation to each statement the figures provide three pieces of information: the proportion of the sample of men and women respondents who agree with the question, the proportion of young men and women who disagree with the question and the proportion of those who are uncertain about their position. The last questions are for those who agreed to be interviewed and are set purposely for comparisons.

After the introduction to the problem, the study will be divided into three main parts. The first part will deal with historical events in Rwanda. It is concerned with the background of the conflict in its broadest sense, on the level of the questionnaire survey or from local voices and from observation and listening to the ways in which Rwandans think about the conflict. Firstly, Belgian rule and European missionaries' influence marked a fundamental shift from the Rwandan way of thinking and doing things. Secondly, this shift from the way Rwandans lived and the way they did things to a new culture of individualism, emphasising immediacy and self-actualisation, profoundly affected people. Thirdly, the economic system inculcated and the political structures fostered did not fit in with the Rwandan situation,

For the purposes of analysis, interviews and questionnaires on similar themes were drawn together. These themes have been developed into six chapters of the study. To sample the extent of the conflict, I have put forward six specific tables. The first theme entitled 'The question of differential in Rwanda' examines the paradox of the historical events that led people into the conflict. By looking at the distribution of responses to this question, I quickly saw how widespread the ethnic conflict was. The next six themes are designed to gauge attitudes and behaviour and reveal respondents' interpretations of the source of conflict. One question is concerned with the theory of 'natural hatred' referred to as the cause of the conflict between Hutu and Tutsi. How does this relate to what foreign journalists call 'natural hatred'? What goes on when it is put forward as a theory for encouraging conflict and how is it different from what Rwandans are saying to have been the cause of the conflict? At the end of this study, I will map out the level of the Anglican Church's real failure and the way the Anglican Church can help people today in the process of reconciliation and look forward to a reconciled future.

The second part analyses the role of the Anglican Church in Rwanda in reconciling the people. It is concerned with concepts surrounding the search for reconciliation. The main focus is put on interpreting the causes of conflict in Rwanda from the beginning, in order to develop understanding of the issues that need to be addressed in the process of reconciliation. An assessment is made of different interpretations of the conflict. Also assessed are the challenges the Anglican Church faced after the genocide in restoring its credibility, in order for it to engage in the process of reconciliation. The role of the Anglican Church will be analysed, based on three aspects of change, in order to investigate theories that were developed as to the causes of the conflict. This is seen as an important part of trying to establish the ways in which ethnic identities were formed and intimately shaped by the powerful influences of Belgian ideology and missionary endeavour under Belgian rule in Rwanda.

The thesis will therefore attempt to give an account of the Belgian ideological ethnic distinction theories under which ethnic conflict later developed. It will analyse how ethnic distinction theory developed in the country, to see whether it was effectively ethnic distinction theory that influenced the Anglican Church leadership in taking part in the ethnic conflict. Chapters Two to Three will give a detailed account of the Belgian rule in Rwanda to find out whether the Belgian period produced the political situation in which the Anglican Church may have found itself part of the ethnic conflict. The study looks at explanations of the nature of social change and historical development, in order to ask whether the Anglican Church was caught in a process of increasing the rationalisation of ethnicity. Were Anglican Church leaders driven by political development or by different social structures adjusting to each other? Or, if none of these answers is correct, whether it was just that the Anglican Church leadership's political naivety combined with their failure to keep away from playing with partisan politics. The purpose of tracing Belgian history in Rwanda is to explain how and when the Anglican Church became entangled in the ethnic conflict, as even now it is still hard to understand how people who speak the same language, share the same culture and profess Christianity could kill one another.

Many attempts have been made to examine the causes of this conflict. This has led to several different interpretations of those causes and shows how difficult it is to fully understand the Rwandan conflict. Even trying to grasp the obscurantism involved does not explain the reality of what exactly took place. Certain questions remain unanswerable, such as: What happened to make Anglican Church leaders act in the way that they did, according to reports in the media or through witnesses? This is because here in the Rwandan conflict is a situation in which it is thought the cause was traceable to the 'natural hatred' between Hutu and Tutsi. However, after the genocide, one elderly Rwandan was asked the reason for this conflict. He commented that in the past, before the Belgian period, there were disputes over things like land ownership and sometimes there were insignificant fights; but there was nothing like that which then proceeded to happen.

The New Yorker magazine observed that this type of conflict was the most shameful and 'dispiriting aspect that challenged conventional wisdom and the whole situation was described as so often ends with a variety of interpretations'.[6]

The fourth chapter provides different interpretations of the genocide and a brief account of witnesses of killings from both Catholic and Anglican Churches. Chapter Five describes the challenges Anglican Churches faced in the aftermath of the genocide, including witnesses criticising the Anglican Church leadership during the killings.

A basis for reconciliation and its application will be explored in Chapters Six, Seven and Eight to see if the Anglican Church has a role to play in reconciling the ethnic groups and building a peaceful future in which coexistence is possible. I will therefore attempt to assess what constitutes a qualitative approach to the study of the role of the Anglican Church in Rwanda.

As with any investigation into understanding exactly what happened, this study is in the form of an inquiry into the historical role of political practices and ideological strategies, in order to understand the origin and source of the conflict. An analysis of history will be made in order to see where the causes of conflict lie and to understand what might have led people in Rwanda to this grave situation. I will also examine the Belgian presence and the changes that established political structures that functioned until independence, in order to assess whether or not they were associated with the genocide and to see whether there was a form of institutional racism that might have taken another

---

[6]Quoted in the New Yorker Magazine, 26 May 1998, p.4.

identity throughout Belgian history in Rwanda. I hope to assess the historical reasons for underdevelopment there and, connected with this, analysis will be carried out through examination of social-economic structures and the Catholic Church's role under Belgian rule in Rwanda. Past experiences elsewhere in the world, such as legal segregation in the southern states of the USA and apartheid in South Africa, may provide an important historical context for this terrifying example of genocide and ethnic cleansing in Rwanda.

The Holocaust, in which the Nazis systematically disposed of an estimated six thousand Jews, Gypsies, Slavs and members of other ethnic groups, remains a terrifying reminder of a similar human potential for destruction. Recent events in Rwanda bear some of the signs of this. Therefore, this study looks beyond the interplay of cultural and institutional change that generated new modes of action. A broader approach will question many of the assumptions made about the role of Belgian rule and the new type of politics that was formed in Rwanda. This past, associated with Belgian ideological theories, will be further analysed in later chapters to show that there was nothing that was free from the earlier prejudice reflected in subsequent policies in the colonies. The aim of this is to highlight what were argued as being the possible causes of the conflict and how Rwandans were trying to restore peace, or regain what respondents considered their birthright.[7]

1.2 Research Objective

The main objective of this study is to trace the causes of the ethnic conflict and the meanings that have been

---

[7] Interviewing lecturers and students at Butare National University of Rwanda, July 1997.

attributed to them in Rwanda and to identify the interactive relations within the Anglican Church in the country to see if there are any generative attitudes regarding the reconciliation debate. In order to identify and examine how the Anglican Church has responded to the crisis, it seems important to assess the role of the Anglican Church initially in terms of the process of rehabilitation. It is necessary to examine the role of the Anglican Church in providing the means for people to heal and the means for survivors to recover from both fear and frustration, having suffered the loss of their loved ones. It is also necessary to examine objectively the procedures that are being adopted by both the Anglican Church and the RPF government to reconcile the people. I will also examine the Anglican Church's strategic plans for the future, to identify how the Anglican Church in Rwanda has prepared itself for the task of working out the framework of a reconciliation programme.

In other words, the ethnic conflict crisis will be analysed from the point of view of the dramatic structural changes in society and the relationships between the clergy after independence will be analysed from the point of view of a search for reconciliation. I will additionally examine what happened during the genocide and its aftermath, while emphasising the role of the Anglican Church in Rwanda in an effort to develop a contextual theology of reconciliation. The focus will be from a reconciliatory theological perspective, argued in a Rwandan context and rooted in the theological work that is being done (or is not being done) there in order to enable the use of culture and the traditional mode of effective communication in the process of reconciliation. I will also examine the role of the Anglican Church in the way it has organised itself towards enhancing equality and diversity in Church appointments.

1.3 The Hypotheses

The above objectives are based on two hypotheses, which I wish to examine or advance. These hypotheses are:

(1) Whether group inequalities in colonial social settings, such as in the Belgian economic rule in Rwanda, were not likely to cause conflict. To test whether the conflict is an ideological construct and has a direct bearing on the Belgians' theories; in particular, of divide and rule and Belgian economic objectives. To analyse responses that seem to suggest that these hypotheses have something to contribute to an explanation of the Rwandan conflict; a viable means of assessing hypotheses as to whether the horizontal inequalities most likely to lead to conflict were substantial, consistent and increasing over time.

(2) To test the hypothesis that, when people have recognised the problem, efforts at theoretical, institutional and practical levels must be made to reverse the situation, but, also, that there is more to be done. To advance the argument that the Revival Heritage and the Anglican Church in general have a role to play in the process of reconciliation; to heal the relations and to improve the socio-economic conditions of those in poverty-stricken areas such as rural communities and those still trapped in refugee camps.[8]

---

[8] http://www.rudyfoto.com/Rwanda Bibliography Page.html/11/11/2003

1.4 Methodology of Data Collection

The methodology adopted in the collection of data or information to meet the objectives was the use of three main sources: primary, secondary and observations:

1.5 Primary Sources

This has to do with the collection of data from the Anglican Church leaders and groups involved in the area of research and trips to sites of activities related to the research. Due to the nature of the research, a multiplicity of methods of data collection was adopted. My first visit to Rwanda was in July 1994 and the data collection itself began July 1997 to May 2004. The data collection took a period of seven years in order to observe, in depth, the situation in the country. In this case, the methods were as follows.

1.6 Research Questionnaires

The questionnaires and research interviews were an important part of information gathering for the study's enquiry into the significance of the role of the Anglican Church and how it was engaged in the process of reconciliation in Rwanda. All the questionnaires presented to Anglican Church leaders in this study made use of the experience and expertise gained in their Church ministry. Before the results could be computerised, they had to be collected and that collection meant sending out questionnaires and letters introducing those questionnaires in parishes.

In July1997, each Anglican Church worker was sent a questionnaire and invited to complete it anonymously. Three hundred and eighty questionnaires and a letter (see sample Appendix 1) were sent out to dioceses. The size of the Anglican Church in Rwanda was first checked in the Anglican Communion Crockford's Clerical Directory 1994, to locate diocesan offices, archdeaconries and parishes in each diocese. All incumbents, priests in charge, deacons, curates and lay leaders received a copy of the questionnaire and a note briefly explaining the purpose of the study and inviting their comments

The questionnaires were broken up into three distinctive sections and were divided into those that must be answered and those that were considered discretionary or supplementary. Selected Anglican lay and Church leaders were invited to interviews to give their views on some issues that would not be covered; for instance, expression of individual disagreements, signs of sorrow and hope. All these would not be provided clearly in questionnaires. The questions presented in the interviews in this study made use of respondents' experience and expertise gained from working with the Anglican Church. They were grouped in such a way as to indicate the main themes or issues covered by each chapter. In all, the questionnaires totalled three hundred respondents from nine dioceses. These three hundred respondents came from assessable areas where the Anglican Church functioned; forty-nine per cent were male and fifty-one per cent were female (see Appendix 11).

This was not a simple process. It was assisted by Anglican Church leaders at diocesan level, not only with the collection, but also by issuing reminders and revisiting those directly involved in the completion of questionnaires. In addition, there were visits to sites of Anglican Church leaders' seminars and meetings dealing with reconciliation strategy for interviews. In this case, the methods of collecting the data were as follows. To ensure that no one was excluded, questionnaires were translated into Kinyarwanda, the language most commonly used in the country.

There were three main sections to the questionnaire. The first parts of the questionnaire asked for general information about the respondents: his/her background, what his/her parents did and what position he/she held in the Anglican Church, just to establish whether he/she was a long-term Anglican Church member. The second part deals with the approach to the Anglican Church in the community and the third with Anglican Church members' feelings about the role of the Anglican Church in the reconciliation process. The questionnaire also covered a wide range of issues, from specific Anglican Church services such as spiritual guidance, pastoral, social community involvement and education, to wider concerns such as how people perceived the Anglican Church and what experiences they had had when they encountered the Anglican Church's leadership.

Anglican Bishops were exceptionally helpful and posted them back on time. There were an estimated two hundred Anglican Churches operating at the time of the study and completed questionnaire replies were initially received from ninety-three. A further eighty-nine questionnaires were received after a reminder was sent out along with two visits to Rwanda. However, eighteen Anglican parish churches in the northwest of the country said that they were unable to respond to the questionnaires because of continuing armed insurgency.[9]

While I was in Rwanda, I discovered that there were areas to which previous questionnaires had been sent, but where they had not yet been received for reasons of security. I organised a meeting with Anglican Church elders from areas where no services were held and there were no leaders to give an account of the political situation in their area. Also, after receiving one hundred and eighty-two questionnaires from the clergy, I soon discovered that

---

[9]Report from Anglican Churches in the Ruhengeri area in July 1995.

women and lay people were unrepresented and I had to interview a selected number of people who represented the voices that were missing; these included civil leaders, academics, bankers, development workers in nongovernmental agencies and informal discussions with political leaders involved in Gacaca programmes.

1.7 Interviews

In order to gain an exact comparison between interviews and questionnaire issues, interview questions were frequently put into statements with the same stem: How long have you been serving the Church in Rwanda? What are the main social and religious problems in the area? How far has your Church, fellowship or organisation addressed problems like those of reconciliation, caring for orphans and support for survivors?

The structure of the interviews was designed to facilitate open-ended questioning. Also, in the process there was a degree of latitude to ask further questions in response to what were seen as significant replies. In addition, the interviewer's other purpose was to assess the feelings or attitudes of both Hutu and Tutsi toward reconciliation. The questions had been compiled after listening to Anglican Church leaders from the nine dioceses and parishes.

The focus of these interviews was to examine Anglican Church members, men and women of all ages, to ask them questions about a specific situation caused by the conflict in Rwanda and about their personal experiences during the crisis. The questions did not suggest certain kinds of answers to respondents. Interview questions were employed to 'test' respondents' knowledge of whom they blamed for the conflict. The interview, therefore, was essentially characterised by factual questions concerned with issues of which respondents had a level of knowledge and issues of which their understanding could be tapped. A request was attached to the questionnaires sent to selected individuals who were likely to be interested in taking part in the interviews. A total of one hundred respondent interviewees were asked to say something about what they saw and heard during the genocide, their feelings and their comments on the conflict (see Appendix 111).

One hundred and twenty-six other responses in live interviews were intentionally for comparing with three hundred questionnaires returned. In many cases, especially where stories were elicited, respondents dealt with many different themes in the same statement. The statements themselves were in a random order so that, for example, the references to Belgian rule or the Anglican Church experience allowed a flow of discussion that would not block or confuse the answers. The order of questioning also allowed interpretation of the conflict.

1.8 Observations

Research was carried out through a combination of triangulation of qualitative and ethnographic approaches using participant observation and semi-structured interviews. I had to visit Rwanda in July 1997, 1998 and May 2004 to monitor the Anglican dioceses where reconciliation programmes were initially forming in order to get first hand information on how work was being carried out and what was being done by the Anglican Church and the government. During all these visits, my concern was to identify people's reaction to the idea of reconciliation, how it was perceived by survivors and by a cross-section of both Hutu and Tutsi Anglican Church leaders and members in Rwanda. It would seem an obvious solution to identify people's problems directly, rather than relying on the research instrument of questionnaires to elicit necessary information. This was done to supplement questionnaires and to achieve a more accurate and honest response.

Another aim was to assess the problems of meaning, omission and memory, where respondents may vary in their interpretations of key issues in a question. There is also the social desirability effect: respondents reply in ways that are designed to fit in with their perception of what is admissible and what isn't around certain issues.

1.9 Secondary Sources

The methodology also consists of desk-based research into the theoretical literature. Prior to carrying out the interviews that form the body of this research, I made a comprehensive analysis of a wide range of secondary sources, including journal reports on the Rwandan conflict and legal procedures of both local Gacaca courts and the International Tribunal, in order to identify arguments that reappear in the voices of authors who championed influential theories concerning the ideology associated with Rwandan ethnic politics. All these are taken into account. In fact, there are many books, articles and journalistic reports from both foreign and local reporters relating to my field of study. Unfortunately, most of these publications do not deal directly with the topic of the role of the Anglican Church in Rwandan reconciliation and most of them approach the issue from the perspective of ethnic hatred.

The approach to written material was examined systematically, attempting to combine all the different types of material that would make consistent sense of the historical events relating to the way that the ethnic crisis escalated in Rwanda. The purpose of this was to examine both primary sources and secondary sources to find out any differences between descriptions from both sides of the cause of the conflict in Rwanda. For example, there was a systematic examination of journalistic and historical publications, which have so often viewed the conflict from a distorted perspective. Many of the early reports of missionaries gave a one-sided view of religion and politics at times, as if there was nothing on the other side. These views are based almost entirely on missionary and Belgian sources, but these sources contain inaccuracies that unfortunately have crept into books and articles.

However, these books and materials offer a great insight into more general issues relating to the history of the Anglican Church in Rwanda and to some extent in the area of Anglican missionary work in Rwanda; particularly sources found at both the Church Missionary Society and in the Rwanda Mission headquarters, Waterloo. This study therefore made use of the essential materials available from the library of literature that exists on issues relating to missionary work in Rwanda, conversion and Revival Heritage.

1.10 Analysis

At the end, findings were very carefully analysed and compared with several other sources to ensure that they contained true, reliable information in order to qualify as part of this study. In a number of cases it was necessary to check figures that at first seemed to be too large. In almost every case, however, further analysis showed that the claims were based on a reality of some kind.

In order to gain an exact comparison between interviews and questionnaire issues, questions were frequently put into statements with the same stem: 'Are you worried about....' or 'Was it wrong to....' These questions were carefully used to assess respondents' knowledge of the area. The procedure also allowed comparisons to be made from different groups, in order to assess the validity of claims and whether the claims were replicable. I set out a profile of respondents who were representative of a cross-section of the Anglican Church.

The purpose of this approach was to test different viewpoints on a number of issues such as history, politics, the Revival Heritage (Anglican Church) teaching and the general atmosphere before and after the genocide. It is a form of approach that relates mainly to the question of whether a conclusion that incorporates a causal relationship between two or more variables holds water. In the quantifying process, answers were analysed, followed by a summary of each question, according to the majority of respondents' views. First, the question of differential; second, the question of social structure; third, different interpretation of genocide; fourth, the question of Église Épiscopale au Rwanda's presence; fifth, Anglican missionary teaching Christianity in Rwanda and, sixth, the question of reconciliation and forgiveness.

1.11 Codifying Data

The collected information was computerised. The totals for each component were grossed up according to the response rate of three hundred. The data scores from both interviews and questionnaire respondents are classified as variable numbers. The numbers allocated to each answer were then used in the computer processing of the data. The coding is a three position identifier, with two digits to represent male and female respondents and a third number character identifying the group type of each question, whether it covers the history of conflict, the Church in society, or the question of reconciliation. In every case, questions within a particular grouping have a particular code. Numbers 1-6 of the table of questions were categorised under six themes. They generated responses that guided my analysis of the data. Each variable number corresponds to the group questions. The coding frame entailed formulating distinctive themes in three hundred replies. Each theme was given a code. For instance, (var00001) is question 1, (var00002) is question 2, (var00003) is question 3 and so on. The totals for each component were grossed up according to the response rate of three hundred.

In the final analysis, the study formed a structure of a set of tables representing six themes for analysis discussed in each chapter, which provides a total of three hundred numbers of interpretations of genocide in general. These themes were grouped into six tables for ease of analysis. For the sake of clarity, comparisons are made between primary and secondary sources to show whether evidence from primary sources coincides with that from secondary sources. One per cent of responses represent three respondents in the Anglican Church of Rwanda. This means that ten per cent of the sample represents thirty respondents and one hundred per cent represents three hundred respondents respectively. To take a more or less arbitrary example of responses, twenty-five per cent were equally worried about the lack of peace and security. Consequently, if we use the above formula, this should be understood to show that approximately one hundred and ninety-five respondents in the Anglican Church are affected by this concern. Looked at this way, the percentage figures take on a greater significance.

Statistics that appear in the tables are used to assess the validity of respondents' claims. The first table appears in Chapter Two, to provide four pieces of information. The first is the proportion of respondents who agree with the statement, the second is the proportion of respondents who disagree with the statement and the third piece of information concerns those who are uncertain about their position. This careful procedure also allows comparisons to be made with cross-references with different voices in written works. As a result, analysis is drawn from contrasts on similar themes discussed in six chapters. The discussion of the findings features in each chapter, from Chapter Two onwards; initially with the debate that is concerned with examining the paradox of the historical theory of ethnic distinction that dominated Belgian rule in Rwanda.

Therefore, data analysis is based upon a contingency of both different voices and responses, and those scored as 'agree' counted as positive responses, whilst 'disagree' counted as negative responses; and 'uncertain' those who had no ideas about what happened. Similarly, those interview questions that asked the extent to which respondents felt a statement applied to the situation or to the Anglican Church had a similar response. The general practice was to use the first position of the category code, as themes from 1 to 6 to identify the six specific topics under examination.

1.12 Issues of Confidentiality and Ethics

The instruments of data collection were constructed with regard to the ethical guidelines and advice received from my first supervisor, Professor Leslie Francis, in the Department of Theology and Religious Studies at the University of Wales, Bangor. During data collection in 1998, strategies were employed to minimise unforeseen problems as identified by Diener and Crandall, such as the humiliation of participants, lack of informed consent or making respondents feel threatened.[10]

Interviews were restricted to the Anglican Church, largely because there can be difficulties in researching sensitive issues and gaining access to sensitive areas. Being an Anglican clergyman made it possible for me to communicate with Anglican Church officials and members

---

[10]Cfr.Diener, E. and Crandall, R. (1978), Ethics in Social and Behavioural Research, Chicago: University of Chicago Press, p.19.

in Rwanda without being mistrusted by my respondents. It was important to avoid any misunderstanding and suspicion in a country where suspicion is still evident.

As matter of confidentiality I had to take great care to ensure that any critical remarks would not lead to future adverse treatment for the person who made them; and there were concerns everywhere that this might occur. The whole atmosphere in the country was still fraught with anxiety and tension. For the protection of individual identities, I will not reveal the names, identities or locations of any of those who objected. I will only mention a few names of those who did not object; for instance, a few Anglican Church leaders. Where people's names are mentioned, it is only where the information is in the public domain. Respondents' identities and privacy were strictly respected and protected in order to encourage their confidence and not to undermine it. In fact, it was explained in advance that disclosures were restricted to relevant information and were not to be misused in any way.

There were also discussions with some Anglican Church leaders such as Archdeacons, Deans and clergy in administrative positions. It was agreed that the data would only be used to explain their experiences before and after the genocide in order to describe the crisis. There are three reasons behind this approach; firstly, to provide an original picture of the conflict, based on local representation of Rwanda as a whole; secondly, to show the widespread responses regarding views that must be taken seriously by Anglican Church leaders and politicians alike and, finally, to examine the validity and reliability of the respondents' concerns about the Anglican Church's missionary theology, which has been criticised as outdated in that the Anglican Church needs a theology that can reconcile and liberate Rwandans in this political and economic crisis.

Any criticism, therefore, had then to be treated discreetly and sensitively with any relevant organisation in order that it could be adequately assessed. In order to counter any suggestion that this might be a biased sample, the selection of interviewees included both Hutu and Tutsi; this was with a view to generating a representative sample to take part in this study. In my view it was important not only to find a way to convey both the fear and the frustration of survivors and those who suffered as a result of the ethnic cleansing policy, but also to examine the objective procedure that the Anglican Church was suggesting adopting and which was evolved to help them. In addition, I wish to make it clear that my respondents refused to be recorded or photographed. I further explained in detail about protection and confidentiality to ensure that they were properly prepared and that they agreed to be involved. If suitability was in doubt, or if there was a conflict of interests, it was suggested that they should withdraw from interviews. The only permission asked was to make notes of the discussions, parts of which I have included in the footnotes. No one was interviewed against his/her will. Those interviewees who had expressed fear were assured that the data elicited would remain confidential and that neither the individuals nor their names would be identifiable.

1.13 Significance of the Study

This study, it is hoped, will be of great significance in many ways. Its intentions are to contribute to knowledge by adding to the literature available in this particular area of study and to argue that, without an understanding of the Belgian rule in Rwanda, it is not possible to consider the role of ethnic distinction as an ideology. By looking at the different ways those involved in the conflict have related to and acknowledged themselves as being part of an ethnic group, some degree of consensus is apparent. An ethnic interpretation of the conflict, however, runs counter to a socio-economic and political interpretation of events, evident in both the actions of people involved at the time and in current scholarship on the conflict in Rwanda. This is not another study about ethnic conflict in Rwanda in particular, but focuses on the role of the Anglican Church in Rwanda and how it could engage in the process of reconciliation. Therefore I will be drawing on what the Anglican Church in Rwanda did during Belgian rule, after independence and what it is currently doing about reconciliation in order to analyse how it is engaged in the process of reconciliation.

There is also hope that this study will be a catalyst in the efforts of the Anglican Church in working towards the development of a contextual theology from a cultural perspective. This is because the Anglican Church doctrine is still irrelevant to Rwandan society. This study, therefore, hopes to trace the Anglican Church's task and role of contextual theology in contemporary society. I believe this will prompt the Anglican Church to emerge from its somewhat irrelevant position to offer an effective ministry as its role in people's everyday life and society in general.

The Anglican Church in Rwanda can shift from teaching with an ethnic distinction bias towards diversity, equality and inclusion-centred teaching of the Christian gospel. I hope that this study will add to knowledge as one of the materials in the study of the African mode of reconciliation.

1.14 Organisation of the Thesis

The thesis is organised in eight main chapters and in two main parts. Chapter One gives a general introduction to the study; this includes the background of the problem, research objectives and hypotheses, methodologies and relevance of the study.

The second chapter, concerned with the core of the thesis itself, deals generally with the history of the

Anglican Church during Belgian rule in Rwanda and the Belgian ideological policies in relation to the introduction of the ethnic distinction. Special emphasis is placed later in this chapter on arguing the changes and development of ethnic identity in Rwanda, including a brief discussion on how changes there created differences among the same people and later in the conflict in the country. This could be seen as a brief history of ethnic conflict in Rwanda. A discussion follows on how ethnic identities developed and how these identities were highlighted by the Anglican Church leadership. This discourse will include an investigation of the social procedures that were used in the period of Belgian rule in the country and their influence on the development of ethnic differences.

Chapters Three and Four concentrate on the main area of how changes endangered the traditional social structures and beliefs in Rwanda. These chapters attempt to examine a paradigmatic change in people's relationships and theories behind the ethnic conflict and local interpretations of causes of the genocide. Here, the discussion is centred both on local explanations of the effect of Belgian ethnic ideology and around the root of ethnic conflict.

Chapters Five and Six deal with challenges facing the Anglican Church in Rwanda and the analysis of contextual and pastoral theology. These chapters look at the reasons upon which this perception of the Anglican Church's role in reconciliation is founded. They examine the theological role of the Anglican Church in Rwanda by examining its concerns and methodological approach. Special attention is paid to past methods of conversion.

The final chapters, Seven and Eight, explore the theology and practice of reconciliation in Anglican Churches in Rwanda and then discuss the Anglican Church's strategies for reconciliation. They stress the need for greater inclusiveness and the reduction of ethnic differences as important factors in the process of reconciliation. The chapters also stress the importance of showing what the Anglican Church in Rwanda is doing at present towards the practical realisation of national reconciliation goals. The final chapter provides a general conclusion and deals with a discussion of data, a consideration of the pertinent issues raised in the thesis and their implications for the Anglican Church as a focus for its ministry in the country.

1.15 The Study Area

The area of this study traces the diverse influences leading to the political crisis and examines the role of the Anglican Church in the process of reconciliation, from a theological perspective. This topic has been selected due to Rwandan discussions regarding it. In Rwanda, efforts are being made by both the government and the churches, including Anglicans, to engage church members in the reconciliation process. Observing that there is a need to involve the Anglicans in the reconciliation process in order to push forward a credible and sustainable reconciliation network, this study sets out its objective through a social and theological framework in order to show how the Anglican Church in Rwanda can actively participate in such an effort.

During the initial stages of this study it was necessary to develop a wide social network of contacts with Anglican Church leaders, community workers in non-government agencies and survivors of the genocide in order to examine their views on reconciliation. All visits included private meetings to create an atmosphere in which the interviewee would feel safe to share confidences without interruption. As they spoke, I listened carefully to their views and I quickly realised the danger of empathising with the experiences and comments of respondents. I decided to make a dispassionate examination of each of their comments, in order to avoid simply taking their statements for granted without considering the potentially one-sided influences that may have informed them.

On arrival in the field, however, I found myself faced with a vastly different reality. It was not about how people reacted in the face of the chaos that originated after the genocide, but rather about a strong process of innovation within the Anglican Church already apparent at the meeting of the Anglican Church leaders. There were many individuals and groups with emergent new ideas, organisations, actors and spheres of action. This presented particular challenges. Interviews for this type of research have to be relatively unstructured and very informal in order to gain the trust of the interviewee and to allow him or her to feel safe to express criticism or resentment without fear of reprisal. Such criticism must be put directly, but sensitively to any relevant individuals, or to the Anglican Church, in order that it can be adequately tested.

In this study, attention is given particularly to tracing and examining the diverse influences leading to the political crisis to including an analysis of contextual theology and the role of the Anglican Church in securing reconciliation in Rwanda. This is because I believe that resolution of the Rwandan conflict will require more than a military solution. The evidence upon which this study is therefore based is drawn primarily from the experiences of survivors of ethnic conflict, who agreed to participate in a series of interviews and ethnographic observations carried out from July 1997 to May 2004. The research method was qualitative rather than quantitative in nature.

Let us look at the choice of a qualitative approach aimed at testing the emotional response of the participants in respect of how they were recovering from the trauma of genocide. For this reason, an appendix to this study outlines the methods by which the research was carried out: (see Appendix 1 and 11). There were two reasons for this qualitative choice: first, it was to develop a research method that was capable of generating and analysing high-quality sensitive data; second, it was to secure the confidence of my respondents.

The role of Catholic missionaries in Rwanda during Belgian rule will also be briefly mentioned, as there were several claims that they had been influenced by Belgian authorities regarding changes in society and human relationships. This examination is carried out as an attempt to understand the way the Anglican Church might engage in the search for reconciliation. It would benefit us to examine what the causes of ethnic conflict are and the role of the missionaries, a role that has been criticised by respondents as one form of social exclusion and that also has been associated with Belgian ethnocentric dehumanisation of an entire group of people.

Chapter Two

The Belgian Ethnicity Debate (Analysis of Interviews)

2.0 Introduction

Rwanda is situated in central East Africa, bordering the Democratic Republic of Congo (formerly Zaire), Burundi, Uganda and Tanzania. It is one of Africa's smallest countries, covering an area of 10,169 square miles. It is a landlocked country, relying heavily on neighbouring countries such as Uganda and particularly upon areas such as Mombasa in Kenya and Dar-es-Salaam in Tanzania as areas for trade. In the last sixty years a large section of the population has been involved in the subsistence farming of crops such as bananas, sorghum, cassava and beans as their main food, as well as cattle rearing. Cash crops include pyrethrum, coffee and tea. Administratively, the country is divided into twelve prefectures composed of 145 municipalities, each of which is headed by a Government-appointed Governor.

Although Rwanda is a small country, according to local sources it is rich in resources, with potential reserves of tin, tungsten, beryl and gold; a tin-smelting plant has been in operation at Karuma since 1981. Statistics show that infant mortality (at less than one year) is 118 per 1,000 live births, while the under-five mortality is 203 per 1,000 live births. The maternal mortality rate is estimated to be 1400 per 100,000 live births. Before the 1994 war, Rwanda was one of the most densely populated countries in the whole continent of Africa, having three ethnic groups: Hutu, 90%; Tutsi 10% and the Twa, a tribe of hunters and gatherers, representing less than 1%.

The adult literacy rate is estimated to be between 69% and 70% and the Gross National Income (GNI) per capita is about US$220.[11] It was very hard to be accurate about the growth rate because the annual estimates depend mostly on readily available data and political assumptions. The population government figures given was estimated at 8.3 million in 2003, but for decades it has remained a densely populated and poor country, victimised by bad Government and plagued by furious ethnic conflict.[12]

The task of this chapter is to examine the paradox within the historical events that led Rwanda into genocide, by means of an investigation of social process procedures used in the Belgian period. This will be from the viewpoint of local people affected by these procedures and, thereby, having an influence on their sense of identity. It involves looking at the underlying methods that were used during the Belgian rule to discover whether any role was played by the Anglican missionary Church (Revival Heritage) in the operation and, if so, how these changes shaped a new political system and formed structures of a type of ideologically constructed ethnic identity.[13]

From the outset, I will state that this study is not aimed in any way at the Rwandan Catholic Church, but one underlying reason for its inclusion in this chapter is the church's role under Belgian rule in Rwanda, a point that needs to be made quite explicitly. The aim behind this inclusion is to examine the role political tactics played during Belgian rule. I shall also attempt to examine the role of the Catholic Church and the nature and extent of the effect that this and Belgian ideological ethnic distinctions might have had throughout this period in being used as a tool to create a relationship of tension and hatred between Hutu and Tutsi. This hatred was created originally from

---

[11] http://www.careinternational.org.uk/Rwanda+statistics+3278twl.
[12] http://wwww.careinternational.org.uk/Rwanda+stastics+3278twl.
[13] Cfr. http://www.Sussex.ac.uk/users/hafa3/kaldor.htm

outside Rwanda and fostered by an ideology of colonial white supremacy. Rwandans came to feel that these colonial ways might be the only viable way to exist.

2.1 Pre-Belgian Identity of Rwanda

Historians have described the pre-colonial division between Hutu, Tutsi and Twa as both a class and a caste division, though neither term is wholly accurate.[14] In Kinyarwanda tradition, the Umwami (King) was the head of the state, the focus of the national unity. The Umwami was, therefore, at the top of the hierarchical order but assisted by three main chiefs. The first was a military chief, similar to the modern-day army commander, or 'Chief of General Staff', who was responsible for the army, ensuring territorial integrity and expansion. The second was the cattle chief, who oversaw all matters pertaining to cattle husbandry, grazing and the settling of related disputes. The third was the land chief, who was responsible for agricultural land, produce and related affairs.[15]

Their predecessors appointed family and clan heads, while the chiefs were, in the main, appointed by the King. Although this was not necessarily the rule, the King often chose his chiefs from the clan (defined as a group with a common ancestor), particularly if clan heads were backed by a sound traditional education. The period of German rule that lasted until after the First World War was one that entrusted responsibility to Rwandan institutions. It is thought that this was because there was a limited number of men. Mbanda quotes Linden to show how minimal the influence of the Germans had been in Rwanda; he states

---

[14] Cfr. Longman, Timothy. "Nation, Race, or Class? Defining the Hutu and Tutsi of East Africa". In the Global Colour Line: Racial and Ethnic Inequality and struggle from a Global Perspective Research in Politics and Society, vol.6, 1999, pp. 3-11

[15] http://www.rwandagateway.org/mot.php3?id_mot=20

that: 'German rule, never in reality more than a handful of soldiers and administrators, did not change the nature of the Rwandan state.'[16]

As previously mentioned, Rwandans shared the same language and culture, which was important not only in itself, but also because it shaped people's attitudes towards each other, the distinctions between the different groups being less well defined. It was further argued by respondents that, before the arrival of outsiders in Rwanda, they had a strong mythological belief about Kanyarwanda, the father of all Rwandans. Generally, historians are divided on the origins of Rwanda's three ethnic groups: Hutu; Tutsi and Twa. However, considering the Rwandan mythology, Kinyarwanda had three children named Gahutu, Gatutsi and Gatwa.[17] Mbanda further asserted that historically, the average Rwandan knew himself or herself by this story and that they identified with one or other of Kanyarwanda's children. Emphasis was placed on what they shared or had in common, rather than on what divided them or was different.[18]

Gerard Prunier and R. Lemarchand both present excellent historical views of Rwanda from the Belgian era to the present, stating that it was even possible for individuals from one group or the other to 'change' their classification. Through a mechanism called 'Ubuhake' by the Tutsi or 'Umuheto' by the Hutu, this conversion could be made.[19]

---

[16] Linden, Ian, (1978). Church and Revolution in Rwanda, Manchester: Manchester University Press, p. 2.
[17] http://www.rwandagateway.org/mot.php3?id_mot=20/9/07
[18] Mbanda, L., (1998). Committed to Conflict, The Destruction of the Anglican Church in Rwanda, London: SPCK, p. 4.
[19] Prunier, G., (1995). The Rwanda Crisis: History of a genocide, New York: Columbia University Press, pp.130-31; Lemarchand, R., (1970), Rwanda and Burundi. London: Pall Mall, pp. 2 – 7.

According to the Kinyarwanda tradition, a Hutu owning ten or more cows could become a Tutsi (KwiHutura).[20] Furthermore, Mbanda explains that, in like manner, if a Tutsi lost his cattle, or turned to farming for a living and married into a Hutu family, he could become Hutu.[21] Rwandans had a common belief: 'Umwami'nu Umukobwa ntibagira Ubwoko' meaning, 'A King and a young woman belong to no tribe and have no ethnic identity'. This makes sense, since women were free to marry into any ethnic group and a King reigned for Hutu, Tutsi and Twa.[22] The King was honoured as standing above the tribal differences that could separate the Rwandan people.

Both the Germans and the Belgians found a unique leadership in Rwanda. The Banyarwanda (people of Rwanda) had, for centuries, developed a highly centralised form of administration protected by strong standing armies, a trained bureaucracy and an economy rooted in land and cattle. The Banyarwanda had a reverence for all things stemming from their strongly rooted, mystical affinity with nature and a desire to be successful in life. Itorero (recruits) was the Kingdom's institution of formal education; the curriculum of Iterero included poetry, composition and rendition, rhetoric, political science, diplomacy, customary law, administration, history, geography, singing and song composition, dancing, sports and military training. The graduate of Itorero, called Intore (the chosen one) had to excel in all these subjects in order to acquire the title.

---

[20]Mbanda, L., (1998). Committed to Conflict, The Destruction of the Anglican Church in Rwanda, London: SPCK, p.4
[21] Ibid.
[22]Ibid.

Figure 5.2 King Mutara III shaking hands with King Baudoin of Belgium in 1946.[23]

Source: Ibid.

A strict code of conduct within the army ensured state security and state expansion. The Umwami (King) was at the top of the hierarchical order, followed by regional chiefs, sub-chiefs, village chiefs and clan heads. Family and clan heads were appointed by their predecessors, while the chiefs were, in the main, appointed by the King. Since family and clan heads were often the best that families and clans could present, Rwanda's system of administration under Kingship manifested itself in a form of people's democracy.

---

[23] http://www.rwandagateway.org/article.php3?16article=115/7/9/07 According to the historical records King Leopold 11 was a man whose ambitions preoccupied with interest in founding an overseas empire, which had started in the 1850s and 1860's when as Duke of Brabant he travelled to Egypt, Formosa, Fiji and Sarawak and as far as the New Hebrides.

Rwandans had belief in the 'Supreme Being' (Imandwa); the 'Eternal God' (Imana) was the state religion, which I shall refer to as traditional religion. It was upon this religious heritage that subsequent religious traditions such as Christianity and Islam established themselves. Though there are many traditional Rwandan beliefs, they have always shared common features. They never sanctioned sorcery or the misuse of any powers of nature. These beliefs always emphasised healing, the driving out of evil spirits and the reconciliation of people within the communities. This is the religion that had always been part and parcel of the Banyarwanda culture. There was never any dualistic tension between faith and politics in Rwanda. Such co-existence had also been possible mainly because of deeper cultural values, as the sense of community, the clan, the traditional leadership and the mechanism in social relations were natural cultural restraints.

Belgian rule was rendered increasingly unhappy by the traditional beliefs and the education system that had ensured the stability of social and political orders celebrating the King's authority. In the view of many respondents, their religious tradition takes them back to roots that spoke with an innocence and directness and which have much appeal in our cynical age. According to local sources, the time between 1879 and 1898 is known as the first period, during which political events in Rwanda were still managed by the King and his subjects. By 1899 to 1959, this was when political power passed from the hands of the King and his supporters into the hands of Belgian agents. German penetration into Rwanda and Burundi started in 1892 when an expedition reached Rwanda and was formalised in 1898. According to local assertions, the Germans inherited a highly organised country.[24]

Before the Germans arrived, Rwanda had three ethnic groups: Hutu; Tutsi and Twa.[25] These three ethnic groups knew themselves as 'Banyarwanda', who had lived together amicably for decades. In addition, there is no evidence to suggest that there was any serious ethnic conflict in Rwanda before Belgian rule. According to Mbanda, the Belgian view of the situation differed from that of the German administrators, which created a strained relationship that both sides manipulated at the expense of Rwandan society.[26]

After the First World War, the Germans left and the Belgians took over the administration of Rwanda, which they would retain until the eve of independence. 1916, is when Belgium (in the form of Congolese Force Publique) invaded and the Belgian troops occupied Rwanda, Burundi and the northern part of present-day Tanzania, which included Karagwe Kingdom. The Belgians had wanted to use Rwanda and other parts of German East Africa as a bargaining tool to gain a prestigious position in Europe.[27] However, it is worth noting that this study does not intend to discuss any ethnic conflict in Burundi, even if the historical and political developments are more or less the same.[28]

---

[24] Cfr. Mbanda, L., (1998). Committed to Conflict, The Destruction of the Anglican Church in Rwanda, London: SPCK, p.11

[25] http://www.historyworld.net/wrldhis/PlainTextHistories.asp?histyid=ad24

[26] Mbanda, L., (1998). Committed to Conflict, The Destruction of the Anglican Church in Rwanda, London: SPCK, p.11

[27] UN Document E/CN.4/1994/7/Add.1, paragraph 171.

[28] Lemarchand, Rene, (1994). Managing Transition Anarchies: Rwanda, Burundi and South Africa in Comparative Perspective, The Journal of Modern African Studies, 32, 4, Cambridge: University Press, pp. 2-7.

In fact, elderly respondents noted that Belgium's arrival in the region was the start of a systematic violation of human rights.[29] Despite that, the United Nations was still responsible for the administration of Rwanda and Burundi. Rwanda, Burundi and Karagwe were the only countries that had been assigned to the heavy hand of German rule in East Africa, because in them the Germans had ostensibly found established order and security.[30] Perhaps because they were replacing another Western power, whose influence they reckoned had taken effect and because of the well-established nature of the leadership they had inherited, the Belgians were less at ease than the Germans.[31]

In Rwanda, Burundi and Bukoba (Tanzania) there had been strong local rule for centuries. When the Germans arrived in Rwanda, they established a form of indirect rule. Mbanda argued that German administrators and the leadership as a whole respected the traditional structures out of a desire to maintain peace,[32] whereas in Tanganyika (today known as Tanzania) governance was from Berlin. At the centre of German rule was the Governor, assisted by an Advisory Council.

In 1919, when the League of Nations was formed after the First World War, Belgium was disappointed at not having acquired any territory in Europe. After some negotiation, Belgium was allowed to retain Rwanda and Burundi as one 'Mandate State'. Karagwe and other northern parts of former German East Africa were joined with the rest of the territory and given to Britain as a Mandate State. Mbanda noted that, throughout the period of

---

[29]Interviews with elders in the neighbourhood of the King's Palace at Nyanza guarded by military personally as publicans had no access to the Palace July 1998I
[30]UN Document E/CN.4/1994/7/Add.1, paragraph 171.
[31]Ibid.
[32]Mbanda, L., (1998). Committed to Conflict, The Destruction of the Anglican Church in Rwanda, London: SPCK, p.11

the German rule and then that of the Belgians, traditional institutions and social structures remained unchallenged until 1926.[33]

2.2 Creating a New Identity in Rwanda

Let us see how this came about. According to respondents, de Waal and Chretien the creation of ethnic identity was deeply influenced by the history of colonial ideology. First, German and the Belgian colonial servants, missionaries and (social) anthropologists had an eminent part in the construction of this supposedly 'natural' contrast between Hutu and Tutsi.[34] The first Christian Church to arrive in Rwanda came with Catholic missionaries, popularly known as the 'White Fathers', who introduced Christianity to the country in 1895 under the Catholic Church leadership of Bishop Hirth and some other senior German military officials. In 1900, the first Roman Catholic missionary in Rwanda, Bishop Hirth, espoused the tactic of suggesting that the Tutsi were a refined people. According to McCullum, the Belgian administration and missionaries saw a possible way to take root in the kingdom, if they used the Tutsi.[35] One way of assembling evidence about the set of political developments in Rwanda is to ask whether ethnic distinction was accidental, or whether the Belgian ideological policies designed it purposely to meet their political objectives.

---

[33] Ibid. p. 12.
[34] de Wall, A., (1994). The genocidal state: Hutu extremism and the origins of the 'final solution' in Rwanda, Times Literary Supplement, July, p.3; Chretien, J.-P., :(1991), "Presse libre" et propaganda raciste au Rwanda: Kangura et 'les 10 commandements du Hutu', Politique Africaine 42:p.114
[35] McCullum, Hugh, (1995). The Angels Have Left Us. The Rwanda Tragedy and the Anglican Churches, with a foreword by Desmond Tutu, Geneva: World Council of Anglican Churches, p. 4.

In order to address the issues raised, I will explore the question of ideologies and political cleavages to see what responses are suggested.

Table 1: The Question of Differential in Rwanda

Agree %	Disagree %	Uncertain %
Is conflict in Rwanda caused by ethnic discrimination?		
34	61	05
Is conflict in Rwanda caused by power struggle?		
51	43	06
Violence is a common problem in the country		
75	21	04
I think it is important to work with all people		
71	26	03

The response shows that 61% of Anglican Church members disagreed with the idea of discrimination and prejudice. It follows, therefore, that in relationship to the question of political differential, 34% agreed that the ethnic distinction concept was extremely prominent in the Belgian rule and the policy of 'divide and rule'. On the other hand, bearing in mind the relationship Anglican Church respondents had with missionaries, the level among respondents of 34% who agreed that ethnic discrimination had resulted in conflict was understandable, compared with 61% who disagreed and the 5% who were uncertain. Perhaps this explains the good relationship that Anglican Church members had with the Anglican (Revivalist Heritage) missionaries, although it does not suggest that discrimination didn't exist under Belgian rule. This phenomenon is seen mostly starkly in the lower percentage response. This response could have been influenced by the question possibly being interpreted by Anglican respondents to mean missionaries rather than the Belgian rule was responsible for divisions.

In another piece of supporting evidence, those interviewed at Gahini Mission think that the hate relationship between Hutu and Tutsi had to do with policies of 'divide and rule',[36] whereas 71% of responses by elderly Anglican members to the question of people working together disagreed with the criticism of Anglican Church missionaries for failing to help them when they needed assistance in the period before Belgian administrators had introduced divisive policies.[37] During interviews, respondents argued that the Catholic missionaries could have halted ideological developments in Rwanda if they had not decided to collude with their fellow Europeans (the Belgian administrators). The idea of the 'divide and rule' policy widened the divisions they had already introduced. Several of the respondents expressed the view that the Catholic Church had colluded with the Belgians in Rwanda in encouraging ethnic distinctions, a view endorsed by Rene Lemarchand, who observes that in Rwanda, people shared the same customs and lived in relative harmony with each other for centuries before the advent of colonial rule.[38]

Seeing the changes that occurred during the Belgian rule, this leads me to the view that the element in Belgian policy of 'divide and rule' had a considerable influence and a major impact on the Rwandan people in how they viewed themselves. The respondents saw this influence as being largely destructive and negative. The accurate identification

---

[36]Interviewing elderly Anglican members at Gahini Mission August 1998.
[37]Ibid.
[38]Lemarchand, Rene, (1994). Managing Transition Anarchies: Rwanda, Burundi and South Africa in Comparative Perspective, The Journal of Modern African Studies, 32, 4, Cambridge: University Press, p. 589; Also, in article 'Les chefs du Rwanda experiment leur loyalisme envers le Mwami', Le Courrier d'Afrique (1 October 1956), in Nkundabagenzi, Rwanda Politique, p. 34.

of such a phenomenon has wider ramifications; during the past decade the issue of ethnic distinction conflict in Rwanda was an integral part of the planning of social policies. It was less considered by researchers who have, in many respects, often overlooked the long-term legacy of these policies and failed to shed any light either on the nature of Belgian rule, which seems to have had this exact impact on social relationships, or on the effect of divisive changes in Rwanda. 43% disagreed with the idea of a power struggle. Instead, they think this policy disempowered the minority. 26% represented those who thought that all these developments were the result of Europeans coming, not only to change people spiritually, but also to change everything else 'for the sake of saving heathen society', a process that caused pain to so many Rwandans[40].

At this point it is perhaps appropriate to remember the Catholic missionaries' role in Belgian rule. In these circumstances, it is not even right to emphasise that the Catholic missionaries' collusion ought to be seen in the context of the effects of those policies on the country and the Rwandan people. I will go a little further to suggest that these effects might not necessarily have been a result of collusion, but from the lack of opposition from all missionaries and in particular the Catholic Church, with its visible presence in the country. From the respondents' point of view, the Belgian administrators understood that it was a betrayal of the Rwandans. They asked why, throughout the Belgian rule in Rwanda, there was no united Christian voice from missionaries to oppose these divisive policies (fuzzy sets) of ethnic distinction.[39] It is undoubtedly an area of contention between Rwandans and all missionary Churches. The Catholic Church, effectively supporting the

---

[39]Interviews in Butare Diocese August 1998

creation of a Hutu identity and nationalism', thus became linked with the Hutu movement. The mission witnessed mass conversions of Rwandan Hutus, making Catholicism the dominant religion in Rwanda.

Trying to assess perceptions of what people might say about the violence in the country, posed a disagreeing state of 'violence as a problem in the country'. Three-quarters, 75% agreed, a fifth, 21%, thought that people cared and 4% were uncertain. Whereas one survivor from among the genocide respondents thought that, 'no one cares anymore for their neighbours'. With reference to the history of the ethnic divides in Rwanda, the role of Anglican Church leadership was seriously criticised by its member respondents, who stressed that from 1959 until the time of the 1994 genocide, Church leaders from all denominations, both Protestants and Catholics, had never, either officially or explicitly, condemned the violence and massacres of the innocent. On the contrary, they noted that local Church leaders and missionaries, men and women, have been part of these humiliating acts either by helping, by passively accepting or by justifying the unacceptable.[40]

This period reveals that Belgian structural development was indeed one sided, because it did not allow people the right of self-determination as to political future and/or ethnicity, which was necessary to enable Rwandan political developments to mature. It is therefore argued that Belgian ideological practices were seen as a complete mismatch with their ideas of the philosophical theories of 'rule by the best.'[41] For that matter, being stronger sanctioned the Belgians to vandalise the institutions of Rwanda (paraphrased).[42] Mario Aguilar describes colonialism as

---

[40]Cfr. http://faculty.vassar.edu/tilongma/Church&Genocide.html/7/01.
[41]http://www.philosophypages.com/hy/2g.htm/5/9/07.
[42]http://www.wsu.edu/~dee/GREECE/ARIST.HTM/21/9/07.

being like a science; a well developed ideology in itself.[43] He argues that Belgian powers created new boundaries and carved out new places where missionaries could preach God's word. The aim of the Belgian administrators and missionaries was to govern Rwanda and to control the minds of the local population.[44] Following on from these developments, some respondents commented that they suspected a certain tactic had been officially legalised in 1933. It took the form of an ethnic identity card; a physical, tangible device to cleave the population. As we will see later, the Belgian authorities insisted on the introduction of an ethnic distinction strategy. According to Mbanda,

'Dr Smith from the Anglican mission and colleagues from the organisation opposed the issuing of identity cards and encouraged Church followers not to accept them. Dr Smith did not stop there, but also worked to request an open-school policy for all Rwandan children and in 1944, Protestant children were finally given a place in what was largely a Catholic institution, the majority of whose children were from noble families'.[45]

On the other hand, the problem with ethnic identity cards was linked to the severe restrictions upon the movement of minorities within the country. This period was criticised by many respondents, saying that the greatest mistake was to replace everything that had made sense and was valued, such as the abolition of traditional social structures, without consulting with the people involved, which was illegal. 'Ryangombe' was the ritual for all the

---

[43]Mudimbe, V.Y., (1994). The Idea of Africa, Bloomington and Indianapolis: Indiana University Press, London: James Curey, pp. 118 - 123.

[44] Aguilar, M. I., (1996). The Rwanda Genocide and the Call to Deepen Christianity in Africa, Uganda: AMECEA GABA Publications Spearhead Nos. 148 – 150, p. xii.

[45] Mbanda, L., (1998). Committed to Conflict, The Destruction of the Anglican Church in Rwanda, London: SPCK, p. 25.

Banyarwanda, without ethnic distinction and was celebrated by all. It is even documented that the 'Uburetwa' system structured relations between people where the poor Hutu and Tutsi had access to the use of land and cattle, but had also to render service to the King and chiefs. It is described as a friendly system, since the whole population was involved in it by consent. [46]

The use of the identity card determined where a person was permitted to live and work, restricting freedom of movement. Threats of confiscation of identity cards and consequent restriction from movement were simply a means of control and power. The restrictions in the process significantly hindered the minority Rwandans' ability to live a normal life in a sense where people could visit a relative in another location without having to apply for permission. The brief definition of the new ethnically distinct identity was a combination of different social characteristics, which excluded Rwandans from the common culture and social identity that had given the minority and the majority different social groupings; a common consciousness that was intended to divide or separate them in some way from each other in a form of social grouping or segregation. The mechanism 'Balkanised' Rwandan society – the 'backlash' awoke its collective conscience, but this was not unification'.[47]

Years later, the strategy of ethnic distinction formed the root of the genocide. This strategic theory of differentiation reflected Belgian ideology, which was implanted in a progressive process. However, in all of this, Hutu saw Tutsi, rather than the Belgian policy, as the oppressor and the enemy. The important thing to remember is that previously there had been no racial, social or cultural

---

[46] Interviewing elderly Anglican members at Gahini Mission August 1998.
[47] Perry, B., (2002). Hate Crime and Identity Politics, London: Thousand Oaks, pp. 480- 9.

differences and economic differences between Hutu and Tutsi were gradually narrowing. Bankers and lecturers in Kigali and Butare National University argued that these differences were artificially imposed on Rwanda.[48] Artificial or not, the division established a very serious difference between Hutu and Tutsi. It was during this period that the politics of ethnicity attracted the attention of the Hutus and became divisive, splitting relationships.

It was argued by the Vice Rector administration at Butare National University that these divisions were not only signs for change, but were the desired implementation of a Belgian rule, which aimed at planting a new order of exploitation and domination on the traditional institutions including the King.[49] At this stage, the Belgian authorities believed that managing the country in their own manner could only be achieved if the King, the traditional religion and Itorero, which supported his rule, were removed. At this time, Belgian administrators and Catholic missionaries were the real masters of the country after the disbanding of Itorero and its replacement with European education. Respondents felt there was here an element of exploitation of Rwanda. Instead of registering people as Banyarwanda in the National Registry, the Belgians registered them as Hutu, Tutsi or Twa. The Catholic Church seemed then to be in the vanguard of encouraging ethnic differences between Rwandans, to the extent that they kept separate lists of Hutu and Tutsi students in their school records.[50]

Despite the Anglican Church having identified with the concern of the Tutsi about imposed identity cards, Anglican missionaries kept a count of those Tutsis who were baptised, confirmed or married in the Church. Respondents

---

[48] Interviews at Gahini Mission and Butare National University, August 1998
[49] Interviews at Gahini Mission and Butare National University, August 1998
[50] Interviews at Gahini Mission August 1998.

added that although it was a normal procedure to keep Anglican Church records for parishioners, specific recording of Tutsis was always viewed with suspicion. On the other hand, the use of this method by all missionaries can be argued as being interplay between ethnic identities. Subjective reconstruction or manipulation by the missionaries was seen by some respondents as unnecessary interference largely designed to create divisions between the same people.[51] All these tactics were criticised. Belgian rule and its artificial differentiations were treated as if they were normal. On the contrary, these manufactured divisions between people encouraged opposition and conflict. This is of course what some respondents criticised, i.e. that this interference and reconstruction of traditional institutions might be considered, in the long run, a recipe for disaster.

However, Hastings objects to the assertion that before the arrival of the Belgian administrators and missionaries, Rwanda was just one happy family in which each group knew its place - before everything fell apart.[52] Hastings points out that Mbanda repeatedly asserts that because the 'White Fathers' favour the Hutu, this produces 'a widening of the divisions.'[53] Unlike Hastings, Roosens, E. does not in the least appear to agree with the idea of alleviating the Hutu majority, but saw it as about the tactics used to consolidate social control policy (Ethnogenesis) in the form of an ethnic identity card.[54] David Newbury shows that while the term "Hutu and Tutsi" existed in pre-colonial time, they were not as entrenched[55] Gana, A.T., observes that missionary Churches during Belgian rule saw the

---

[51] Interviews with Kigali Diocesan staff, August 1998.
[52]Hastings, A., "The Tribal Contest behind Africa's Bloodbath" The Tablet, 5 September 1998, p. 1152.
[53] Ibid.
[54]Roosens, E., (1989). Creating Ethnicity: The process of Ethnogenesis, Newbury Park: Sage Publications, p. 14.
[55]Newbury, D., (1998). "Understanding Genocide", ASR 41

Church of Christ as collaborating with the brutal assault on the psyche of Africa rather than resisting it, thereby facilitating the entrenchment of what one might call 'copycats' in all spheres of human activity – whether in economics or politics.[56] Marvin Markowitz adds that the Catholic Party was far more powerful in Belgium and that it had continued to participate in every government throughout the interwar period; being particularly influential in the ministry of its colonies.[57]

Of equal significance, is that only 26% disagreed with differentiation between the Rwandan people and 71%, who agreed it was important to work with all people, argued that it was a deliberate intention to create confusion among the same people. The argument put forward by respondents was that the introduction of the new order plainly included constructive divisive measures, which put Hutu and Tutsi into an almost impossible position as a result of ethnically distinctive policies. In addition, 68% of both Tutsi and Hutu broadly confirm the Vice Rector's argument at Butare National University that a 'Balkanisation' policy was the real problem.[58] It was people's experience that this particular setting was where the roots of conflict lay and it spoiled their relationships, excluding them from each other and turning them into instruments of conflict.

Since then, Rwandan politicians manoeuvring for power have repeatedly manipulated ethnic rivalries for political ends, without any fear of being accountable for their actions. One of the interviewees who agreed to disclose his identity, Nayinzira, added that differences were simply engineered. During colonisation and the post-

---

[56]Gana, A. T., (1994). The African Political Crisis and the Anglican Church in Africa, London: SPCK, p.228.
[57]Markowitz, M. D. (1973). Cross and Sword: the Political Role of Christianity Mission in the Belgian Congo, 1908-1960. Stanford, p. 92.
[58] Interviews at Gahini Mission and Butare National University, August 1998.

Belgian period, divisions were encouraged, leading to hatred.[59] Many respondents saw the reason for the lack of appropriate action from missionaries to oppose these ideological policies that constructed divisive measures as the collusion of the Catholic Church during the Belgian rule in Rwanda.

An elderly respondent at Gahini Mission described the missionaries in general like this: 'A missionary was at least three people in one. He was a devout Christian, a Belgian representing the values of a civilisation (in this case the Belgian interest) and he was an elder brother in Christ to the local people.'[60] Nevertheless, Hastings admits that 'Undoubtedly the White Fathers oscillated between cultivating the ruling Tutsis and endeavouring to alleviate the oppressed state of the Hutu (85 percent of the population).'[61] In addition, elderly Anglican Church members lamented that political changes caused pain and hurt so much, while Tutsi respondents further claimed that, at this period, some Tutsis disowned the Catholic Church and returned to traditional belief.[62]

However, it appears that the problem does not in the least appear to have been Catholicism or Christianity. The forces that breached old boundaries and created Rwanda as a fractured society with fused identities largely eclipsed missionary politics. This is the reason I should re-visit the Belgian days to see whether there is any sign of an organised collaborative enterprise or if was entirely accidental. At this point I tend to agree with Tschury and Roosens that, as proved by what developed later, it was not

---

[59]Interviews at Kigali July 1998.
[60]Interviews at Gahini Mission, July 1998.
[61]Hastings, A., "The Tribal Contest behind Africa's Bloodbath" The Tablet, 5 September 1998, p. 1152.
[62]Ibid.

liberation.[63] The political bases for these policies were viewed as being born out of innovations of the Belgian rule, which were the main obstacles and were widely criticised by many respondents as unnecessary divisions created among the Rwandan people. These artificial divisions prevented them from uniting and ensured that they did not demand their rights as one group. All along, the Belgian administrators had a political agenda for the Tutsi to be seen as carrying out oppressive acts.

A notable influence from the start, the Belgian education system began the steady and continual downgrading of the country's history, feeding young minds with European values and skills as well as Western achievements. Throughout this period, the problematic obstacle expressed by respondents was that the aim of ethnic distinction was to prevent Rwandans from uniting in things such as common ritual celebrations that had previously brought them together. This was done in the belief that if Rwandans did unite they would resist Belgian changes. They further argued that, being so enamoured of missionary influences, including those of the Anglican Church that at this period was already visible at Gahini Mission, they would neglect Rwandan history. All mission schools taught only European history, while Rwandan history was never mentioned, discussed or included in the education curriculum. Respondents argued that missionaries from all denominations, including the Anglican Church, did not oppose the Belgian policies whose targets for changing young Rwandans, churches, schools and medical centres were the channels of change that made steady headway.

It was further observed by lecturers at Butare National University that, at this period, the influence to change was

---

[63]Tschury, Theo, (1998), Ethnic Conflict and Religion, Challenge to the Churches, Geneva: WCC Publications,
pp 152-156.

aimed at the traditional beliefs and at moving the King, who was seen as an obstacle to change.[64] As stated at the outset, whilst the aim here is to establish the history of genocide in Rwanda, this leads to a process that clearly explains how the European influence in changing Rwandan society was determined to get ahead of the system that was in place and the way that Belgian rule dealt with any visible obstacle it encountered. In the view of many local observers, this period was not seen as a strange episode. Would anyone imagine that missionaries would disassociate themselves from Belgian policies when those were the policies of their fellow Europeans? Many respondents added that, during this period, almost all missionaries sympathised with fellow Europeans, which was the reason that they could not raise their voices to oppose the Belgian repression of Rwandan people at the time.

In fact, it was even argued by the elderly respondents at Nyamatimba and Gahini Mission that, irrespective of denomination, in principle, all missionaries cared little to oppose the education curriculum.[65] Therefore no missionary Church can hold up clean hands; the fundamental influence of the changes in Rwanda that occurred is argued as the basis of the current political state. In fact, these events are the source of the Belgian ideas, assumptions and beliefs that help to explain a systematic plan aimed at making Rwandans lose their common ground. Jean Pierre Chrétien blames Belgian policies for interfering with the way in which people had lived quite peacefully together, sharing many common factors including cultural unity, language and religion together with major social organisations like the clan as well as

---

[64] Interviews at Gahini Mission and Butare National University, August 1998.
[65] Interviews at Gatuna, Nyamatimba and Gahini Mission, July 1989.

family habits such as intermarriage.[66] Out of the encounter between the West and Rwandan society came: 'A classic piece of Victorian anthropology, influenced by social Darwinism, placed the Tutsi aristocracy as part of a 'Hamitic invasion' from Ethiopia and the northeast, supposedly superior to Bantu autochthones.'[67]

If this is the case, it clearly underlines the anthropologists' contribution to this examination of these dramatic changes, which included the degradation of Hutu, unifying them and triggering a feeling that Hutus must liberate themselves from Tutsi domination, effectively concealing a more complex Belgian agenda.[68] And it is this that is one of the objects being analysed in this chapter.

Analysis of economic perspectives and historical materials shows that these measures carried a serious human cost in that, in their attempt to look at Rwandan problems, Belgians still saw the situation through Western lenses. It was not until the 1950s that the Catholic Church switched its allegiance completely from the Tutsi leadership to the Hutu majority, which then left them open to new accusations of ethnic favouritism.[69] However, it is important to recognise the fact that the phrase 'the Tutsi are enemies of the country' was in common use; it is impossible to dismiss the problems presented by the impact of the political pressure. It was always likely to affect human relations; respondents even argued that the huge

---

[66]Chrétien, J. P., (1991). 'Presse libre' et Propagande Raciste au Rwanda: Kangura et 'Les 10 Commandements du Hutu, Politique Africaine 42, pp. 15 – 16.
[67] Ibid.., p. 15.
[68]McCullum, Hugh, (1995). The Angels Have Left Us. The Rwanda Tragedy and the Anglican Churches, with a foreword by Desmond Tutu, Geneva: World Council of Anglican Churches, p. 14
[69]Ibid.., p. 4.

pressure that followed later led to total collapse of the authority of traditional institutions.[70]

Respondents recalled how Catholic missionaries claimed to be 'fulfilling God's law' and further, that Belgian rule represented the continuation of God's creation.[71] This openness to such a viewpoint, of course, might be deemed to undermine the process of democracy as evidenced in allied terms such as 'freedom', 'equality' and 'participation'. Respondents argued that Rwanda's system of leadership under kingship manifested itself in a form of democracy, because it had a well-organised and respected system that was accountable to Rwandans.[72]

At the start, the Tutsi were given education, later taking posts in the Belgian administration.[73] As well as giving privilege to the Tutsi group and ruling through them to begin with, the Belgians used the traditional structure of Tutsi chiefs to administer the country. Their approach, however, strengthened the ethnic distinction by educating only the sons of Tutsi chiefs. Sanders points out that 'By this time colonialists had developed a concept that the Tutsi were born leaders, a perspective encouraged by the early anthropologists' and musicologists' belief that the Tutsi were partially of European extraction and therefore able to lead.'[74]

McCullum describes this as follows: 'The past racist theories of the early colonisers in the 18th century persuaded them that physical appearances – Tutsis [were] tall and slim with straight noses and long fingers ('more

---

[70] Interviews at Gahini Mission and Butare National University, August 1998.
[71] Ibid.
[72] Interviews at Kigali July 1998.
[73] Bowen, R., (1995). "Rwanda, Missionary Reflections on a Catastrophe", London: SPCK, pp. 15-18.
[74] Sanders, E. R., (1966). "The Hamitic Hypothesis: its Origin and Unctions in Time Perspective", Journal of African History 10, 4: 521 – 532, pp. 521- 32.

like us'), Hutus, on the other hand, were more 'Bantu' in appearance, shorter, with broad noses and stubby fingers – were an indicator of intelligence and ability.'[75]

Prunier observed that the struggle for cultural dominance and subjugation among the Hutu and Tutsi - the central players in the recent massacres - was exploited by racially obsessed Europeans.[76] In fact, from 1930 up to the 1940s, Catholic missionaries taught mainly Tutsis, claiming that they were the only ones with the ability to learn.[77] The Hutu chiefs and deputy- chiefs were removed and replaced by Tutsi. Catholic Bishop Monsignor Classe in 1930 issued a warning: 'The greatest harm the government could possibly inflict on itself and on the country would be to do away with Mututsi caste. Such revolution would lead the country into anarchy and towards ant- European communism far from reaching progress. As a rule, cannot possibly have chiefs who would be better, more intelligent, active, more capable of understanding idea of progress and even more likely to be accepted by the population than Batutsi.' (Classe, 1930).

The theory highlighted differences that first began under the Germans but were not implemented as policy. Later, Belgian administrators, missionaries and social anthropologists contributed to the construction of this supposedly natural contrast between Hutu and Tutsi abilities. This reconstruction of both biological and ideological differences was again expressed clearly by Chrétien. He attributes this theory to the similarities between the Hutu and Tutsi dichotomy and the Gaulois

---

[75] See appendix: IV and McCullum, Hugh, (1995). The Angels Have Left Us. The Rwanda Tragedy and the Anglican Churches, with a foreword by Desmond Tutu, Geneva: World Council of Anglican Churches, p. 2.
[76] Prunier, Gerard. (1995). The Rwanda Crisis: History of a Genocide, New York: Columbia University Press, pp. 130 - 31
[77] Interviews, Kigali and Butare, July 1998.

Francs dichotomy, which was a dominant philosophical and political discourse in France from the sixteenth to the nineteenth centuries.[78] At that time, missionaries in support of Belgian ideology portrayed Tutsi as being more intelligent than Hutu, creating a very serious inferiority complex among the latter.

Dramatic social change occurred even before the United Nations ended its trusteeship.[79] It is important to note that in Rwanda since that time there has been a smooth succession into Government. Minasse Haile observes that the compelling evidence for this is that international human rights were not universal and, during colonialism, human rights were not part of the Western law brought to Africa.[80] In Rwanda, the suppression of Belgian unrest was characterised by punitive measures, which included forced labour, exile and imprisonment without trial, collective fines, collective punishment and loss of property. Tschury explains that: 'It was the same way as racism against European Jews in the 1930s and 1940s. Such a transformation of values is indicative of the similar heightened racism against blacks in South Africa [which] frequently shows the collusion of the Church and other religious organisations with powers engaged in the theory of oppressive and conflict.'[81]

One aspect of this theory is the charge that Belgian rule promoted ethnocentric attitudes. Tschury argues that in Rwanda: 'From the progressive integration of pre-

---

[78]Chrétien, J. P., (1991). 'Presse libre' et Propagande Raciste au Rwanda: Kangura et 'Les 10 Commandements du Hutu, Politique Africaine 42, p. 114.

[79] Amnesty International Index: IOR 41/02/94.

[80] Minasse, H., (1961). United Nations Consideration of domestic questions and of their International Effects, Columbia University, pp. 591- 92.

[81] Tschury, Theo, (1998), Ethnic Conflict and Religion, Challenge to the Churches, Geneva: WCC Publications, p. 13. Interviews at Butare National University July 1998

colonial times, the colonial government, encouraged by the hierarchy, thus created an apartheid state in which the seeds of ethnic conflict lay. By 1958, the Tutsis held 88% of all administrative posts. In addition, 95% of all chiefs were Tutsis, while 90% of Rwanda's Population was Hutu.'[82]

In 1931 the King was baptised to Christianity. Subsequently, after he had embraced the Christian faith he urged his people to do the same. At this time the Catholic Church identified with the King's leadership.[83] It was even noted then that, because of the great conversion, neighbouring countries referred to Rwanda as a 'Christian Kingdom in central Africa'.[84] As Ian Linden observes, 'While the Tutsis started out rejecting the Church, they later embraced it and 'cornered it for themselves'.[85] However, according to a respondent who was at that time a trainee in Itorero, the King co-operated with these changes, although admittedly under pressure from Bishop Classe.[86] According to local observation it was under these tactics that the Belgian authorities and the Catholic Church switched favours from the Tutsi minority to the Hutu majority.[87] The King was arrested with his family and was exiled by the Belgian administration to Shaba province in the Democratic Republic of Congo (Zaire) where, after a short while, he died. While the Belgian authorities celebrated their victory over the monarchy, missionaries realised that it was going to be very difficult to manage the Rwandans without their tried and tested system of

---

[82] Ibid. p. 43.
[83] Cfr. McCullum, Hugh, (1995). The Angels Have Left Us. The Rwanda Tragedy and the Anglican Churches, with a foreword by Desmond Tutu, Geneva: World Council of Anglican Churches, p.3.
[84] Interviews at Gahini Diocese, July 1998.
[85] Linden, Ian, (1978). Church and Revolution in Rwanda, Manchester: Manchester University Press, p. 243.
[86] Interviewing elderly people in the neighbourhood of Inyanza Palace, August 1998.
[87] Interviews at Gahini, Byumba, Kigali, July 1998.

leadership. Bishop Classe changed his mind again, choosing Prince Rudahigwa for the vacant throne. King Mutara III Rudahigwa was crowned in 1933.

By this time, the Catholic Church had become very influential and powerful. The King tried to ensure that the Belgian administration did not use the tactic of divide and rule that it had introduced earlier. He called for clan alliance rather than ethnic alliance since the three strands of Rwanda shared the same clans. It is these shifts and perhaps discontinuities of the King's authority in the turbulent late 1950s and early 1960s that appear to be the starting point for the impression that, from then on, the Belgian authorities and the Catholic missionaries had hidden offstage while the Tutsi became the visible oppressors in the eyes of the Hutu. The Belgian ethnocentrism will be analysed in the next chapter to explain the belief that one's own race or ethnic group is the most important and that some or all of the aspects of its culture are superior to those of other groups. This belief exposes the genesis of entrenched racism in Belgian rule in Rwanda at every level, where there were no representative institutions for a very long time and there was no freedom of association.

What is 'racism'? Briefly, racism is an ethnocentric pride in one's own racial group and preference for the distinctive characteristics of the group; a belief that those characteristics are fundamentally biological in nature and are thus transmitted to succeeding generations. This is accompanied by strong negative feeling towards other groups who do not share these characteristics. It is these characteristics, coupled with the thrust to exclude the other group from full participation in the life of the society; in other wards 'racism' has in no small measure determined the people that they are, while preventing others from reaching their potential or belonging. The ethnic distinction policy in the Belgian rule in Rwanda created resentment and in some instances was equally entrenched in its attitudes among Hutu towards what they saw as repression from Tutsi. Overall, this kind of policy left a scar on the country and the policies of racism scarred the Rwandan population during this period.[88]

An alternative approach to the conflict must begin by attempting to understand the role of ideology and the economy in the Belgian rule. This requires consideration, both of ethnic distinction as ideology and economy as politics. This approach carried within it considerable problems and, in itself, is open to criticism in what is revealed. Respondents at Butare National University widely criticised the Catholic Church's role during the Belgian rule and described its involvement as a failure to challenge ideological policies, which meant to challenge the very structures of the ideology of ethnic distinction in political rule.[89] By its very nature, everything institutional, structural and systematic was built around racism; ideology, economy and cultural politics conflicting at a deep level. It is further argued by Professor Rutiba that such discrimination sprang from a belief in racism, which was defined as 'the result of the [way] Belgian rule ordered the law and the way it was used in and through the structures of Rwandan society.'[90]

Things were organised in favour of the Belgians and against the Rwandans upon whom, at this point, the Belgian administrators had imposed domination. This was to be seen in the way they disbanded the traditional army and replaced it with Belgian-trained Congolese soldiers who terrorised Rwandans.[91] The Congolese were under the command of Belgian officers, which marked the end of self-rule for Rwanda. Thus a period of government by

---

[88] Cfr. Brixton (1986). Anglican and Racism, British Council of Churches Report.
[89] Interviews at Butare National University July 1998
[90] Interviewing John Rutiba at Makerere University, Kampala, Uganda, July 1998.
[91] Ibid.

traditional institution was ended, while that of ethnic opposition to Belgian ideological propaganda had not yet begun. First, the power of the King was weakened step by step. Second, Belgian administrators felt hindered by the huge Rwandan army whose indomitability had made the kingdom a force to be reckoned with in the politics of the interlacustine (traditional region) of East Africa.[92]

According to Michael Kayihura, who was by then Prime Minister (and the last holder of the office), 'The reigning monarch, King Yuhi 1V Musinga, vehemently opposed the connivance of the Catholic Church and Belgian authorities to undermine traditional religion and his own leadership, but he was later denounced by Bishop Classe'.[93]

The Belgian authorities also opposed the King's political master programme.[94] The King died in 1959 in Bujumbura, the capital of Burundi, in the midst of disagreement with the Belgian authorities. According to local respondents, many Rwandans at the time believed that the Belgian authorities had killed the King. The Belgian authorities had hoped that with the death of King Mutara III Rudahigwa in 1959, the institution of Kingship was over. However, the Rwandan masses present at the burial refused to have the deceased buried before the new King was announced to the nation. Belgian authorities took this to be a humiliating defeat and were able to impose restrictive conditions on the King. The Bishop's decision was seen as an attempt to avoid immediate bloodshed,[95] and, as Michael Kayihura points out, under the monarchy, the Belgian

---

[92] Interviews at Gahini Mission, Kigali and Butare July 1998.
[93] Interviewing the last Prime minister of Rwanda Michael Kayihura Michael July 1998.
[94] Interview, Kigali and Butare, July 1998.
[95] Interviews at Gahini Mission July 1998.

administrators had reluctantly accepted Bishop Classe's advice to install the new King.[96]

Respondents argued that this reluctant acceptance was the reason for the Belgian administrators' change of mind, because the Catholic Church had come to Rwanda via Uganda after the religious troubles in that Kingdom. There, converts were burned alive, culminating in the death of the celebrated Ugandan Martyrs. The White Father Missionaries who escaped from Uganda to Rwanda saw direct alignment with the Hutu as being the only sure way to avoid a recurrence of future troubles similar to those experienced in Uganda. Harley, the Belgian Governor, acceded in order to avoid violent confrontation and Chief Michael Kayihura asked Chief Kayumba to announce the new King. Prince Jean Baptist Ndahindurwa was subsequently crowned as King Jean Baptist Kigeli V Ndahindurwa.[97]

According to respondents this was the genesis of the Belgian classic theory of dominance in practice; ideological theory informing the dominant culture, the result in this case being the creation of the dual culture of 'Kiboko' (whip) decadence that brought with it a philosophy of violence accompanied by new methods and practices. The Kiboko culture allowed Belgians to diversify their policies for forced labour. Under this culture, Rwandans were ordered to provide free labour as porters for Belgian officers, as well as being required to provide them with food.[98] The analysis of these measures shows how violence was embedded in the structural and cultural content within which groups interacted. The inappropriate choice of the Belgian political ideology of ethnic distinction, based on coercion and subjugation of one people by another and the

---

[96] Interviewing the last Prime minister of Rwanda Michael Kayihura July 1998.
[97] Ibid.
[98] Interviews at Gahini Mission July 1998.

imposition of that ideology in this matter, was not at all concerned with democratic rule in Rwanda.

In addition, the struggle for human rights became caught up within the struggle for Belgian policies from there on. This very point was echoed by 43% of respondents. This 43% agreed that the main drive of the Belgian rule was to establish a system of leadership in their favour that, in the long run, would allow them to do whatever they wanted without hindrance.[99] To suggest anything to the contrary is simply evading the evidence that appears and re-appears elsewhere. In France, the debate about tier-modernism led many French intellectuals to attack Libertés sans Frontiers as an expression of this line of thought.[100] Libertés sans Frontiers was attacked for supporting the liberation of third world countries, which seems to confirm the claims of those who say that Belgian administrators had no intention of handing over power in the colonies.[101] In part, the use of force reflected a conscious denial of the people's rights for the sake of advancing desirable Belgian political convenience.

The demand for high taxes and, among other things, for the daily supply of eggs to Belgian families resident in the country, forced hundreds of thousands of Rwandans into exile. As a result of both these demands and the brutal treatment given out, military garrisons under Belgian officers were put in place to deal with any revolt.[102] However, Mbanda argues that the traditional structures that used to accomplish national progress were not favoured by the Catholic missionaries who called them 'oppressive',

---

[99] Analysis of questions and interviews carried out July 1998- May 2005.
[100] Kaldor, Mary, (2003). Global Civil Society, An Answer to War, Oxford: Blackwell Publishers Ltd, p.131.
[101] Interviews with Bankers at Kigali, August 1998.
[102] Cfr. Oliver, R., & Fage, J. B., (1962). A Short History of Africa, London: Penguin African Library AP2, p. 206.

while the Anglican Church tried to stay out of politics.[103] In general, respondents shared a more critical view of all missionaries' performance under Belgian rule and argued that they disliked the Rwandan traditional institutions and culture, which explains why missionaries barely said anything when the traditional leadership was abolished. Respondents interpreted the missionaries' decision to support the colonisers as a political move and in a variety of responses critics described how the Belgian administrators (in this case Catholic missionaries) knowingly worked hard to undermine the King's authority and all that Rwandans held as important.[104]

In this respect the Catholic Church introduced its own beliefs, culture and values that prepared the ground for creating differences among Rwandans. Traditional rituals were forbidden. The lack of freedom to worship and to observe their own culture was described by respondents as a 'sell out' by all missionaries.[105] To ensure their position after abolishing the cultural celebrations of Imandwa, the Catholic missionaries, supported by a group of Hutu Christian intellectuals, replaced it with Christianity, changing the character of Rwandan society and its rituals. The point often overlooked was the role Ryangombe played in uniting Rwandans. Perhaps in their European reality, the Belgians were confusing the interpretation of the ritual with politics.

During this period, Catholic missionaries and Hutu jointly drew up a manifesto that provided the intellectual framework to promote the ideology of ethnic distinction. The ethnic-oriented Hutu Manifesto criticised the submission of the Hutus to the Tutsi King, criticised the traditional rituals and went on to denigrate the whole

---

[103]Mbanda, L., (1998). Committed to Conflict, The Destruction of the Anglican Church in Rwanda, London: SPCK, p. 9.
[104] Interviews at Gahini Mission July 1998.
[105] Ibid.

traditional system. According to local people, such tradition that had both ensured the stability of social order and celebrated the King's authority was undermined.[106] This meant that the King was regarded as an obstacle both to Belgian rule and to the Hutu, so his power was quickly restricted. At the same time the celebrated rituals including social responsibilities and guidelines for community involvement that had united Rwandans and which had been enforced by the Kingdom, were either ignored or abolished. Elderly respondents argued that the King had been under increasing political pressure to abolish the institution of Ubuhake, which the Belgian administration system had transformed from the status of economic alignment to that of slavery, so he had demanded independence for his people and country.[107]

It is argued that the Belgian rejection of the established system in Rwanda was a clear abuse and abrogation of people's right to self-determination. It is therefore, important to highlight how the Belgian use of the ideological theory of divide and rule explains how Belgian rule was determined to get past any visible obstacle in its way. Firstly, the power of the Rwandan King was weakened step by step. Secondly, the people felt hindered by the huge Rwandan army, whose indomitability had made the Kingdom a force to be reckoned with in the politics of the interlacustine (traditional religion) of East Africa.[108] At this time the demand for independence began, mainly by the same previously favoured Tutsi elite gathered as a political party, Union Nationale Rwandaise (UNAR). And one respondent, who cannot be named, described something unconventional about the subversive

---

[106] Interviewing elderly Anglican members at Gahini Mission August 1998.
[107] Ibid.
[108] Interviews at Gahini Mission, Kigali and Butare July 1998.

nature of political dimensions during this period.[109] It was here that efforts were made by Belgian administrators and missionaries to create political parties, but the resulting constitutional compromise left loopholes, which later enabled Belgium to intervene increasingly in Rwandan affairs.[110] The widespread struggle for independence was in response to the formation of UNAR (Rwandese Africa National Union), which had previously been the desire of the deceased King Mutara III Rudahigwa, who had demanded independence for the country.[111]

2.3 The Root of Conflict

Political manoeuvring climaxed during this period when both the Catholic Church and the Belgian authorities switched sides for the sake of convenience, thereby abandoning the Tutsi and founding new alliances with the Hutu. In 1957, the Hutu catechist Gregoire Kayibanda was influenced by the ideological patronage of J.P. Harroy, the Belgian Governor of Rwanda and Archbishop. Perraudin, a Swiss White Father, head of the Roman Catholic Church in Rwanda, published the 'Hutu Manifesto', demanding that political authority be granted to the Hutu majority. The King's death triggered widespread violence by his supporters against the Hutu and against anyone who sympathised with Belgians and missionaries. Hutu supported by Belgium succeeded in overthrowing the monarchy in a violent coup, which resulted in thousands of deaths[112] after the Hutu rise to power.

In 1959 the Hutu, supported by Belgium, achieved the violent overthrow of the Tutsi leadership, which resulted in

---

[109] Interviews at Butare, Gahini and Kigali August 1998
[110] Ibíd.
[111] http://www.jha.greatlakes/July 20, 2000
[112] Kritzinger, J. J., (1996). The Rwandan Tragedy as Public Indictment of Christian Mission, London, SPCK, p.342.

thousands of deaths after the Hutu rise to power. The United Nations organised elections in 1961, leading to self-government and Rwandan independence in 1962. As Rwanda prepared for its political independence, Belgium played a significant part in the preparation of the constitution and the politics for the forthcoming elections. As the radical Hutus gained power in Rwanda at independence in 1962, Catholic and Anglican clergy found themselves with personal friends in all levels of governance and with good access to the centres of power. According to respondents, Catholic Bishops and priests specifically represented Rwanda in foreign missions, while Parti du Mouvement de l'Emancipation du Peuple Hutu (Party for Hutu Emancipation) ideology was preached in Catholic Churches in a process where the experience of a hostile act of ethnic nature was transformed into a tangible agenda affected by the politics of division. The Parti du Mouvement de l'Emancipation du Peuple Hutu (Party for Hutu Emancipation), for its part, demanded that Belgian rule should continue in the country for eight more years from 1960.[113].

In pursuit of the common enemy and assisted by the Catholic Church, the Belgian authorities heightened the ethnic differences by using politically active ex-seminarian Hutu to form a sectarian political party called ParmeHutu. The first presidential election in Rwanda was won by Grégoire Kayibanda, the leader of the interim provisional government in 1959. Grégoire Kayibanda, who was Archbishop Andre Perraudin's Secretary General and editor of the newspaper Kinyamateka and the name of his party, the Parti du Mouvement de l'Emancipation du Peuple Hutu (Party for Hutu Emancipation), makes all too plain what is to be the central plank of government policy.[114]

---

[113] Interviews at Butare, Gahini and Kigali August 1998.
[114] Interviews at Butare National University and Kigali August 1998

To an extent, Parti du Mouvement de l'Emancipation du Peuple Hutu (Party for Hutu Emancipation) looked as if it was the Hutu 'peasant revolution' or a 'rural grassroots democracy' that had abolished traditional politics and replaced it with the new leadership.[115] According to respondents at Gahini Mission and questionnaires returned, 51% agreed that, it was from that period that the open struggle for policies of ethnic distinction had full effect on Tutsi; party politics, representing the majority Hutu, firmly marginalised the Tutsi.[116] Outright revolt by the Hutu was followed by harsh repression, leaving the Tutsi with a strong sense of grievance and from that period distinct ethnic identity cards were used to monitor Tutsi movements within the country and those leaving. As already observed, from this time an organised campaign of violence was carried out during which the Tutsi were referred to as 'cockroaches' and 'the enemy'.[117]

From this time, messages of hatred for Tutsi were effectively promulgated through Radio Libre Mille Collines station, which was responsible for the broadcasts that exhorted every Hutu to kill Tutsi. This radio station broadcast inflammatory anti-Tutsi programmes and advised its listeners to kill Tutsi children by saying: 'To get the rats you have to kill them when they are small'.[118] The sectarian party safeguarding the interests of Hutu (PermeHutu) had been established in 1957, urging all Hutu to fight their common enemy, the Tutsi.

The British philosopher Bernard Russell called the murder of the Tutsi in Rwanda during that period 'the worst human tragedy the world had occasion to witness since the

---

[115] Appel a' la conscience des Bahutu' in Chrétien (1995), p.116.
[116] Interviews at Butare, Gahini and Kigali August 1998.
[117] Cfr. Amnesty International Index: AFR 47/17/94 Distr :SC/CO//CC, p. 15
[118] Ibid.

extermination of the Jews by the Nazis.'[119] The Times in London reported on 3rd February 1964 that when the United Nations was asked for help, it was reported to have taken the attitude that 'the matter was for the internal affairs of the Rwanda government and no concern to them'.[120] The official figure of the number of dead was put at 100,000, but the local people believe the figure is much higher than that. From the time the open struggle for power among Rwandans began, the political party representing the Hutu majority firmly took over power. The first open ethnic conflict took place from 1957 to 1994 and forced a large number of Rwandans out of the country, most of them fleeing to neighbouring Uganda.

In all these political developments, the Anglican Church mission remained neutral and at times played an interventionist role in political developments under the Revivalist Heritage. It was even noted that it could have been its characteristic, with born-again brethren spirits counselling restraint from taking sides. In this case, tensions and differences were being overcome within the Revivalist fellowship. Evidence for this was noted by Mbanda: 'Honest Christians, Godly people, the saved, (in the Kinyarwanda language, 'Abarokore') were holding evening and weekend meetings characterised by groups engaging in prayer, fasting, confession of sins, predictions of what might come, rich Bible studies, willing to certain deep thoughts, singing heavenly songs and concern for one another.'[121]

During this period, revivalists contributed something which may appear small, yet in a way speaks volumes about how shared religious convictions had suppressed

---

[119] Russell, B., (1968). The Autobiography of Bertrand Russell, 3 Vols, London: George Press, p. 3.
[120] The Times, London, February 3, 1964, p.10
[121] Mbanda, L., (1998). Committed to Conflict, The Destruction of the Anglican Church in Rwanda, London: SPCK, p.77.

political visions. During the political turmoil, Revivalist missionaries at Gahini mission sympathised with displaced Tutsi and hid many from their pursuers, including the Queen Mother who was sheltered at Gahini mission. This sympathy was criticised by Logiest who asserted that when the Catholics later changed their politics and dropped their support of the Tutsi hierarchy, the Protestant Churches rushed to fill the void. One of the administrators, Logiest admits having difficulties with the Protestants' learning.[122]

At this point the Anglican missionaries sympathised with Tutsi and supported displaced internal refugees. In 1959, when revivalist converts were killed because of their unwavering and uncompromising commitment to Christian teaching, because they saw that the political conditions were restricting them from the demands of Christian discipline, they fled to Uganda and Burundi.

The conflict between Hutu and Tutsi persisted after independence, with further large numbers of Tutsi killed in 1960, 1963, 1973, 1990 and 1994. Rwanda experienced killings and the exodus of refugees into neighbouring countries in fear for their lives. Ordinary Hutus became immune from prosecution for killing the Tutsi 'enemies of the State'.[123] In fact, the leadership rewarded them for doing so. Doubtless, the situation was made worse by the war, which had created permanent divisions among the Banyarwanda. Throughout their thirty-three years in exile, Tutsi had made many attempts to return to their country. Such attempts, whether peaceful or violent, were always met with aggression from the Habyarimana's Government. Diplomatic attempts were made to persuade the Government to change its position but they were always frustrated by the regime's adamant refusal to move.

---

[122] Ibid. p. 25.
[123] Ibid.

Repeatedly, the reason given by the regime as an appeasement to the international community regarding refugees was that the country was overpopulated. For many years, whenever the Head of State felt compassionate enough and made reference to refugees in his address to the nation, Habyarimana's terse four-word sentence, 'Stay where you are', became the regime's cliché. Once, when a local journalist confronted him, arguing that the refugees have a right to a nationality, Habyarimana responded, 'They have the right but there is no place.'[124] Amnesty International pointed out that 'The international community failed to act in the face of periodic and widespread politically motivated killings, which occurred in the lead up to and after independence.'[125]

Conclusion

This chapter has revealed that Rwanda has undergone tremendous change over the last one hundred years. It has described the history of Belgian rule in the 'Belgian period' and the measures that carried a serious human cost. It has expressed respondents' views that stressed that the Belgian rule and missionaries still saw matters from a Western perspective and, as a result, were unable to understand the Rwandans' needs. In some cases the justification for the gradual exclusion of Tutsi lies behind the conflict that led people in what was a politically driven slaughter. It is this history, the very hallmark of Belgian rule, which explains why the traditional system, enshrined in beliefs and values, was lauded by almost all respondents.

The next chapter assesses how the Belgian administration and Catholic missionaries built a new society in Rwanda. It amplifies questions about Belgian

---

[124] Interviews with RPF soldiers at Byumba, July 1998.
[125] United Nations High Commission for Refugees' Report, 1959.

ideology and the failure of this powerful influence to promote human rights in Rwanda. The aim of this is to examine whether the Belgian presence enhanced a just rule and to assess the validity of respondents' claims that Belgian economic pressure had led Rwandans to engage in conflict. The chapter will also examine the relationship between the socio-economic structures and how they were introduced and administered in Rwanda in order to assess the developmental theories aimed at promoting the economic interests of an imposed order and the role of legitimising or maintaining, constructing or destroying the existing order. It will attempt to assess the Belgian socio-economic structures in comparison with the Rwandan Uburetwa. The Rwandan traditional economic organisational approach was argued as having failed the development of Rwanda after independence. The nature of the socio-economic exclusion, in highlighting these measures, perpetuated social inequality that was aimed at separating Rwandans and escalating the ethnic conflict.

Chapter Three

A Paradigmatic Change of Structure and People's Relationships in Rwanda

3.0 Introduction

This chapter seeks to examine the theories behind the historical development of the economic structure and the human relations' change that made genocide possible. The basic aim is to examine how the new order under the foreign influence consolidated all existing social structures for care and social protection into a unified new structure of registration, along with traditional institutions to end their roles in Rwandan society. Statistics suggest that many of those interviewed for this study have greatly enhanced the knowledge and understanding of the ideological influence of economic policies, which could have contributed both directly and indirectly to what appears today in Rwanda. These policies include the effects of violence and the lack of political discernment by the Anglican Church after independence. Even where religion became entangled in politics, for instance in the Belgian era, the Catholic Church in Rwanda perhaps had little awareness of the role it played in influencing the structure of Belgian rule in Rwandan society.

The purpose of this is to demonstrate the Belgian economic structures, to assess their negative impact on development and to look at the theory, problems and practices of Belgian economic development. An examination follows of interviewee respondents, Kigali bankers and economic lecturers from Butare National University. They describe how such economic development, lacking a realistic consideration of the long-term implications of future development and combined with unjust economic policies, isolated the ethnic minority amongst Rwandans. In this context, the changes that took place in Rwanda during Belgian rule are the main focus of this chapter. However, it is not necessary to discuss the Rwandan economy to explore how the changes in the Rwandan historical structure created a dysfunctional economy that was criticised as having created differences among similar people in Rwandan society in the interests of that rule.

The main purpose here is to identify the effect of abolishing the traditional institutions and social economic structures, to see how this might have contributed to the political problems, since traditional economic structures were a political component of social relationships in Rwandan society. It is therefore important to make an in-depth analysis of these developments to explain how the present ethnic conflict began. David Newbury offers insight into the history of pre-Belgian Rwanda. He argues that Belgian policies were the very source of ethnic tensions underlying the genocide. These tensions blossomed during the Belgian era, but did not exist in the pre-Belgian period.[126] Ian Linden observes that 'The European historical experience of profound transformations has either been too terrible or involved too much disillusionment.'[127]

In order to identify a variety of possible explanations that have been described in the Belgian policies in Rwanda, some of them would seem to have implications for understanding the relationship between Belgian administrators, Catholic missionaries and Rwandans during Belgian rule. Despite that it is problematic to use memories collected in the 1990s to tell the history of the 1950s, but findings from three sources: observation, questionnaires

---

[126] Cfr. Newbury, D., Practical Anthropology, Vol.16n. 4, July-Aug. 1969.
[127] http://www.sedos.org/english/linden 2.htm

and interviews from bankers and Rwandan economists' responses have a common feature: they start with a view concerning poverty and unemployment, which argues that Belgian policies created inequalities in Rwanda. Paul Kagame recently stated that in Rwanda we appreciate the fact that, 'Since 2004, the World Bank Group has been at the forefront of shifting towards programmatic support with an intention of strengthening country policy ownership. This shift was based on the realisation that policy prescriptions and blue prints from the outside have never worked'.[128] The questions on social structure show that 87% agree about the poor economy in the country and another 89% agree with lack of development after independence.

Table 2: The Question of Social Structure

Agree %	Disagree %	Uncertain %
Why did the economic development fail in Rwanda?		
87	12	01
Was there any economic development after independence?		
89	06	05
Is employment related to the past Belgian rule?		
76	24	00
Did the Anglican Church provide social care?		
41	05	52
Ws the conflict related to economy?		
66	32	02

Analysis of these figures confirms that Belgian policies are the crux of the matter when economic structures changed in the early years. Criticism from bankers and

---

[128] New Times, the English newspaper on 15 September 2008, p.1

economists in Kigali and Butare National University often focused on society, culture and traditional institutions as having set patterns of rules and behaviour, which was how Rwandan society functioned. God is known, not by thinking out ideas about him/her, but by seeking and doing His will as made known to people and by a consciousness of right and wrong. They argued that new sources of income that were introduced by the Belgian administration and Asian merchants undermined the existing economic system.[129]

Also, it is essential to realise that according to Biblical teachings our knowledge of God is not reached by abstract speculation, as in Greek philosophy, but in the actual everyday business of living and of social relationships. What is important is that because there were such dramatic changes and loss of power of traditional institutions within a short period, the elements of tolerance or intolerance within the Belgian regime began to reverse the traditional structures and the traditional order of reality. There is a spiritual realisation that people's political conflicts do not exist in isolation. The question to ask became, 'What should the role of the missionary Churches have been during this period?' What could the Christian Churches have done when Rwandans were denied rights in the process of the changes? Respondents from the Anglican provincial office clarified that any denial of people's participation rights would have an obvious and drastic effect on the missionary churches, because the same people make up the Church. The theory subscribes to the belief that it was a matter of Church responsibility to stand firm on the truth and speak out for those denied their rights.[130]

This theory stems directly from the notion of Belgian superiority. The economic structure gave rise to the belief

---

[129] Interviews with Bankers at Kigali and Butare National University August 1998.

[130] Interviews at the Anglican provincial offices in Kigali, August 1998.

that the nature of the Belgian administration and its structure lacked ethical principles. In addition to its current effects, this led to controversies, conflict and the dysfunction of the economic structure after independence; all of which explains the problems the Belgian administration had to face and their refusal to engage Rwandans in being involved in the reality of interpreting and forming the required economic development.

This policy might be interpreted as 'ethnocentrism', in which the influence of discriminative development was channelled into the construction of a one-sided development in Rwanda. This development reveals a state machine embarked upon production, paving the way for a process of political conflict in the country. It is the introduction of this structural development that reflects a chronic subsequent failure of the country to achieve productivity. It is further argued by bankers and economists that everybody necessarily had an interest in the development and that the Belgian administrators and Rwandan authorities required a form of 'playing the game by the same rules'.[131]

In connection with responses to the question of economy, 66% agreed with the conflict being related to a poor economy and a lack of equality of participation in Belgian economics. This situation was seen as one bearing the seeds of conflict and exploitation and meant that people lost their value to their communities and the outside world in the form of unequal pay for workers, becoming objects of their colonisers and constantly being required to provide raw materials.[132]

Similarly, 89% agreed with the wider criticism of the form of developmental arrangements, which were described as inhumane, unjust and unnatural. At best, the process was

---

[131] Interviews with Bankers at Kigali and Butare National University August 1998,
[132] Questionnaires, August 1998.

described as an illustration of the Belgian attitude towards colonies, creating a situation said to be inextricably associated with underdevelopment and poverty and which subsequently exacerbated the conflict in Rwanda that ended in genocide. Uncertainty figures do not vary by more than 1% or 7% between these groups with regard to any response statements. 66% particularly agreed with criticism of the economic structure that seemed to have been associated with power, ethnocentrism and racial injustice in the 1950s to 1960s. This was a period in the colonies heralded as providing more than just an increase in the production of new knowledge and a proliferation of the new mode of ideological theories of rule and exploitation. It also saw a new destruction of Rwandan knowledge on a scale that had previously not been possible and which even damaged people's ability to operate in society. It is therefore the purpose of the analysis to assess whether the Belgian development had a direct bearing on people's lack of progress with reference to the lack of progress of Rwandan development in general.

Mbanda sees this as the germ of an idea in the earliest stage of Belgian development, having 'put the yeast to the ethnic tensions and nurtured them into fully blown hatred of each other.'[133] It is his explanation of how the use of ideological theories prepared the ground for exploitative constructs of economy and infrastructure in Rwanda during colonialism. It is this transformation, characterised by economic strategies within the social structures, which emanated from the Belgian ideology. It meant changing everything that previously had a meaning for people and had the effect of changing their reasons for being, which in a sense resulted in the old structures falling away. It is argued that a healthy relationship creates a positive impact

---

[133] Mbanda, L., (1998). Committed to Conflict, The Destruction of the Anglican Church in Rwanda, London: SPCK, p.39.

on social well-being and on other areas of general well-being as documented in 'The Human'. At this point, it is appropriate to start by examining a little more closely the assumption that the line of cause of economic conflict was as cited in J.M. Bernstein's analysis of 'grand narrative theory' or 'meta-narratives'.[134]

3.1 The Grand Narrative Theory

Of course, the line of causes of ethnic conflict in Rwanda is cited to exist in many areas. For instance there was the lack of respect towards Rwandan culture and traditional structures, ethnocentric theory and the capitalist theory of exploiting the poor. However, at this point the concern is not to diagnose the cause of change, but to ask the question, 'Why did Rwanda not develop like other industrial societies?' I can trace this question only by analysing the Belgian economic structure that was put in place. Mario Aguilar's analysis suggests that the potential for conflict originally started from the controversial grand narratives of the migration and origins of the Tutsi, the emphasis on Hutus as indigenous people and the total overshadowing of the Twa people of Rwanda.[135]

This theory of the Hutu as being the indigenous people of Rwanda was very much used during Habyarimana's regime when he told the Tutsi to return to Ethiopia, their homeland. Bernstein's idea of the 'grand narrative' theory provides an alternative explanation, mainly used as a development theory to maintain the argument that the problem for poor countries is related to their citizens' lack of will to be modern. The developmental theory argues that people did not embrace the idea of progress and that they

---

[134] Aguilar, M. I., (1996). The Rwanda Genocide and the Call to Deepen Christianity in Africa, Uganda: AMECEA GABA Publications Spearhead Nos. 148 – 150, p.2.
[135] Ibid.

lacked the kind of initiative that made the wealthy nations powerful.

Analysis of Belgian interests uncovers two categories: on the one hand there are the greedy 'rightists' who push the line that Western interests must be defended by force. On the other hand are the liberal conceptions that distortedly propagated the view that Rwandans did not have interests of their own; that Africans only existed to push the interests of others. Respondents said that missionaries used to ask young Christians whether they were pro-capitalist or pro-communist.[136] They further said that it was a liberalist misunderstanding of Rwandans to assume that they did not have their own interests; that if they did anything they would do it because they have been told to do so by the colonisers. That view still persists.[137] They added that the answer to the 'pro-capitalist or pro-communist' question was always 'We are pro-ourselves.'[138]

The Rwandan political developments can be understood by reference to psychoanalytical theory, which explains that people's relationships are elaborately entangled and fundamentally bound up within the enriched social and cultural environment. The paradigm of poor countries not being competitive within the modern world economy essentially focuses upon the methodological capitalist tools of economy and political order, argued as having created the Rwandan fate of being destined to supply the industrial world with agricultural and mineral resources, creating exploitation and a situation of dependency.[139]

---

[136] Interviews at Butare National University August 1998.
[137] Interviews at Gahini, Kigali and Butare National University August 1998.
[138] Ibid.
[139] Nash, M. (1967). In Tribal & Peasant Economies, Readings in Economic Anthropology Texas, Press Sourcebooks in Anthropology, London: University of Texas Press, pp.11-15.

Bishop Alexis Birindabagabo's view was that, 'by the end of the 1950s, the issue of racial discrimination in Rwanda had arrived in the Belgian policy agenda within social economy was embedded and operated within the Belgian economic system and continued to operate even after independence'.[140] Thus, in Rwanda the prevalence of Belgian racism promulgated ethnic discrimination, which played an insidious role in the economy isolation.

The central theme in this discrimination theory explains underachievement in the colonial economy. The racist theory was a set of attitudes and behaviour towards people of another race and culture, reinforced by belief of superiority and was championed in the twentieth century - notably based on the belief that races are distinct and can be graded as 'superior' or 'inferior'.

The argument became centred on understanding who possessed power and with it the ability to make people do things, which was seen as a consequence of the abolition of Rwandan traditional structure. It was also argued by A. T. Gana, that the influences for abolition of the Rwandan traditional structure were the three results of a broad theoretical concept. The liberally conceptualised economic structure as the facilitator of the good life was a life characterised by: (1) justice (2) security (3) freedom.[141] However, it is argued that the influence of that theoretical concept was a result of the need for manufacturing industries to underpin the Belgian capitalist economy. This economic structure was unfamiliar to Rwandans. When people were denied the use of the traditional structural system, Rwandans became like lost sheep, thrown on the street by the unwelcoming job market. Yet these changes responded to economical justice that observed results in

---

[140]An interview with Bishop Alexis Birindabagabo in Kigali, August 1998
[141]Cfr. Gana, A. T., (1994). The African Political Crisis and the Anglican Church in Africa, London: SPCK, p.232.

terms of outcomes; the relative distribution of wealth in terms of justifying fair play. To play under economic rules and policies set by the Belgian capitalist concepts was crucial, as we will further illustrate by reference to the World Bank debt.

Recent co-operative studies by the World Bank argued forcefully against embracing this fundamental misrepresentation of the historical facts.[142] It lacks the chronological order of events and the strategies applied in order to reconstruct the type of economy introduced in colonies. In a real sense, what does it mean to 'embrace or choose?' Those two words are best explained through analysis of the Belgian system and the way in which it operated. In fact, during the Belgian rule in Rwanda there was no choice of whether to embrace the changes or not; the process was one-sided, relying heavily upon the use of law and force. It follows from this that the theoretical analysis of change brings us back to the fact that making choices about the Belgian economy in the colonies tended to perpetuate the myth of legal objectivity. Its objective of neutrality should therefore be regarded with a degree of scepticism.

In practice, economic neutrality would have ensured that individuals competed on equal terms for goods, benefits and life chances, even though the outcomes may have been different. This was a way of promoting the ideal objective of providing services for all, with equal access to the means of competing to achieve in life. Fage argues that the theory of colonial rule did not include any financial assistance to stimulate the economic development of the local economy in colonial territories from the outset.[143] At the same time, the Belgian urge for the economic objective

---

[142]World Bank, "World Bank Debt Tables 1989/90 First Supplement 1989", Washington DC: World Bank, pp.157-158

[143]Oliver, R., & Fage, J. B., (1962). A Short History of Africa, London: Penguin African Library AP2.

of neutrality was replaced by the purely market-governed and impersonal laws of supply and demand.[144] It was especially debilitating for Rwandans to be denied a key role, but they did recognise that changes in their society were both inevitable and acceptable provided that the aim was developmental. However, one banker's view was that the lack of development was regarded as a weakness on the side of Belgian administrators. What was pointed out as being the Belgian administrators' weakness was that it was not realistic to offer Rwandans the opportunity to take responsibility to choose what they wanted to do. It is important to look at both sides of the argument. The fact is that during the Belgian rule in Rwanda the option for people to embrace was denied and was regarded as irrelevant by the Belgian administrators.

Whether or not that is true, high priority was given to the ideology of the capitalist economic structure. This affected all aspects of Rwandan development, with people denied any role in decision-making, clearly signalling that there were no prospects for equal opportunities. It is argued that there are consequences to increased latitude for local decision-making. As complex rationing decisions become more frequent, adherence to centralised and traditional rationing values may simply leave the world's poorest citizens with limited, unrealistic and culturally insensitive developmental options. This demanded that Rwandan people needed to develop their own rationing models with consideration for local social conditions and taking all the variables into consideration in the rationing equation.

However, their failure in not considering the importance of ethical notions in the Belgian rule in Rwandan social structures is argued as having distorted and

---

[144]Cfr. Brogden, M., (1982). The Police: Autonomy and Consent, London: Academic Press, p.55.

concealed the features of Belgian exploitation. Otherwise, there was no reason why Rwandans were denied the opportunity of working out their own future. Freedom, rights, equality and social justice all remained essential in a society that was based on a moral collective conscience and whose human relationships were subject to the traditional conceptions of common responsibility to each other as a community. The notion of shared values is at the heart of the views of most respondents who observed the lack of rational choice as a serious failure on the part of the social structure. It is argued that when one is allowed to engage in societal productivity, the human relationships of those involved will influence and interact with whatever other processes are occurring in relation to their daily working and general well-being.

I do wish, however, to highlight certain critical comments that it was not very inspiring and especially that the speed of change did not correspond with the realities in Rwanda. One advocate of this view submits that participation of the people would have enhanced the system in the process of change, if the proportional representation of all ethnic groups had allowed them to feel part of the changing society.

Harvey Cox is relevant here and is quite right to argue that wherever these rapid changes were introduced without care as to which party they would affect, this was 'simply a euphemism for revolution.'[145] In Rwanda this was indeed true and the evidence of it is the 1959 political revolution. This type of rationale provides a concept of either rationality or irrationality that represents the analytical understanding of the breakdown of people's relations during the changes in society under Belgian rule, while the elements of social reality show the Belgian administrators' objective was to dominate the colony. It is further argued

---

[145] Harvey, Cox, (1965). The Secular City, London: SCM Press, p. 107.

that these were theoretical ideas, produced and received in a colonial capitalist setting and which promoted the idea that knowledge either permitted or limited local people in their participation in developmental social structures. Thus, the decision of Belgian rule in avoiding fundamentally to engage Rwandan people in the transitional period of social structural changes, suggests that it was a climate in which differences were heightened and wherein 'ethnic distinction' was further entrenched.

Ethnic policy gradually created fear and loathing. Promoted as part of the politics and seen as the cause of considerable problems, it informs how Belgian ideology established a very serious difference among Rwandans. As has been argued above, the penultimate analysis of Belgian rule in Rwanda concludes that attitudes and behaviours changed in a way that had a deleterious effect and contributed to the situation underlining the social problems that followed later. If all this seems rather remote from an analysis of people's relations, it is not because two issues of greater spiritual significance had happened. It was related intimately to the earlier interpretations of Belgians as a political system of change, considering that what people went through was intolerable and that it created contradictions in society that left people spiritually weak and disintegrating. Archbishop Kolini described the earlier work of missionaries from all denominations and Belgian administration as not seeming to have discovered or to have deliberately chosen to ignore the rituals and religious beliefs that were enshrined in traditional structures, politics and economy.

It is here that the role of the traditional structure was important for people, taking into account causal factors explained by respondents, one after the other, as deficiencies in the Belgian economic structure, isolating and depriving people from participation in the new economic structural changes. Bishop Alexis Birindabagabo quoted the report of Bishop Sangu who expressed this concern at the 1974 Rome Synod. Bishop Sangu argued that too many innovations were the work of missionaries who disregarded the great traditions of the continent and wanted to change things after their own ideas. In addition, Bishop Alexis said the work of a missionary or the work of any expatriate might miss the point if he/she does not first try to gain an insight into people's ideas of what they feel needs to be changed. The approach to change of the Belgian administrators and missionaries was very much criticised in that they came with the intent of changing everything that existed in the country. It is argued by elderly Anglican Church members at Kigali diocese that underlying scepticism was widely discounted as the influence of the Belgian agenda mostly obscured or denied the traditional heritage. Mystical celebrations were treated as if they were magic, curses, witchcraft or to do with ancestral spirits; an attitude found offensive and hurtful by Rwandans.[146]

According to respondents, the Belgian impact began to have its influence on the course of political developments as expected and all such developments were interpreted as infringements of human rights. It was in this period that Rwandan culture, rituals and traditional institutions were treated as primitive beliefs, which had no place in Christianity or in modern society. Actually that was not the case, but even if it had been, the beliefs could have been respected as part of the legitimate pride that people take in their society. This argument will be explained later in Chapter Six. Adrian Hastings notes that missionaries considered themselves to be messengers of change.[147] However, Welbourn argues that missionaries brought with them not only the Christian Gospel, but also an attitude that

---

[146]Interviews in Kigali August 1998.
[147]Hastings, A., (1979). A History of African Christianity 1950-1975, Cambridge: Cambridge University Press, UK, p. 22.

was more characteristic of nineteenth century scientific rationalisation.[148] The European missionaries from all denominations saw their role as having come to abolish satanic worship and ritual celebrations in Rwanda. Hence, returning to the missionary interpretation of Ryangombe, this ritual was soon exaggerated and politicised as the Hutu's submission to the King of Tutsi.

Nevertheless, this rationalisation is discounted by Desouter who studied the traditional ritual, based on the mythical story of a certain Ryangombe, which played an important role in the understanding and celebration of the unity of the Rwandan population.[149] Furthermore, Kimenyi explains the traditional Ryangombe ritual, which is based on the mythical story of a man of that name. From his findings he stated that it 'played an important role in the understanding and celebration of the unity of the Rwandan population.'[150] This had been identified as perhaps a hidden ethnocentric sense of superiority and, at this period, racism did not allow Catholic missionaries to see the true role of the Ryangombe ritual.[151]

This shows that mystical celebrations were often misunderstood by missionaries. In this instance, they confused the idea of Ryangombe with traditional leadership. The characteristic of Ryangombe as a ritual is sacred to all Rwandans and Max Gluckman refers to the ritual performance as being highly conventionalised and by which people believe that they are helped, by mystical means outside of sensory observations and control, to

---

[148]Cfr. Welbourn, F. B., (1965). East African Christian, London: Oxford University Press, p. 37.

[149]Desouter, Serge A. (1995). Tyangombe-rituelen als buffer tussen de machtigen en horigen in het oude Rwanda. *Wereld en Zending* 24(2):58- 64

[150]Kimenyi, A., (1989). Kinyarwanda and Kirundi Names, The Edwin Millen Press, pp. 47-48

[151]Cfr. Pirouet, L., (1989). Christianity Worldwide, Anglican Church History 4: AD1800 Onwards, London: SPCK, p.168.

protect, purify or enrich the participants and their group.[152] The ritual gave expression to the relationship that is purported to exist between people and the surrounding world. Moreover, the ritual established a bond between those who performed the rites. In fact, respondents argued that the dislike of these rites by Belgian administrators and missionaries was mostly to do with the way that they brought together Hutu, Tutsi and Twa during ritual celebrations.

Two of the things that impressed and attracted people were the ways in which rituals were conducted and the sacredness of the ceremony. During the occasion, all people became one, united without differences between Tutsi, Hutu or Twa, while the celebrant's focus was on the ritualistic ceremony. A similar example of such a ritual would be the Islamic ritual ceremony of Mecca, which unites Muslims all over the world. Rituals have many functions, both at the level of the individual and for groups. They can channel and express emotions, guide and reinforce forms of behaviour, support or subvert the status quo, being about change, or restore harmony and balance. Rituals also have a very important role in healing. They may be used to maintain the life forces and fertility of the earth and to ensure right relationships with the unseen world, whether of spirits, ancestors, deities, or other supernatural forces.[153]

John Taylor, in The Primal Vision, is again relevant here. Taylor vividly describes the network of rituals that gave security and meaning to life in Africa. He explains the vertical relationships going back through father and grandfather to the ancestors so that people felt they were an

---

[152]Gluckman, Max, (1966), "Politics, Law and Ritual in Tribal Society", Oxford: Blackwell, p.224.
[153]Cfr. Bowie, F. (2000). "Ritual Theory, rites of passage and ritual violence", The Anthropology of Religion, Oxford: Basil Blackwell, 151-85. ISBN 0631 20848, p.150

integral part of the community.[154] Returning to developments in Rwanda, respondents lamented the speed of change.[155]

Traditionally, when people decided what was good and what was wrong they were guided by the approval or disapproval of their community, rather than by personal appreciation. This tradition gave stability and security in an unsafe world, with respondents believing that, as anything new was seen to be dangerous, this perpetuated the Rwandans' reliance on Ryangombe consultation in decision-making. The study on Belgian influence attaches importance to major issues, including the lack of consideration for people's fundamental values and the rapid change in Rwandan society brought about by Belgian rule, as well as the influence of European missionaries.

These rapid changes raised two major points of concern: Firstly, it was argued that Rwandans were treated as if they did not matter, or had nothing to offer. Belgium, Britain, France and Germany had much more influence than the Rwandan Kings, who were not even consulted at the time.[156] According to a group of elderly Rwandans, 'The Rwandan was always told what to do and felt insulted.'[157] Secondly, the Rwandans were angered by the absurdity of changing every structure in the country, when the changes did not necessarily solve their social problems. The concern about change surfaced in the various discourses of respondents, who believed that, if the Catholic Church and the Belgians had allowed the King and chiefs to act as the custodians of Rwandan traditional culture and customary values, there would have been a

---

[154] Taylor, J. V., (1963). The Primal Vision, London: S.C.M), chapter 8.
[155] Interview at Butare National University, August 1998.
[156] Mbanda, L., (1998). Committed to Conflict, The Destruction of the Anglican Church in Rwanda, London: SPCK, p. 38.
[157] Interviewing elderly Anglican Church members at Gahini Mission, July 1998.

different Rwanda.[158] In their view, the trouble was that at this stage, the Belgian administrators were clearly participating fully in the creation of bureaucratic and political power in their own interest. An elderly respondent put it succinctly, saying that these changes in Rwandan society sowed seeds of fear, hatred, envy and helplessness by uprooting old knowledge and values without replacing them with anything relevant and viable.[159]

This is the kind of the situation Bishop Sheppard describes: 'To go to such an area from Europe, imagining that you know everything and that the people there can't help themselves, would destroy the value of going.'[160] Certainly, during this period of Belgian rule in Rwanda, the Catholic Church's missionaries, in particular, failed to slow the political drive of the Belgians. Ian Corrine Brown adds that 'No culture or custom is odd to the people who practice it.'[161] The point being made is that individuals live within institutions. If these institutions are traditionally structured, they will produce individuals with a consciousness of their societal values that is dictated by their daily lives.

The Catholic missionaries' Christian belief in the sanctity of established authority suggests that they failed to persuade their fellow countrymen and women to preserve the traditional institutions and treasured cultural values of the Rwandan people. There was no excuse for missionaries not to act against the Belgian practice of control over the way that people governed themselves. There was no consideration of, or listening to what the Rwandans would suggest. It is even right to agree with respondents that the assumption on the part of the Belgian administrators was

---

[158]Interviews Byumba, Butare August 1998.
[159]Ibid.
[160]Sheppard, D., (1983). Bias to the Poor, London: Hodder and Stoughton, p. 22.
[161]Brown, I. C., (1963). "Understanding Other Cultures", Prentice Hall, Inc., Englewood Cliffs, New Jersey, pp. 14 – 5.

that the Belgian system would operate forever. Respondents stressed the absence of the missionaries' consideration of local values, as demonstrated by laying down their own rules. They were widely criticised for behaving as if missionaries had come to change uncivilised society and to nurture accepted Western behaviour as being suitable for Rwandans.[162]

On the other hand, it is argued that what was required in the process of change was anthropological understanding of the people to whom Belgian administrators and missionaries sought to bring change. Luzbetak argues how necessary it was for the missionaries to 'know something about the mythopoeic mentality; about family relations, structures and obligations; about the concept of hierarchy and authority.'[163] However, it is argued in the social theory of change that, once you have the idea of society, there exists the possibility of asking what sort of change is possible or desirable, for consideration can be given to the values that people espouse wherever they live in the world. Nothomb argues that 'by trying to limit the African mentality to only one of them, one would end with a partial and one-sided understanding.'[164]

Likewise, Frankel observes that 'the real task is not to force change but to include it in a manner, which will be meaningful to the members of the societies it affects.'[165] The point is clearly made by the Belgians' insistence on teaching Flemish to Rwandans, despite it being of no use in

---

[162]Ibid.
[163]Luzbetak, L. J. (1963), "The Church and Culture", an applied anthropology for the religious worker. Divine Word Publication Techny. Illinois USA, p. 6.
[164]Nothomb, D., (1965). "Un Humanism African", Editions Lumen Vitae, Bruxelles, p.16.
[165]Frankel, S. H., (1955). The Economic Impact on Underdeveloped Societies, Cambridge: Harvard University Press, pp. 78- 9.

their everyday lives.[166] On the other hand, this suggests that, unlike today, most missionaries from all Christian denominations during the period had no training in how to relate to other cultures before recruitment for missionary work. Whilst it is true that every cultural group is to some degree ethnocentric, the Belgian administration of this period allowed missionaries to instil the belief that European leadership was superior. A term to describe this was coined by Amin Summer, a social evolutionist, who defined it as the viewpoint that, 'One's own group is the centre of everything,' against which all other groups are judged.[167]

3.2 A Critical Analysis of the Belgian Administrative Social Structure

The concept of economic development is rather hydra-headed, in that it can be approached from various fronts and disciplines. Just like the concept of religion, which is also difficult to define precisely, development is not easily defined or described as being this or that. This is simply because it cuts through many disciplines and several facets of life, such that the 'definitions are contextual and contingent upon the ideological, epistemological or methodological orientation of their purveyors.'[168] This is why it is very difficult to give a precise answer to the question 'What is development?' Often, someone might be tempted to ask in response, 'What kind of development?' The implication is that within the scope of the argument in this chapter, I will focus on the socio-economic development of humans, where a definition of development

---

[166]Barham, E. L., (1961). Ruanda, a Bird's Eye View, London: Ruanda Mission CMS, p. 6.
[167]http://www.en.wikipedia.org/wiki/Ethnocentrism/17/9/07
[168]Simon, D. & Anders, N., (Eds), "Development as Theory and Practice", Harlow. Longmann, 1999, p.19

cannot easily be found for its framework and direction, especially when it relates to economic development and conflict theories.

In this case, Simon David and Anders Norman have produced an economic definition for Rwandan development that considers the basic needs and quality of life of Rwandan people and the aspirations of the people to meet these needs, as well as 'enhancing their living standards and emulating advanced industrialised countries in some variant of classical modernisation strategies'.[169] Therefore, this chapter argues that any phenomenon that impedes the full sustainable realisation of the basic needs and quality of life for people is not development-orientated. The intention of this study from the outset is to base my argument on the subjective local experience and human suffering, the violence and the struggle that was embedded in the Belgian economy seen as perceptually contributing to the Rwandan conflict.

Nevertheless, what seems to be true is that most poor countries like Rwanda have been reduced, as one respondent described it, to 'the status of economic slaves and beggars.[170] It is for this reason that, at the centre of this chapter, I have decided to assess Rwandan economic history to see whether the lack of Rwandan economic development is linked to the causes of genocide. The intention is to amplify different voices that have thrown valuable light on the Belgian-constructed economic reality, in order to assess the trustworthiness of these criticisms, particularly from those who have argued that the Belgian economy created massive problems that led the country into political crisis. This is because it presents a situation where it is often thought that the issues of Rwandan

---

[169]Ibid.
[170]Interviews with Bankers at Kigali August 1998.

conflict can be tackled in isolation, kept apart from the economic issues.

3.3 The Lack of Ethnics in the Social Structure of Belgian Rule

Emphasis is laid on analysing the form of injustice embodied in the development. For instance, to consider criticisms, if one pursues the constructionist view of the development as being directly responsible for Belgian power and capitalist reality, the process unveils strategies for perpetuating capitalist interests and exploitation on a wider scale. Furthermore, it is argued that a proper perspective on the concept of development is imperative in order to allay the result of failure of economic development in Rwanda. Thus, development must be seen as the building-up of people so that they can forge a future for themselves. Denis Goulet is one of the rare economic scholars who provides a crystal-clear concept of development. Goulet argues that authentic development must aim at the total realisation of human capabilities. Promoting positive methodology, he further adds that 'Development is simply a means to the human ascent...all humanity is viewed as receiving a summons to assume its own identity'.[171]

The criticism of the classic Belgian social theorist's drive of economic rationality, which appeared as the main vehicle of ethnic distinction conflict, was imported into ethnocentric theories of market that so often involved the exclusion of Rwandans from decision making in their own country. It turned them into labourers in industry, where they were 'supervised' but never 'supervisor'. Therefore, this thesis explores people's views about Rwandan social

---

[171]Goulet, Denis, (1971). The Cruel Choice: A New Concept in the Theory of Development, Centre for the study of development and social change, New York: Atheneum, pp. 295-312.

structures and focuses on criticisms from local respondents. It looks at rights and wrongs and places the blame for the political consequences of dramatic polarisation in Rwanda upon the Belgian belief in a superstructure, which failed to support the traditional institutions in functioning as a whole.

I wish to argue that, if the objective of the Belgian administration in Rwanda was to create a superstructure, then it was obliged to ensure that all people were protected and secured from 'cradle to grave'. In other words, issues surrounding the superstructure theory have been said to have had a terrible impact on the country as a whole and have influenced how people relate to each other. The effect of under development is directly upon the people. If it is, then I am persuaded to argue that if a building is created on shaky foundations, it is bound to crumble, however good the materials used in the superstructure.

The actual criticism of who advanced this theory was that its design was unrealistic for a development that could not service all Rwandans and instead reduced them to entrenched inequalities, where young Rwandans were pushed on to the streets in a search for unavailable jobs. In effect, the analysis of one of the areas, if not the most dominant and in which race bias has been clearly perpetuated, is the development process of countries, societies and humanity as a whole. It is argued that the concept of development must focus upon human values, raising several factors necessary for the basic process of development: (i) growth in output of goods and services; (ii) satisfactory progress towards social goals; (iii) relative equity in the distribution of the benefits of development and (iv) a liberating progress and humanisation. In this way, I will argue that to ignore the importance of a long-term liberating strategy at the early stage of economic structuring was to enable a few to exploit the majority. In this case, ignoring the participation of all was a conspicuous theory that, in the long-term development process, favoured some people and disadvantaged others.

Peter Uvin specifically draws attention to the fact that for the vast majority of poor Rwandans, life was characterised by great 'structural violence' as evidenced by extreme inequality, absence of life chances, social exclusion and deprivation of self-respect.[172] He argues that the exclusion of equal, ethical values had a negative effect on long-term performance and economic policies. The superstructure conception is therefore seen as a result of a myriad of factors, with the over-arching element being the structural violence of the Belgian economic superstructure. This laid the groundwork for the conflict as a result of the pursuit of ideological policies that contained polarised theories of conflict during the Belgian rule in Rwanda. The consequences of this were far-reaching, characterised by Rwanda producing what Rwandans did not consume, yet consuming what they did not produce, exporting raw materials and importing finished goods.

Elderly respondents of Gahini argued that the political structure that was introduced by the Belgian administrators seriously undermined the traditional structures and the chief's order of authority.[173] In this respect, the Belgian economy meant a loss of the country's sovereignty, which in turn meant the distortion of production. It is this idea of creating a social structure, but limiting its exercise, which is particularity distinctive of Belgian economic interests and, in a way, the control of people.

It is also important to note that other influences were behind much that was happening in Rwanda during the Belgian rule. A good example is found in Maquet's views, which tend to obscure the real agenda of the Belgians.

---

[172]Uvin, P. and Warren, M. A. C., 1994, Aiding Violence: The Development Enterprise in Rwanda, Forwarded, London: Anglican Church Missionary Society, pp.3 - 7.
[173]Elderly survivors at Gahini Mission interviewed July 1998.

Anthropologist scholars like Maquet argue about the theory of ethnic differences between Hutu and Tutsi. It is even arguable that, ethnic conflict has its roots in Maquet theories. Maquet raises suspicion about the traditional arrangements, arguing that they served only the Tutsi in dominating the Hutus. Maquet characterises the traditional ritual arrangements as a 'caste system'. The two principal castes referred to are Hutu agriculturalists and Tutsi herders.[174] Maquet points out two methods used by Tutsis to exploit Hutus: (i) The Tutsis only made up ten percent of the population, which enabled the minority to be served by the majority. (ii) The physical appearance of the Tutsis, with their slender figure and light skin, was used as a sign of superiority over the Hutus, who are of ordinary stature.

This clearly illustrates how even scholars defended the Belgian policies and ideology of ethnicity, suggesting that ethnic division had existed even before the advent of Belgian rule in Rwanda.[175] The overall picture that emerges from the development of these negative observations suggests that ethnic distinction was in the interest of the Rwandans. However, unlike the writings of some scholars, 'Ubuhake or Umuheto' (a mechanism called 'Ubuhake' by the Tutsi or 'Umuheto' by the Hutu) was mainly an economic system, which enabled a sort of symbiotic relationship between the wealthy and privileged on one hand and the less privileged on the other. It was a system in which ordinary Hutu, Tutsi and Twa participated and mutually benefited.[176]

Maquet's assertion was disputed as misleading by some respondents. In other words, it is important to gain insight into the criticisms raised about the nature of Belgian

---

[174]Maquet, J. J., (1954). Le Système des Relations Sociales dans le Rwanda Ancien. Tervuren: Musée, (Annales du Musée royale du Congo belge, Sciences de l'homme, ethnocide, 1), p.81.
[175]http://www.jha.greatlakes/July 20, 2000
[176]http://www.rwangagateway.org/mot.php3?id;mot=20

economic development in terms of the national economic growth and human development required for a stable society, with 'law and order' as its prime concern. Ubuhake was voluntarily subscribed to and was entered into for many reasons; including protection and anticipation, as well as getting favours from the most affluent and powerful. Maquet's criticism seems to have missed the point that the arrangements had not aimed only at Hutus serving Tutsis. Furthermore, the problem with Maquet's claim is that he seems to have looked at just one side of the Ubuhake arrangements without considering the whole process and how it served Rwandans in general. In its defence, Mbanda argued that Ubuhake 'created strong close relationships'.[177]

One of Mbanda's examples is that of a Tutsi who recalled stories from his parents, who had left their homes in search of Ubuhake and the wealth that the Rwandan culture could offer. Those recruited in the Ubuhake system learned a lot from the Kings and the chiefs during their Ubuhake period of contracted employment and, when the time came, they returned home with herds of cattle to impress their families and peers.[178] However, Maquet seems to be less concerned with understanding its role, in favour of locating it in the 'caste system'. A more pressing question is 'Why does Maquet not mention that the poor Tutsi also served Hutus, becoming wealthier in the process?' Furthermore, Maquet contradicts the observations made earlier by Bishop Classe, who stated, 'The term "Tutsi" often refers not to origin, but to social conditions or wealth, especially as regards cattle. Whoever is chief, or is rich will often be referred to as Tutsi.'[179]

---

[177]See Mbanda, L., (1998). Committed to Conflict, The Destruction of the Anglican Church in Rwanda, London: SPCK, p.10.
[178]Ibid.
[179]Clacce, L. P., (1935). Ils Trébuchaient dans les Ténèbres. Grands Lacs, no. special, 1 March.

The underlying assumption here is that Maquet's political ideas were rooted in a capitalist system precisely because it was so diffused in its operation and political design and the dealings seemed neutral. Given that there was widespread use of Belgian economic interests distinguished by exploitation, Maquet was unable to question the capitalists' lack of care that was geared for exploitation and, at the same time, created an underclass that was socially excluded and living in poverty.

Instead, Maquet chose to criticise the Ubuhake, overshadowed by the Belgian view of capitalism that made a few individual Rwandans richer, while the majority became poorer. In other words, Rwandans were relegated to a subordinate position that this thesis wishes to highlight. The local criticism of the Belgian policies, which are partly seen as the source of conflict, was embedded in a Rwandan economic structure that created human suffering, violence and the struggle of one people against another. As outlined above, the ideas of social structural functionalism theory offer an explanation that has been highly influential in the 1950's and 1960's in shaping, what Talbot Parsons correctly observed in his theory of structural function, as promotion of the idea of supremacy.

The idea of supremacy meant that the Belgian ideological economic structure was associated with an ethnocentric belief of supremacy hidden in the use of biological theory and opened the door to the creation of exploitative economic structures.[180] Analysis of the history of Belgian rule so far, indicates that there was a sidelining of Rwandans' roles; the process of socio-economic development was no exception to the racial trend. It seemed rather to be one of the core areas, where the polarised nature of human development was clearly manifested and it

---

[180]Parsons, T., (1969). Politics and Social Structures, New York: The Free Press. p. 64 also sees Rwanda Documentary, Appendix IV.

received much attention. This exclusion was expressed by local interviewees in terms of them being treated as if they had inferior brainpower or a lack of leadership qualities. The use of this biological theory convincingly explains the approach and practice of the Belgian phenomenon, as analysed appears similar to Berger and Luckmann's theory of constructed reality. In relation to Belgian economic development in Rwanda, Berger and Luckmann's theory of how reality is constructed, ordered and maintained, commits the familiar error of attempting to divorce the concept from the problem of the natural human fear of uncertainty. The economic system introduced into Rwanda was, from the viewpoint of the Rwandan economists who defined development structures in the country, not acceptable. Perhaps this lack of acceptance could be described as Berger has described it as 'a psychological fear of the future'. [181]

It therefore calls for an analysis of psychological economic theories, since the device, in an age of colonial questions bequeathed by modernity, provides a sense of connection to the earlier period of the Belgian rule in Rwanda. So, for example, architectural design incorporated ideas in the extreme form, approaches that concentrated on characteristics of the biological or psychological in the focus of developing Rwandan economic structures. If differences could be found, it is thought that the influence of the early work of Lombroso, (November 6, 1836 – October 19, 1909) an Italian criminologist who became famous and then infamous, for his attempts to find biological differences among people, would provide a lead. Although Lombroso's specific ideas were largely

---

[181]Berger Peter, (1966). Invitation to Sociology: London: Penguin, p. 104.

discredited, this did not stop the continuation of the search for biological differences between colonies.[182]

It is argued that the theory of biological differences might be due to the influence of the nature of rationality and subjectivity embedded in the ethnic distinction theory, a subtle combination of both the ethnocentric and also the ideological, a mechanism of economic exploitation that was used in colonial days.[183] This is seen as a theory that was 'conflict making', which is to say that ideally the period was a convergence of post colonialist and postmodernist programmes in new cultural politics. Bankers in Rwanda were led by capitalist interests to generate new theoretical perspectives that challenged Rwandan traditionally established institutions and in practical terms, it is argued by Rwandan economists that this is why the Belgian ethnocentric belief around economic interests became the colony's economic reality.

However, this ethnocentric belief created divisions that seem to have been aimed at disparities of group power in the country, evidenced by the lack of naturalisation and neutralisation of the market. This strikingly reveals how the reconstruction of the economic system seemed to have had no long-term meaningful purpose for Rwanda. Therefore, a situation analogous to that of the Belgian economic development in Rwanda is regarded as having been based on the concept of ethnocentric economic structure or superstructure.[184]

---

[182]Cfr. http://www.d.umn.edu/~jhamlin1/biological.html/14/7/07; Coleman, Alice (1988). 'Design Disadvantage and Design Improvement; The Criminologist, vol. 12, p.20
[183]Lakeland, (1998), Post Modernity: Christian Identity in a Fragmented Age, Minneapolis, Minn.: Fortress, p.12
[184]Cf. Pocock, J.G.A., "Burke and the Ancient Constitution: A Problem in the History of Ideas (1960)"J.G.A. Pocock, Vol. 3, No. 2, in The Historical Journal, xiiv, 2 (1969), pp. 285–301.

Because it operates through ethnocentric theories, the psychological fear that can be traced as being linked with the Belgian policies was designed to discriminate against Rwandans, as they did not accommodate the circumstances of social groups or plans for long-term economic development in Rwanda. This is why the Belgian economic reality construction theory is open to a number of criticisms.[185] Accordingly, Rwandan Bankers argue that people lose the incentive for innovation, knowing that any benefits that resulted from their inventions and discoveries will simply be appropriated by the governing class, which in this case was the Belgian administration. In particular, a common criticism in table 2 on page 73, (figures agreed by 87% of respondents), was the way the transformation of traditional economic structures lacked ethical operating principles for social responsibility and values that took account of social welfare. Michael Tedaro argues that development is 'the process of improving human lives'.[186] Also, 76% in table 2 argued with bankers interviewed that, having abolished the Rwandan traditional system of alignment of the economy to cater for the social wellbeing of the population, it was important to provide 'tools to the pool', in order to promote future economic management and avoid creating the mass unemployment that exists in Rwanda today.

A positive, pragmatic structured and functional approach was essential because, as in every society and as previously detailed, Rwanda had beliefs and systems in operation, in this case based in part on a sense of economic collective duty known as 'Uburetwa'. The system is described by Dalton as 'the bonds of kinship, which

---

[185]Cfr. http://www.cpnm.org/new/English/articles_news/rootcause_karma.htm
[186] Tedaro, M. P., (1977). Economics for a Developing World, an Introduction to Principles, Problems and Policies for Development, London & New York: Longman, p. 6.

structure families, clans and Kings, are often the bonds which organise economic activities'.[187] Moreover, unlike the hunter-gatherer societies, Uburetwa had a well-organised operational system to apply social welfare and private ownership before it was greatly distorted and undermined by the Belgian administration. The accurate identification of these developments had wider ramifications. Linden argues from the point that 'The transformation of a complex 'feudal' social mobility into a bureaucratic Belgian State hardened social and economic differences into rigid class differences and finally resulted in 'tribal conflict'.[188]

Rene Lemarchand adds that, to the contrary, the image projected by the media of the patterns of exclusion brought to light during and after independence cannot be justified as 'deep-seated, ancestral enmities'.[189] This is true. Tracing the origin of ethnic conflict within the Belgian administrative economic structure shows the likelihood of conflict being created in the long run, in any sort of economy where it does not take account of the local view. Linden further argues that the economic predicament of Rwanda was certainly a primary factor.[190]

In respect of human improvement, this chapter has argued that social changes were related to economic interests in Belgians who had a greatly distorted view of the Rwandan people's relationships. It was further argued that

---

[187]Dalton, G., (Ed.), (1967). Tribal & Peasant Economics, Readings in Economic Anthropology, Texas: Press Sourcebooks in Anthropology, p. 8
[188]Linden, Ian, (1998). "The Church and Genocide, Lessons from Rwandese Tragedy", in Baum, Gregory & Wells, Harold (Des), The Reconciliation of peoples, Challenges to the Churches, Maryknoll, NY: Obis Books; Geneva: WCC Publications, pp.41-43.
[189]Lemarchand, Rene (1994). Managing Transition Anarchies: Rwanda, Burundi and South Africa in Comparative Perspective, The Journal of Modern African Studies, 32, 4, Cambridge: University Press, p.598.
[190]Ibid. p.45.

it was essential for local people to participate in the process of their own future. Three important aspects were raised by the Rwandan economists, suggesting that it was essential for the Belgian development to take certain steps. Firstly, people's income, food consumption levels, shelter, clothing, medical services and education must be raised. Secondly, conditions that provided basic needs and maintaining people's self-esteem through the establishment of structures that promoted human dignity and respect must be created. Thirdly, people's freedom to choose must be increased, because it is argued that participation is the practice of freedom and that failure to encourage this and to enable local people to participate fully in the development process would be loss of opportunity for long-term development.

Conclusion

In conclusion, the relevance of the legitimisation of Rwanda's cultural economic structures from the above explanations suggests that the production of knowledge can be a collective and social process in a stronger and more active sense than Berger and Luckmann considered. The problem of the choice of economic structure in Rwanda and the refusal to engage Rwandans in the interpretative social economic reality is argued by Lenski to be an ethnocentric belief, but one that provides a better explanation of relationship between race and Belgian development than that provided by earlier racist theorists.[191] It is therefore argued that, in effect, the refusal amounted to privileging only colonisers as far as development was concerned in Rwanda. Yet the renewal of traditional structures was needed, not their abolition, providing liberation into

---

[191] Lenski, G., Nolan, P. and Lenski, J., (1995). Human Societies, an Introduction to Macro Sociology, Seventh Edition, New York: McGrawHill, Inc.,p.174

responsibility for specific, though limited, aims in connection with the lives of Rwandans and the needs of the static developmental sections of the population, notably children and old people.

Internationally standardised rules and regulations needed to ensure that, in theory at least, all people were treated equally, were either not available or not considered important in Rwanda. On the other hand, it is argued that the equality of treatment in the Belgian administration was necessary, so as to offer opportunities for emphasis to be placed upon rules guaranteeing equality of treatment. The lack of local participation was seen as an infringement of people's rights. Any process that undervalues people and discounts their participation as a fundamental feature of its reality should be treated with profound suspicion. In fact, most people from Rwanda have overwhelmingly argued that such a fundamental desire should have been realised. It was further argued that this was Belgian discrimination of the highest order, as it lacked respect for Rwandans. Respect is a fundamentally important quality for participation as a citizen and a part of the human community.[192]

The next chapter explores the question of differences in the interpretation of the causes of genocide in Rwanda in 1994. The main aim here is to try to highlight differences between interpretations of the Rwandan conflict. Some saw it as an historical African tribal problem, others as hatred between Hutu and Tutsi, while yet another interpretation suggests it was political propaganda during Habyarimana's regime. The focus of the next chapter will be to try to compare alternative claims. For instance the views of journalists and of academia are compared to show how interpretations of the Rwandan conflict and genocide differed between local and foreign agencies.

---

[192]Interviews with Bankers at Kigali, August 1998.

Chapter Four

Part I: Genocide and its Aftermath: Analysis of Interviews and Literature

The Interpretation of Genocide

4.0 Introduction

In seeking to understand the underlying reasons for the Rwandan genocide and to examine local explanations of the effect of Belgian ethnic ideology, the causes of the conflict are discussed and attention is drawn to some of the interpretations that give very passive and superficial reasons for the Rwandan conflict. It would be helpful to know what local people are saying and giving as the reason for the conflict. As for the press, they have never searched hard enough to know what local people say about the conflict. Often overlooked is how many explanations at the time of and indeed after the genocide, paid very little attention to underlying causes, such as ethnic ideology and economic factors.

According to local respondents, it was a power game and poor governance, rather than ethnic hatred and they added that it is wrong to interpret the conflict as just an outbreak of supposedly deep ethnic hatred, nursed over centuries.[193] It was argued by both academia and Anglican Church local respondents at Kigali and Butare (correctly, I believe) that the underlying assumption of the outsider's somewhat pathological interpretive use of 'natural hatred' creates the impression that these are people who are

---

[193] Interviews in Kigali and Butare National University July 1998.

fundamentally different from one another and that these differences were the cause of the conflict.[194]

The aim of this chapter is to consider the complex ethnic conflict associated with the socio-economic basis of the crisis. Some foreign reporters and writers have different interpretations of fundamental, underlying assumptions and misconceptions of facts that are perceived differently from the way in which local representatives view them. However, if these interpretations are inaccurate or false they may end up hindering rather than helping. As foreign journalism describes it, almost the entire conflict is shown as Hutu and Tutsi mutual hatred and since ethnic cleansing has hatred as a characteristic, this has distorted the cause of the conflict. Another error concerns the fact that foreign observers, since they tend to come from the upper echelons of industrialised society, in practice can interpret particular economic issues and political shifts in ways that are unrepresentative of local issues. Other academic writers, to a lesser extent, pass on their prejudices, often based on erroneous information.

The problem is not only to explain and establish the causes of the ethnic crisis in Rwanda, but also to examine critically the explanations that are being offered within the media and the broader public sphere in the hope of establishing the root cause of the political crisis in Rwanda, which we have said has been interpreted as if it was caused by natural dislike between the Hutu and Tutsi.[195] The first step is to consider which theory and interpretation of practice was influential in the Belgian operation. The second step is to closely consider interviews with elderly people, Anglican Church leaders, local politicians, intellectuals, former insurgents and the genocide survivors

---

[194]Ibid.
[195]Brandstetter, Anna-Maria, (1998). 'Ethnic or Socioeconomic Conflict? Political Interpretations of the Rwandan Crisis', Institute for Ethnology and Africa Studies, Germany: Mainz University, p. 432

who have been affected by the violence in order to build up a picture of the consequences of these events and lay bare the political and social context, which has made it so intractable (see appendix 1V). Additionally, through a process of analysis, I will also establish whether the political crisis in Rwanda was caused by the natural dislike of Hutu and Tutsi or whether it had to do with a political ideology of ethnic distinction as used in Belgian policy.

Anna-Maria Brandstetter was correct to argue that it seems to be all the more necessary to trust the interpretations developed by the local actors in the Rwandan arena.[196] And there are three reasons for trusting local interpretation; firstly, that local voices are conspicuously only referred to, but their views are never fully expressed, merely used in passing comments, which appear to endorse the belief that it was hatred that prevented Rwandan people from living together and secondly, that the contribution of local people best fits with the eyewitness accounts justifying the eyewitness role of presence function. Thirdly, I offer an alternative argument that journalistic commentary and other explanations often oversimplified the conflict by suggesting the cause to be 'tribal' or 'ethnic' hatred, thereby ruling out the possibility that the underlying causes might have been a combination of different factors.[197] Thus it is argued that the focus of foreign media tends to be a chain of reasoning and not necessarily a statement of actual facts that respondents believed. It oversimplified complex matters and made an unfair judgement, constructively placed on those areas of interest to an industrial society, but unrepresentative of the reality of the conflict.[198]

Respondents and International Alert both agreed equally that the problem with the foreign media is that they

---

[196]Shriver, W. D., Woodstock Report, March 1996, No. 45.
180 Cfr. http://www.ambarwanda.org.uk/genocide/index.htm/9/6/06
[198]Interviews at Gahini, Butare, Byumba and Kigali July 1998

attempt to provide instant answers to everything. At Butare National University, respondents criticised their pure reasoning and observed that the media needs to exercise responsible journalism 'and seek facts before publishing false stories that misinform the public and impact negatively on the country and Rwandans'.[199] This means that the facts as stated by the Western media fall on one side or only expose abuses of human rights when their own interests are affected.[200]

I will briefly attempt to look more analytically at the interpretation of the reasons for outsiders taking one view; it seems to have been identified by respondents as being due to an inability to interpret events that created the so called 'hatred' in society.[201] Hence it can be argued that the failure of past shortcomings in conventional research included the overriding tendency on the part of journalists not to challenge their own presumptions, a lack of awareness of the actual situation and also a failure to take into account the extent to which they excluded the so called 'uneducated people' who were able to distinguish between 'realistic' and 'unrealistic'.

An example of this is the way in which words such as 'ethnicity' and 'hatred' were repeatedly used by Western reporters to justify the political crisis as having been caused by a natural hatred between Hutu and Tutsi. The latter judgement is extremely important in terms of overlooking the differences embedded in society. Because there are differences in interpretation of the conflict, it is better to distinguish analysis of the conflict from various foreign interpretations of the Rwandan genocide. It was also argued elsewhere in this thesis that much more complex, divisive political propaganda concealed the socio-economic problems that few interpretations have attempted to

---

[199]Interviews in Kigali and Butare National University July 1998
[200]International Alert Report 12-15 September 1994, p. 5.
[201]Interviews at Butare National University, July 1998.

explain, preferring to concentrate on the reciprocal killings, underrepresented as a result of the differences in emphasis on such interpretations. This is how the Rwandan conflict is often viewed. Having explained the local people's interpretation, the next task is to develop different interpretations of the Rwandan conflict.

4.1 Different Interpretations of Genocide

A first hand, detailed account of the international response to the 1994 genocide in Rwanda was recorded by Philip Gourevitch in 'We Wish to Inform You That Tomorrow We Will Be Killed With Our Families: Stories from Rwanda'. Gourevitch's report helped to inform the world of what was happening in Rwanda at that time, but the world chose to do nothing. Everywhere that I went in Rwanda, there were similar criticisms regarding this failure. However, many respondents interpreted the refusal and the choice for ignoring what was happening during this period in Rwanda as covering up by foreign journalists or their lack of information on what was happening. The evidence in Rwanda at this period shows that the small contingent of United Nations troops and the few Belgian peacekeepers at this period had lost control on the ground and, when they began to lose their soldiers, they decided to pull out leaving unprotected civilians to be killed. At this point, the United States of America did not want to involve itself in matters that did not concern it directly.

In fact, at this time, America had just suffered the humiliating experience of its peace mission in Somalia, where the American soldier's body was dragged through the streets of Mogadishu, an event that was televised worldwide. As a result of this American experience in Somalia, President Bill Clinton did not want to make any mistakes. Respondents expressed their disappointment and anger, pointing out that the interpretations of journalists were aimed at creating the impression that the Rwandan genocide had simply been a spontaneous outburst of hatred that had existed for centuries between the 'tribes' of the Hutu and Tutsi.[202] The problem is that there is a general assumption that wars in Africa are to do with tribalism.[203] Regarding this, this chapter's objective is an attempt to find out facts without making value judgments about them. Impartial responses can be helpful in this.

There were a few honest Western journalists who presented a clear picture of what appeared to be a true account of what happened in Rwanda and these are Hugh McCullum, Philip Gourevitch, Alison des Forges and Mark Doyle who soberly described the perversity of the Rwandan ethnic conflict and how the media failed to understand it. Gourevitch brilliantly balanced a compelling historical and political analysis necessary to understand the political crisis in Rwanda. Gourevitch blamed Western governments, in particular France and the United States, the United Nations, the international aid community and the elite Western media for their inaction before, during and after the genocide.[204]

Des Forges added that, 'Policy makers in France, Belgium and the United States and at the United Nations all knew of the preparations for massive slaughter and failed to take the steps needed to prevent it'.[205] On the other hand,

---

[202]Cfr. Destexhe, A. Shawcross, William. Translated by Marschner, Alison, (1996), Rwanda and Genocide in the Twentieth Century, New York University Press, p. 116; also compare with Brandstetter, Anna-Maria, (1998). 'Ethnic or Socioeconomic Conflict? Political Interpretations of the Rwandan Crisis', Institute for Ethnology and Africa Studies, Germany: Mainz University, p. 429.
[203]http://www.makepovertyhistory.org/docs/507.
[204]Gourevitch, Philip, (1998). We Wish to Inform You That Tomorrow We Will Be Killed With Our Families: Stories from Rwanda, New York: Farrar Straus and Giroux, p. 25.
[205]Des Forges, Alison, (1999). Leave None to Tell the Story: Genocide in Rwanda, New York: Federation for Human Rights Leagues, p. 45.

Kofi Annan admitted that the international community failed and that must leave us always with a sense of bitter regret.[206]

Another journalist who was able to look beneath the surface of the conflict was Hugh McCullum. The reason for this may be because he had wide experience of covering Africa since 1968. Having also worked for a Christian organisation, McCullum was prepared to take a more in-depth look into the hidden causes of the conflict than others. At the end of 1994, he even doubted the truthfulness of other journalists that still talked of a country losing its sanity, commenting that this was too simplistic an analysis.[207] Philip Gourevitch further argued that what happened in Rwanda was not a frantic explosion of bloodlust, sparked by the anger of a people whose President was shot, but rather a careful and long-prepared plan.[208]

The next section examines respondents' worries, fears and hopes in the light of trying to trace who was responsible for genocide. This is a careful procedure that allows comparisons to be made between local interpretation of who was responsible for genocide and foreign interpretations. As such, interviews and questionnaires posed questions such as: who did Rwandans 'blame' for the 1994 genocide? Did they blame the perpetrators, or the RPF, or Habyarimana's government for failing to protect them? Or was it society at large? In order to gain answers, an exact comparison is needed between interviews and questions or statements, which are frequently used to show the agreements or disagreements with other sources. It suggests that the answer is neither uniform nor

---

[206]Cfr. http://www.news.bbc.co.uk/1/hi/world/africa/3573229.stm/18/9/07
[207]McCullum, Hugh, (1995). The Angels Have Left Us. The Rwanda Tragedy and the Anglican Churches, with a foreword by Desmond Tutu, Geneva: World Council of Anglican Churches, p. 14.
[208]Ibíd.

straightforward. A significant 44% said they blamed the perpetrators (Interahamwe and army). However, if the judgement of whom to blame for the genocide is made on the basis of the majority, then 56% disagreed with hatred but agreed with Belgian policies. The actual assessments over the range of local identification of blame are seen as having been put down to past policies of ethnicity.

Table 3: Different Interpretations of Genocide

Agree %	Disagree %	Uncertain %
Do you blame anyone for genocide?		
56	44	01
Do you trust your neighbour?		
41	53	06
Do you agree that the source of conflict is tribal hatred?		
25	68	07
Are you scared of resettling in your area?		
55	42	03
I am concerned about the risk of war		
43	56	01
There would be peace and development in the country if people wanted it		
43	51	06

Almost two-thirds of the majority (56%) were of an opinion that was reiterated by several respondents who spent significantly more time talking about how all Churches after independence in Rwanda had failed them, rather than blaming the politicians for the genocide. In a real sense, respondents were not under any illusion about what happened, but the blame was directed to all Churches for not acting neutrally and then toward the Belgians and Habyarimana's political propaganda. Certainly the contrast between 56% and 44% is marked by the 12% gap, where it may be correct to deduce that some respondents particularly blamed all Churches for involvement in party politics. Suffice to say that, at this point, laying the blame in the arena of ethnic conflict is particularly problematic, for a number of reasons. A victim may avoid blaming anyone, as this could be seen as a sign of grievance.

While 56% might have avoided blaming anyone out of a desire to preserve the illusion that they were liked by their neighbours, they might have avoided doing so for fear of the consequences. And blaming is viewed with uncertainty by only 1%. This gives an indication that among the survivors there were those who were still seeking redress, although 44% were unable to define the reason for their victimisation without necessarily laying the blame on Habyarimana's regime or the perpetrators. Another 53% who disagreed, but agreed with respondents interviewed during the initial stages of the conflict that the media distorted this version. They were inclined to disregard Belgian policies as the reason behind the genocide and downgraded the version of events as just one of 'natural hatred'.

By concentrating on some issues rather than others, the media pushed the idea that the genocide ultimately had much more to do with 'ancient tribal hatreds' and, as such, it could have been averted.[209] For example, the 25% who felt worried about the future, agreed with a local view that the use of tribal hatred as a cause of the genocide failed to grasp the multiple facets of Belgian policies that were intrinsically characteristic of Belgian rule and occurred systematically over a long period of time; a process described as 'divide and rule'. In this respect, the history of genocide in Rwanda is better represented as a 'process' rather than as an isolated event. What is more significant,

---

[209] http://faculty.vassar.edu/tilongma/Church&Genocide.html/8/9/07.

however, is that the overwhelming majority (68%) disagree and believe that journalists and academics arrived at incorrect interpretations; they viewed these events under the influence of the climate of political propaganda.

According to local responses, it was not a coincidence that from some of the interpretations, earlier images of the RPF (Rwandan Patriotic Front) reflected distortions and misrepresentations in such a way as to be seen to deliberately have developed effective weapons to destroy the RPF, or at least to belittle it.[210] For instance, each of these interpretations basically differs from each of the others and speculations are at times misleading, assuming that the reason why the RPF was fighting the Habyarimana regime and confusing the RPF use of class rather than ethnicity was to gain favours in Rwanda, which has not yet been proved to be true.

Take, for example, Bennett's interpretation of the self-labelling of the RPF as Inkontanyi as clear proof of the RPF's monarchist restorative intentions.[211] It is now over 14 years after the war and there is no evidence of Kamukama's claims for the RPF's intentions to restore the monarch. Kamukama further interpreted that the difference between the RPF and Habyarimana's regime was the RPF's emphasis on class rather than ethnicity, meaning that 'a class campaign' was opposed to the 'caste' ethnicity campaign used by Habyarimana's regime.[212] In sharp

---

[210]Interviews in Kigali August 1998.
[211]Bennett, J. (1994), Zur Geschicte und Politik der Rwandischen Patriotischen Front, in:Schurings, H., ed., ed. Ein Volk verlaBt sein Land: Krieg und Volkermonrd in Ruanda. Koln: Neuer ISP Verl, pp. 169 – 176; Brandstetter, Anna-Maria, (1998). "Ethnic or Socioeconomic Conflict? Political Interpretations of the Rwandan Crisis", Institute for Ethnology and Africa Studies, Germany: Mainz University, p. 432.
[212]Kamukama, D., (1993). "Pride and Prejudice in ethnic relations, Rwanda", p.155 in: P. Anyango (Ed.) Arms and Daggers in the Heart of Africa: Studies on internal conflict, p. 155.

contrast, according to the RPF, the enemy was not Hutu, but the corruption of the suppressive and discriminative state elite. Linda Melvern identified the real cause of the genocide by saying, 'The Rwandan government corrupt oligarchy pilfered the treasury, fermented violence and planned the extermination of the Tutsi to hold on to power'.[213] Again, Kamukama and Bennett seem to have misunderstood the RPF's use of 'a class campaign' as intentional in the hope of finding support in Rwanda amongst the suppressed classes and justifying their cause at an international level.[214] But Alex de Waal disagrees with Kamukama and Bennett's interpretations. His view was rather that: '……there have been several reasons for playing down ethnicity. On one hand, the ideology of leading members of the RPF had "another intellectual lineage". They traced the descent of their political leanings back to the NRA, to Frelimo in Mozambique where Museveni was first trained and then Mao Tsetung. Maoist theories of guerrilla war emphasise social transformation through the participation in liberating war and they concentrate more on social economic tensions rather than on ethnic solidarity'.[215]

Hastings defended the view of the majority and argued that the absolute refusal of the Tutsi to accept a non-dominant position was the cause of the conflict.[216] To whatever degree this was indisputable, there were other issues intertwined with it and we shall see them in later developments. Of course, if a democratic means had been

---

[213]Melvern, L., (2006). Conspiracy to Murder: The Rwandan Genocide, Verso Books, UK pp. 2-9
[214]Bennett, J. (1994), Zur Geschichte und Politik der Rwandischen Patritischen Front, in: Schurings, H., ed. Ein Volk verlaBt sein Land: Krieg und Volermond in Ruanda. Koln: Neuter ISP Vero., p. 173.
[215]de Waal, Alex, "The Genocidal State", in the Times Literary Supplement, London, 1 July 1994, p.3; Brandstetter, A., (1998), p. 432.
[216]Hastings, A., "The Tribal Contest behind Africa's Bloodbath" The Tablet, 5 September 1998, p. 1152.

available, this would have been the best mechanism. Against this interpretation, Chrétien offers an excellent argument that the genocide in Rwanda was the result of a complex interplay of economic, political and social problems.[217] Another significant argument provided by Alison Des Forges holds water because the Rwandan genocide 'was not an uncontrollable outburst of rage by a people consumed by 'ancient tribal hatreds' or the preordained result of the impersonal forces of poverty, overpopulation and political propaganda climate provided a fertile soil for genocide.[218]

The framing theory of hatred has its roots in this period. This theory holds that the political and ideological aspects reinforced by Des Forges' argument is in agreement with much local opinion that this genocide resulted from the deliberate choice of the modern elite to foster hatred and fear to keep itself in power.[219] Moreover, in the above (table 3) 41% respondents still trusted their neighbours. The emphasis here is not on 'ethnic difference'; rather what was important was the political propaganda that escalated ethnic divisions from as early as 1957 onwards.

Considering the political developments of this period, I would argue that propaganda succeeded in generating a poisonous atmosphere that provoked unrest and fear and that this was exploited by extremists in order to justify their genocidal action. It is argued that the problem was that this kind of framework developed the inherent theory of the Tutsi status in that they had no legitimate place in Rwanda. The State sanctioned a political ideology, which held that

---

[217]Chrétien, J. P., (1991). 'Presse libre' et Propagande Raciste au Rwanda: Kangura et 'Les 10 Commandements du Hutu, Politique Africaine' 42, pp. 109-120.
[218]Des Forges, Alison, (1999). Leave None to Tell the Story: Genocide in Rwanda, New York: Federation for Human Rights Leagues, pp. 43-47.
[219]Ibid.

the Tutsi people were 'foreign invaders' who should be sent 'home' to Ethiopia. The propaganda grabbed attention at a national level as a deep concern (or hatred) of the RPF.

In fact, at this period Habyarimana's political regime progressively become profoundly engaged in creating a xenophobic political climate of fear, suspicion and mistrust. It is clear that they did this by using messages of hatred, disseminated through tracts distributed in villages and sites where Tutsi refugees and those displaced by violence were gathered. The political propaganda message was that Tutsi were 'foreigners' who should leave Rwanda 'before it is too late'.[220] Habyarimana's regime and Hutu extremists wanted the conflict to be seen as an ethnic conflict between Hutu and Tutsi, purposely linked to external propaganda that concealed much more complex social tensions that overshadowed the Arusha Accord negation, grabbed the headlines and hardened the attitudes of many Hutus. The use of these tactics explains the task of Hutu extremists whose central political ambition was to remain in control of the country and in power.

This preying on Hutu fears subsequently reinvigorated extremism in the north. What is important here is not 'ethnic difference', but rather the ideological propaganda messages that seem to have been used as a tool to deepen hatred and fear. The extreme propaganda of the political regime played and picked up on resentment in order to pursue ethnic ideological strategy. It is important to understand that the use of extremist political propaganda reflected the political aspects of indoctrination embedded in ethnicity. Consequently, feelings of hatred were aroused that poisoned relationships among Hutus and Tutsis and eventually consumed reason. It is important to understand that Rwandans were fed a constant stream of anti-RPF

---

[220]The press coverage sees, Amelia, French, "Militias Raid Camps as New Offensive starts in the Killing Fields," The Independent Newspaper, 16 December 1998.

propaganda, making it easier for the Hutu to sympathise with extremism than for the individuals who were directly involved. Equally, the government's emphasis on ethnic differences, associating it with categorisation into a Hutu and Tutsi conflict, does not explain and establish the causes of the genocide. However, it was certainly this propaganda that increased the fear that there was an impending danger to the Hutus.

It is therefore important to link all the divisive measures used to distinguish between the two groups, who in many respects mirrored each other as having triggered violent actions. The argument here is that Habyarimana's ideological Ten Commandments were a product of particular political developments in addition to socio-economic structural changes that led to the collapse of mutual responsibility. In essence, what was central in this ideological propaganda was the achievement of a state of fear and a poisoning of relationships to purposely turn Hutus against Tutsis. (Consequently it was the situation that determined what ultimately happened).

Survivors described such discrimination as originating with the leadership, which they defined as, 'the result of the majority Hutus ordering the law and the way it applied in and through the structures of society and the way things were organised in favour of one group against the other'.[221]

It is worth recalling that the Habyarimana came to power in 1973, a result of a northern Hutu-instigated military coup designed to shift power away from southerners suspected of accumulating more than their fair share of wealth. On the other hand, the combination of the national issue of wealth and the deposition of President Kayibanda was seen as being soft on the Tutsi.[222]

---

[221]Interviewing elderly men and women at Gahini Mission July 1998.
[222]Reyntjens, Filipe, (1995), Rwanda: Trois jours qui ont fait basculer L'histoire. Bruxelles ; Paris : Institut africain-CEDAF/Afrika institut-ASDOC; L''Harmatt, pp. 3-7.

The natives of the Gisenyi and Ruhengeri prefectures and, to a lesser extent, Byumba, exercised a near monopoly of political power and control over the country's limited economic resources. As such, what an entire social structure, sustained through the ordinary vicissitudes of economy, clearly denies the extent of the problem. This, in turn, led to interpretations being taken out of context, categorising the conflict as merely due to hatred, to the extent that it was understood by local people, over simplistically, to be connected to ethnic ideology. Thus was the Rwandan ethnic conflict misinterpreted, with observers misled into confining the genesis of the conflict to some kind of 'natural hatred'. The political propaganda identified the latter as the chief cause, leading observers to focus on tribal animosity, rather than on ideological policy as the real problem.[223]

Thus it could be argued that the reasons for the existence of so many different interpretations are because an ideological conflict was presented as the starting-point to conceal Belgian ideological policies connected to the ethnic conflict, each of which, in turn, 'muddied the waters'. Ethnic distinction policy, however, was viewed as natural, desirable and ordinary, in one sense even 'normal', in contrast with labelling the conflict itself as 'abnormal'.[224] It is argued that if serious attention was given to those powers that manifested themselves in the political nature and ordered political actions, regardless of any other interpretation the argument follows that people perceived Habyarimana's rule to be infused with a belief in earlier ethnic distinction ideological politics. Furthermore, it needs to be borne in mind that Habyarimana's rule was not just a

---

[223]Cfr. Brandstetter, Anna-Maria, (1998). 'Ethnic or Socioeconomic Conflict? Political Interpretations of the Rwandan Crisis', Institute for Ethnology and Africa Studies, Germany: Mainz University, pp. 432 - 436.
[224]Ibid.

product of his own charisma or powers, or of the disorder caused by the Hutu dislike of the Tutsi. This was much more the product of Belgium making an 'easy target' of an earlier political agenda than to blame the Rwandan troubles on the Tutsi.

I will be quick to argue that, considering the agenda setting theory, the media does strongly influence what people think about political matters. In Jean-Pierre Chrétien's view, Habyarimana's regime became the favourite child of Belgian and international cooperation and NGOs; the famous 'pays des mille cooperates'.[225] Pabanel agrees that, in international opinion, the Rwandan government had successfully resolved the ethnic question and dedicated itself to development, thoroughly convinced that it would overcome it.[226] Furthermore, Rene Lemarchand added that France helped to give the Habyarimana regime a degree of credibility that proved totally illusory and thus created false expectations about its commitment to democracy.[227] Above all, at this time, Habyarimana's regime was busy dominating the upper echelons of the army, security services, the civil service, the diplomatic missions and the university.[228] The commanders of the Presidential Guard were drawn exclusively from Habyarimana's relatives and village. Habyarimana came from the commune of Karago, as did his powerful wife, Agathe Habyarimana and her influential

---

[225]Chrétien, J. P., (1991). 'Presse libre' et Propagande Raciste au Rwanda: Kangura et 'Les 10 Commandements du Hutu, Politique Africaine' 42, pp. 127-129.
[226]Pabanel, J.P., (1995). Bilande la Deuxième République Rwandaise: du Modèle de Dévelopemental a la violence générale, Politique Africaine 57: p. 113.
[227]Lemarchand, Rene (1994). Managing Transition Anarchies: Rwanda, Burundi and South Africa in Comparative Perspective, The Journal of Modern African Studies, 32, 4, Cambridge: University Press, p. 603.
[228]Interviews in Byumba, Gisenyi and Kigali July 1998.

brothers.[229] Colette Braeckman argues that this made up a small group known as 'Akazu' (a little household), many of whom were related to Habyarimana's wife.[230]

This explains the close connection between Habyarimana's governance and the Akazu clique. They had access to the best land and houses, the most lucrative business opportunities and easy credit facilities.[231] In spite of this and President Habyarimana's claims 'to have instituted a programme to ease ethnic tensions and to create a balance between the two ethnic groups', most observers saw the programme as perpetuating discrimination against the Tutsi.[232] According to political sources, it was the children who obtained grants to study and train abroad and who were offered the best jobs in the country. In his report on Human Rights and Conflict Resolution in Africa, Nguema refers to the fact that institutional corruption, tribalism and nepotism were the consequences of poor leadership by the Heads of State.

In sharp contrast, the household used absolute power to dispense State resources as if these were their personal property.[233] During interviews, the residents from the Gitarama region said that they were accustomed to thinking that this regime belonged to them. Ethnic and regional segregation had been instilled in the Hutu from Gitarama,

---

[229] Amnesty International Index: (AI 1990 – 1992) and Rwanda: Mass murder by government supporters and troops in April and May 1994.

[230] Akazu close connection clique was excellently described by Colette Braeckmann and A. Guillaume, La Poudriere Rwandaise', in Le Soir (Brussels), 1 June 1994, p.8.

[231] Interviews, Gisenyi, Butare and Kigali, July 1998.

[232] Special Report, Rwanda: Accountability for War Crimes and Genocide, A Report at a United States Institute of Peace Conference, 2001, p. 3.

[233] Nguema, I., The Challenges for Peace Making in Africa, Conflict Resolution, Addis Ababa, Ethiopia, London: International Alert Report, September 1994 p. 7.

to the extent that they would say, 'Any person who did not come from the north was Tutsi'.[234]

Those from Gitarama came to believe their own propaganda, namely that the privileges they enjoyed were a birthright and that they would last forever. Throughout the thirty-three years, many communities were psychologically prepared by propaganda that encouraged hatred of the Tutsi.

However, each regime advancing this ethnic ideology made claims of establishing a pure democracy of the majority that had permanently overcome the minority of the feudal Tutsi. But the new democratic process excluded the Tutsi from national democracy, which referred to Rwanda as the land of the Hutu. This new approach requires consideration; both of democracy under the Hutu, which was firmly associated with the ideology of ethnicity. Such a democratic approach carried with it considerable problems for the Tutsi in Gisenyi and Ruhengeri where Habyarimana's and his clan-mates were known as the 'blessed region'.[235] Similarly, before the genocide in Rwanda, the Hutu were fed a constant diet of manipulative anti-Tutsi propaganda that made Hutus sympathise with the ambitions of their leader to be directly involved in the genocide. Donald Shriver rightly observed that Churchill proved during World War II how rhetoric can be mobilised for war.[236]

All the propaganda words that were redefined and used in interpretations should, in my view, have been handled with care because foreign journalists were under the influence of Habyarimana's propaganda. In addition to this, interpretations from African writers tend to reinterpret the assumptions of Europeans, rather than revealing their

---

[234] Interviews in Gitarama July 1998.
[235] Interviewing Genocide survivors at Ruhengeri and Gisenyi trading centre, July 1998.
[236] Shriver, W. D., Woodstock Report, March 1996, No. 45.

own findings, apart from a few such as Rakiya Omaar from African Rights. The situation therefore conceals the real causes of the Rwandan conflict; in itself a social process framed by Belgians, thus explaining how well planned it was. The fact that Habyarimana's regime had, for so long, concentrated on the use of ideological propaganda was a dangerous move, because it was the kind of framing that used 'ethnicity' and 'hatred' to conceal much greater complex social and economic problems.

Framing effects argues that the way in which Habyarimina's regime used ethnicity politics affected political life itself and the way people see and understand it. Another important issue here is that the examination of the main causes of this conflict and also the critical examination of the framing give it a completely different meaning; explanations that moved Rwandans to heroic actions based on political propaganda.

It is this background of the history of Rwanda that may help to explain the Belgian theory of ethnic distinction, which was later translated by Habyarimana's regime into the Hutu 'Ten Commandments' for political operations. A journalist who visited Rwanda before the genocide and after reported that: 'From the beginning, everything began to go horribly wrong. The clique of northerners around Habyarimana, the Akazu, aware that their power and privilege were close to an end and that they might have to face justice without impunity, deployed every tactic available to derail the accords'.[237]

On the other hand, it is as important to extend this argument to the interpretation of the other side and to individuals who were forced to act upon the response. It could also be argued that, in this circumstance, these people were under conditions not of their own making, who acted

---

[237]McCullum, Hugh, (1995). The Angels Have Left Us. The Rwanda Tragedy and the Anglican Churches, with a foreword by Desmond Tutu, Geneva: World Council of Anglican Churches, p. 11.

in order to pursue a settlement of an old dispute. On the other hand, it is necessary to place the cause of the genocide within the context of political developments following the invasion of the RPF.[238] The strategic position of the RPF was to perpetuate the war until injustice was defeated. If argued from the perspective of liberation, the RPF mission was subverting what Gutierrez called 'an order of justice'.[239] They wanted to combat institutional violence in the 'dominant sectors' controlled by the powerful clique.

Habyarimana's regime was self-defence against the political interference that was determined to dominate and tear down the structures of his power. Thus, Molt argued that, 'the use of terror and propaganda, successfully added fuel to the Hutu's fear of RPF'.[240] On the other hand, Adrian Hastings argued that without the help of Museveni and indeed of America, the RPF could never have threatened Rwanda and there would have been no genocide, bad as the preceding government undoubtedly was.[241]

The help from America and Uganda draws our attention to another issue worthy of examination. Firstly, in view of the refugees' situation, refugees from Uganda saw the help given by President Museveni of Uganda and America to the RPF as an act of compassion and the help given to many others as salvation.[242] I argue that the interpretation of this help from Museveni and America was

---

[238]Cfr. Watson, C., Exile from Rwanda: Background to an Invasion. Washington: The U.S. committee for refugees, Issue paper, February 1991, p. 434; also compare with Brandstetter, A., (1998).
[239]Gutierrez, G., (1988). A Theology of Liberation, 2nd (Edn), Maryknoll, New York: Orbis, p. 13.
[240]Molt, P., (1994a). Der Pyrrhussieg der 'Patritischen Front' in Ruanda, Blatter furDeutsche und Internationale Politik 8, p. 932.
[241]Hastings, A., "The Tribal Contest behind Africa's Bloodbath" The Talet, 5 September 1998, p. 1152.
[242]Interviews Kigali, August 1998, I am grateful to these participants' views and their analysis of the life in exile.

to assist refugees who had tried for so long to find a home in their own homeland.[243] Refugees who had been forced out of Uganda saw the help not as waging war on the Rwandan government, but rather as self-liberation. The refugees' desire for a return to Rwanda has been described as the 'romanticisation' of their lost land.[244]

However, in my view, the 'homeland' idea makes sense and is indisputable since, for many refugees, there is that moment of reflection on the past and the longing to be home that one experiences every day. This could have been one of the reasons as there is always that dream of returning to the homeland, a common experience shared by immigrants or refugees. It is argued that Museveni and America were just responding to the refugees' residential crisis that had been created by the Ugandan People's Congress. The Congress had evicted 19,000 including Rwandan refugees of the 1950s and the migrants of 1959, some of whom were already naturalised citizens after Uganda's independence in 1962. For instance, Bishop Kossia Shalita, the former bishop of Ankole diocese, was not a refugee in Uganda, but being Munyarwanda was thrown out the country.

I will further argue that help should not have come solely from Museveni and America. There was an international obligation to prevent human rights' abuse and it should have been a concern for the wider community. Another reason - as we will find out later - is that the above arguments explain the experiences of the Tutsi. This was still the case in the years before genocide. On top of this, the crises and sporadic persecutions that were to follow years later marked a turning point for the Tutsi in Uganda. In order to understand the background that triggered the

---

[243]Ibid. Kigali, July 1998.
[244]Watson, C., Exile from Rwanda: Background to an Invasion. Washington: The U.S. committee for refugees, Issue paper, February 1991, p. 9; also compare with Brandstetter, A., (1998), p. 434.

formation of the RPF, it is also essential to recall what had happened before the genocide and to enquire as to which party was at fault and for what reasons. People do not slaughter each other for enjoyment. There were unresolved political issues in Rwanda and Uganda leading to the onset of the genocide.

Many young men like Fred Rwigyema and Paul Kagame, who were beginning to feel that the history of Rwanda was old history now that they were Ugandans, suddenly found that people among whom they had lived for over thirty-three years were treating them as hated enemies and despised foreigners. Rogers Bowen is right in arguing that, in Rwanda, lessons had not been learned and that unresolved injustices in one generation would return to haunt the next.[245] Lemarchand interpreted the RPF invasion as 'revenge'. He stated that 'Their revenge, as we now realise, came in 1990 when, under the banner of the Tutsi-dominated Front Patriotique Rwandais (RPF), their sons proceeded to fight their way back as 'refugee warriors.' [246]

There is an element of inaccuracy here in the use of the word 'revenge'. The RPF did not return for revenge. What it is important to realise is that Tutsi exiles from 1959 had never been allowed to return to Rwanda and had remained in exile for thirty-five years as stateless refugees. The argument is that living in a stateless situation creates demand for an instrumental process to find a place to call home and for the status that this provides. This is the staple desire of any normal person for whom it would become an objective and a potent source of focus with sheer determination as the fuel to achieve the goal. Rogers

---

[245]Bowen, R. (1995). "Rwanda, Missionary Reflections on a Catastrophe", London: SPCK, p. 36.
[246]Lemarchand, Rene (1994). "Managing Transition Anarchies: Rwanda, Burundi and South Africa in Comparative Perspective", The Journal of Modern African Studies, 32, 4, Cambridge: University Press, p. 583.

Bowen offers the most convincing argument that the 'Tutsi refugees' frustration both at being in exile and also being stateless (they were not allowed to return to Rwanda and were allowed to take citizenship in the country to which they were exiled), is the background to their invasion'.[247]

It was not until 1980 when the Ugandan government, headed by Milton Obote, demonstrated how precarious were the residential rights of Rwandan refugees living in Uganda, by persecuting them and forcing many to return to Rwanda. From the exact circumstances and reasons for their return it is clear that many young Rwandan refugees living in Uganda who had joined Museveni's National Resistance Army had done so to fight in defence of the rights of the refugees. It is also worth noting that UNHCR had failed to resolve the Rwandan refugee problem between Uganda and Rwanda,[248] where there were an estimated one hundred people killed in no man's land at the border.

In addition, there were many rapes and in total 40,000 people fled towards the border in an attempt to get back into Rwanda.[249] Those who managed to cross were interned in camps on the other side. Those who fared the worst were a group of 810,000 caught on a narrow strip of land at the border, hemmed in by the Rwandan border guards on one side and the Ugandan border guards on the other. These refugees were held there for several months, with only a little Red Cross assistance and slowly dying of infectious diseases or despair. Under foreign pressure, the Ugandan government agreed to a screening exercise to determine

---

[247] Bowen, R. (1995). "Rwanda, Missionary Reflections on a Catastrophe", London: SPCK, p. 36.
[248] Amnesty International May 1994.
[249] UNHCR Report, Kampala, (1984), about the situation of Rwandan's exiles in Uganda had a particularly significant effect on the political situation in Rwanda: in the early 1980s, the Uganda Government forced many Rwandese refugees out of Uganda.

who was a refugee and who was not. The process dragged on inconclusively for many months while persecution of Tutsi refugees by Hutu continued sporadically.[250]

A further point that needs to be considered here is that as the RPF guerrilla war grew in intensity, a serious ethnic political problem began to develop within Rwanda. This came from sources such as 'Kangura' magazine, which literally means 'the voice aimed at awakening ethnic ideology to create disorder and fear among Hutus'.[251] According to respondents, RTLM radio station and Kangura mainly served to promote ethnic propaganda and openly criticised the Tutsi, commonly demonising them as enemies of the country in preparation for execution of the genocide.[252] Lemarchand argued that 'Never at a loss for metaphors of domination, the media consistently sought to portray all Tutsi as members of a feudal, alien minority hell-bent upon reimposing their domination on the Hutu masses'.[253] At this point, Habyarimana's government was besieged from inside and outside its borders as it became apparent that they could not win the war against the RPF. Habyarimana's supporters opted for ethnic cleansing with the intention of eliminating the Tutsi in Rwanda.

4.2 Witness to the Killings

This section describes how the ethnic distinction crisis ended in genocide and provides a detailed account of eye witnesses to the killings. An agreement was signed with the RPF at Arusha, Tanzania, on 6 August 1991. At this

---

[250]Ibid.
[251]Kangura, Kinyarwanda local News paper, January 1994.
[252]Cfr. Prunier, G., (1995). The Rwanda Crisis: History of a genocide, New York: Columbia University Press, pp.130-31
[253]Lemarchand, Rene (1994). Managing Transition Anarchies: Rwanda, Burundi and South Africa in Comparative Perspective, The Journal of Modern African Studies, 32, 4, Cambridge: University Press, p.589.

meeting, Habyarimana agreed to implement the Arusha accords that meant power sharing with the RPF, although the accords also threatened the powerful clique that surrounded him. Filip Reytjens offers a detailed historical debate of the role of Burundi and Rwanda that includes references to the Arusha Accords. Hutu extremists saw the Arusha Accords as an end to their domination; in their eyes their power had been 'stolen' by the RPF that they considered 'Tutsi'.[254] The trigger for the genocide began on 6th April 1994, when the plane returning President Junenal Habyarimana of Rwanda and President Cyprien Ntariyamira of Burundi from Arusha was shot down as it approached Kanombe airport in Rwanda. No one has yet claimed responsibility for either assassination.

According to many foreign observers, this was actually the real start of the genocide, which is generally interpreted as being limited to the period April – June 1994.[255] The shooting down of the aircraft became a politically charged thunderbolt with as much significance in the region as the aircraft that crashed into the World Trade Centre in New York and the Pentagon in Washington D.C., September 11, 2001.

Under these circumstances, it was even seen by survivors that the genocide of the Tutsi was a strategic plan to derail the Arusha accords. They argue that the crash also triggered off the anti-Tutsi incitement broadcasts to arouse the Hutu militia (Interahamwe) that translates in English to 'those who attack together'. The militia was created by Hutu dominated political parties loyal to president Habyarimana. At the Anglican Church parish of Shyogwe, near the new headquarters of the interim government that had established itself after President Habyarimana's death,

---

[254]Reyntjens, Filipe, (1994a). L'Afrique des Grands las en Crise: Rwanda, Burundi, 1988–1994, Paris, pp. 249- 56.
[255]Guichaova, A., (1998). Les Antécédents Politiques de la Crise Rwandaise de 1994, Arusha, pp. 36-37.

survivors witnessed another flashpoint. On 7 April 1994, the Interahamwe (Hutu Militias) in Kigali used Habyarimana's death as a pretext for commencing the systematic genocide of Tutsi and moderate Hutu. The deputy Prime Minister Agathe Uwilingiyimana and ten Belgian peacekeepers were among the first to be killed.[256]

Soon after their deaths, members of the security forces and gangs of Hutu men, many of whom were believed to be members of the Interahamwe, erected roadblocks in Kigali in order to control all movements in the city and to identify their enemies and Tutsi. They claimed that the purpose of the exercise was to weed out RPF spies that were hiding in the city. It soon became clear that the roadblocks were to be used as execution points for anyone whom they suspected was 'an enemy' or who was trying to escape. Similar roadblocks were rapidly erected by Hutu gangs all over Rwanda. On 8 April the 'hardline'

Hutu parliamentarian Sindikubwabo formed an interim government and within one hundred days almost one million Tutsis and moderate Hutu had been killed. On 12 April 1994 the regime moved to Gitarama as fighting between the RPF and the government armed forces (FAR) intensified in Kigali.[257] According to African rights: 'A number of men appointed as Ministers in the interim government, senior politicians of Habyarimana's ruling MRND party, officers in the FAR and some businessmen went to Shyogwe. The group included Eliezer Niyitegeka, Minster of Information, a native of Kibuye, like Musabyimana and a close friend of the Bishop; Daniel

---

[256] de Waal, Alex 'The Genocidal State', in the Times newspaper Literary Supplement (London), 1 July 1994, pp. 3 – 4; Compare with Lemarchand, Rene, 'The Apocalypse in Rwanda', in the Cultural Survival Quarterly July – October 1994.
[257] African Rights, The Protestant Churches and the Genocide, An Appeal to the World Council of Churches contains a copy of the Bishop's Report 1999, p.3

Mangula, Minister of Higher Education, Scientific Research and a member of the central committee of MRND; Edouard Karemera, first Vice President of MRND and a former secretary general of MRND, who was named Minister of the Interior during the genocide and Major Nyirahakizima'. [258]

The most senior attendees from the Anglican Church left for Gitarama in the convoys that accompanied government ministers out of Kigali. These included members of the hierarchy of the Anglican Church leaders who sought refuge there. These included Augustin Nshamihigo, the Archbishop; Bishop Adonia Sebununguri of the diocese of Kigali; Bishop Onesphore Rwaje, the Bishop of Byumba; Augustin Munabawi, the Bishop of Kibungo; Bishop Jonathan Ruhumuriza, coadjutor Bishop of Kigali and many other Anglican Church leaders. The Anglican Church was not, of course, the only Church in Rwanda whose servants were accused of failing to speak out during the genocide and of participating in the killings. Members of other Churches were also suspected of involvement.

From the accounts of survivors, some clerics, nuns and monks were among the killers. One survivor's account was thought to have been exaggerated, but his account was compared before it was accepted. For example, a report by 'African Rights' contains a condemnatory story of one of the survivors who saw a Church leader killing people inside the Church.[259] The report agreed with respondents' accounts that, towards the end of April, very early in the morning... 'I saw Pastor Elizaphan Ntakuritimana, with his

---

[258] African Rights, The Protestant Churches and the Genocide, Appeal to the World Council of Churches contains a copy of the Bishop's Report 1999, p. 3.
[259] African Rights, Rwanda – Killing the Evidence: Murder, Attacks, Arrests and Intimidation of Survivors and Witnesses, April 1996 approximately 105 pages, see on pp. 28-29.

car full of militiamen. He was driving. They went to the Ku Murambi. They killed all the wounded people, all the women and all the children who had joined us. Afterwards, they destroyed the Church and took away the sheets in Ntakuritimana's car.[260]

The survivors expressed both condemnation and disappointment at so cruel an action from a pastor of the Adventist Church. The survivors' words were as follows: '(We) strongly condemn Elizaphan Ntakuritimana. He was a pastor before the genocide, he taught us about loving God and loving one's neighbour. Then he participated in the genocide, becoming a real killer'.[261] All over Rwanda people sought shelter in churches believing that, in the words of one survivor, 'no one could kill somebody in God's house'.[262]

Another group of Methodists placed their fate in the hands of Bishop Aaron Ruhumuriza, who was also the Legal Representative of the Council of Protestant Churches in Rwanda. However, it is just coincidence the name is 'Ruhumuriza'. We should not be misled and confuse the two Bishops with Bishop Jonathan Ruhumuriza who is an Anglican and Bishop Aaron Ruhumuriza who belongs to the Free Methodist Church of Rwanda. These are just similar names without being blood relations, which is very common in Rwanda. African rights Bishop Aaron Ruhumuriza and his colleague Pastor Uzarama appeared to enjoy good relations with the same militiamen from whom they were fleeing. Militiamen frequently visited the Methodist Church where the Bishop helped them to prepare for a massacre.[263]

---

[260]Ibid.
[261] frican Rights, (1995), Death, Despair and Defiance, approximately 1234 pages, p. 328.
[262]Interviewing a survivor of the genocide at Kigali July 1998.
[263]African Rights, (1995), Death, Despair and Defiance, approximately 1234 pages, p. 328.

Pierre Claver Rwabugasa is one of the few people who survived and whose testimony is credible, because he lived in the area throughout and he was half Hutu and half Tutsi and his views were regarded as neutral on the grounds that he had been cited by other respondents, but not in as much detail as in his account. He says Bishop Ruhumuriza was there with the assassins. The killers broke the glass in the windows then began to throw grenades and to shoot into the Methodist Church. 'Because there were a lot of us, we were forced to get out through the windows. I had hardly escaped when I saw that the local population was ready to kill anyone who was fortunate enough to get out alive.'[264]

Bishop Aaron Ruhumuriza saw that the Church was full of corpses and would have believed that no survivor could escape very far because the entire gate of the Methodist Church was full of Interahamwe.[265] Of course, it was a very serious and disturbing allegation for the Bishop to hear that he had been part of murder within the walls of an Anglican Church. Even if it had happened outside the Anglican Church, it is still unacceptable behaviour from a servant of the Lord, clearly pointing to the Anglican Church's failure on the part of the Bishop and the Anglican Church leadership. A backlash among the Rwandan population has resulted in increased conversions from Christianity to Islam, which is seen as being a religion connected with less violence. Survivors stressed that 'the Anglican Church should not thwart human justice but encourage people to repent and forgive'.[266.]

Pierre Claver summed up the role of the two pastors in these words: 'Bishop Aaron Ruhumuriza and his colleague, Pastor Uzarama, were the main planners of the deaths of people at the Methodist Church of Gikondo in Kigali.'[267]

---

[264]Ibid. p. 328.
[265]Ibid. p. 329.
[266]Anglican Communion News Service, 21 March 1998.
[267]Cfr. African Rights Witness to Genocide – Issue 6, June 1998.

Again, according to a witness living near the parish, Bishop Musabyimana's house soon became a regular meeting place for those politicians who presided over the genocide. Mattieu Mutabaruka was the head teacher of Shyogwe Primary School. He lived close to Mapfundo. As a Hutu, he did not need to hide and this gave him the opportunity to observe the vehicles and personalities that frequented Musabyimana's house. According to Mutabaruka, on 13 April 1994 the group of Hutu living in and around Shyogwe fled the violence. They sought refuge at the Anglican parish church where they met large numbers of Hutu who had fled the fighting between the FAR and the RPF in Byumba.[268]

The Bishop, accompanied by Major Anne Marie Kyankwanzi and Eliezer Niyitegeka, turned them away. He told them that they would be better protected at the Catholic Bishopric of Kabgayi, yet, according to the witness, it was commonly known that the route was road blocked by militia. Many of the group were killed by militiamen before they reached Kabgayi. A young pastor called Jean Berchmans Mutimura, who had trained at Shyogwe and who had recently been ordained in August 1993, persuaded Bishop Musabyimana to let about twenty-seven of the survivors hide in the diocesan premises. They were, for the most part, educated men: teachers, civil servants and their families. All of these displaced refugees were known personally to the Bishop; some of them considered him as a friend, others taught in schools sponsored by the diocese.

Those whom the Bishop agreed to hide were placed in different buildings and houses that belonged to the diocese. Reassured about their security by the Bishop himself, they were not immediately suspicious, but they were concerned when Hutu began to make lists of all the refugees, carefully

---

[268]http://www.skepfiles.org/moretext/genocide.htm.

differentiating the Tutsi from the Hutu. Four days later, Ngirinsuti accompanied by Bishop Musabyimana, Niyitegeka and several soldiers came to the refugees. Ngirinshuti read out the names of the Hutu on the list, then the three men supervised as the soldiers beat up the Tutsi refugees and put them in a van to be driven to their deaths. Although he was only twelve years old at the time, Fulegence Mukunzi was forced into the van with other refugees who were to be murdered, but managed to escape. Later, Mukunzi told of how Bishop Musabyimana stood by as the men were taken and remembered one particular incident that revealed the influence that Bishop Musabyimana held over the militia.[269]

Bishop Samuel Musabyimana arrived with Niyitegeka, a giant of a man, to watch as the assassins made them get into the van. He pointed out the wife of the mayor of Nyamabuye, saying: 'I know that woman. Her husband is a Hutu, let her get off.'[270] She was then freed by the assassins and allowed to climb down from the van, solely because Bishop Musabyimana had given the order and they were used to obeying him.[271] Bishop Musabyimana then told the soldiers to go and kill the others outside the parish. The men cried out, begging the Bishop to save them but he didn't say a word. Not only did the Bishop fail to intervene on behalf of the men who had put their trust in him, but he also helped the militia to select their victims. Claudette Nyiransa, a Hutu, was also present as the abductions took place and recalls Bishop Musabyimana's order to take them beyond the parish.[272]

Bishop Musabyimana made no effort to save the family of primary school teacher Speciose Bazubagira and

---

[269]Interviews, Nyamabuye, Kigali, Gisenyi and Nyamata, July 1998.
[270]African Rights Appeal to the World Council of Churches contains a copy of the Bishop's Report, December 1999, p. 5.
[271]Ibid.
[272]Interviews, Shogwe and Kigali, July 1998.

her husband Leonard Kayitare, who taught at Shyogwe secondary school. The family had fled to Shyogwe on 10 April 1994 and as the Bishop had studied with her husband and knew him well, Speciose believed that he could and would protect them. When they reached his home Musabyimana had assured them that they would be safe. On reflection, she believes that he was simply ensuring that educated people from the area, who were a principal target of the genocide, were eliminated.[273] Her husband Leonard was taken away by the militia and was killed on 6 May 1994. Speciose saw him being forced into the van and she also recalls seeing Bishop Musabyimana, together with other men, forcing people to climb into the van at gunpoint.[274]

Elias Nkubito, a Hutu farmer, who had tried to look after Kayitare and his family, was on his way to visit them in the parish that day. He saw the gathering of the militia from Shyogwe and the arrival of Musabyimana's younger brother. He remembers how Musabyimana accompanied a soldier as he put Wellars Kamanzi, a teacher at Nyamabuye primary school and his wife into the van that would take them to their deaths. He narrated how he watched as Ngirinshuti Hutu brought some water and a cloth for the Bishop and washed his hands: 'While he was wiping his hands dry, he said that the blood of these individuals could not curse him any longer. I realised that the Bishop had played a major role in the murder of these people and that he was in favour of the genocide. This was evident from the fact that he saved some people and delivered others into the hands of murderers.' [275]

Pastor Celestin Hategekimana, the diocesan secretary, hid in the Bishop's house. Nevertheless, he does not

---

[273] Ibid.
[274] Ibid.
[275] African Rights Appeal to the World Council of Churches contains a copy of the Bishop's Report, December 1999, p 5.

consider the Bishop to be his saviour. He alleges that on the morning of 28th May 1994, the Bishop deliberately exposed him and his relatives to the militia. Jean Berchmans Mutimura had secretly hidden a small group of refugees in the parish house when the Bishop approached him, asking if there was anyone there in need of help to escape.[276] The refugees, including Mutimura's mother and three nieces, together with Reverend Celestin Hategekimana were taken by Mutimura to the Bishop who told them to wait and said that he would return, but he never appeared again. After he left, the Interahamwe arrived and what happened is described in the Reverend Hategekimana's account*:* 'It was the end of us because the assassins had seen us. We ran into the houses, but nothing worked; they discovered us easily. I hid in the toilet; the others hid in one of the missionaries' houses. The assassins arrived and some of the refugees fled, but the old ones stayed there. The assassins drove them to the communal grave and killed them. I stayed in the toilet until Bishop Samuel (Musabyimana) returned, after the death of the people whom he had exposed to the assassins.'[277]

Later, when the Bishop found Celestin, he told him to disguise himself and took him to Gikongoro. The next day, they left for Gisenyi by helicopter and then entered the former Zaire on foot. The allegations of genocide against Bishop Samuel Musabyimana come not only from former parishioners, but from the colleagues who had been his close friends, for example pastor Celestin Hategekimana and pastor Jean Berchmans Mutimura. The Reverend Jean Berchmans Mutimura was responsible for saving the lives of several Tutsis and said, 'I condemn Bishop Samuel Musabyimana who did nothing for the people who were

---

[276]Ibid.
[277]African Rights; Witness to Genocide, No.3, May 1996.

threatened, through collaborating with the people who were killing many Tutsis.'[278]

Events at the Parish of Shyogwe in 1994 also raise questions about the involvement of two other high-ranking Anglican churchmen, namely Jonathan Ruhumuriza and Adonia Sebununguri. Both of these men were in Shyogwe throughout the period when killings were planned and carried out in the parish. McCullum argues that: 'It was a careful and long prepared plan to destroy a people. Press reports at the end of 1994 were still talking about a country losing its sanity, but that is too simplistic an analysis. What happened in Rwanda was premeditated murder, genocide with clear motives, means and opportunity to carry it out. The plane crash was merely the signal.'[279]

Testimonies gathered from pastors and other survivors suggest that they were present at many meetings held with the Interahamwe and members of the interim government and that they conspired with them. The Reverend Celestin Hategekimana one day heard 'the two (Ruhumuriza and Sebununguri) requesting interim government offices to supply more guns to the forces in Shyogwe'.[280]

When Bishop Samuel Musabyimana travelled abroad, he often appointed Bishop Ruhumuriza to take charge of affairs in his absence. Together with Bishop Adonia Sebununguri, Ruhumuriza safeguarded only Hutus. Celestin recalled the reactions of Bishop Ruhumuriza and Sebununguri when they found three Tutsi who had been hidden by Pastor Mutimura. Bishop Ruhumuriza stood by while Sebununguri told him to expel the refugees. Bishop Adonia Sebununguri told Pastor Mutimura, who had hidden

---

[278]Interview, Kigali, July 1998.
[279]McCullum, Hugh, (1995). The Angels Have Left Us. The Rwanda Tragedy and the Anglican Churches, with a foreword by Desmond Tutu, Geneva: World Council of Anglican Churches, p. 14.
[280]McCullum, H., (1995), p. 14; compare African Rights; Witness to Genocide, No.3, May 1996.

them that he should 'not bother about anything and that even God had accepted that the Tutsi die, because they are a cursed race'.[281] He was told that it was necessary to make them come out and the children (by which he meant the Interahamwe) were going to kill them immediately as there was no pity for these wicked people'.[282] From his base in Gitarama, Bishop Ruhumuriza visited Kigali frequently, but he did not use this freedom of movement as an opportunity to assist his colleagues whose lives were in danger.

Esperance Umurungi lost her husband, Annenie Munana, in the genocide. Ananie worked for the Anglican Church diocese of Kigali and during the first days of the genocide, the family hid in the Anglican Church Cathedral of Kigali, which was the headquarters of both Adonia Sebununguri and Jonathan Ruhumuriza.

The Reverend Alphonse Karuhije was a member of the senior clergy on the Cathedral staff and Semadimba was Bishop Sebununguri's driver for more than twenty five years. When the two decided to leave for Shyogwe on 14 April 1994, they were begged for help but did nothing.

Esperance, who is a survivor, feels bitter about the two who failed to save the lives of their employees who were in trouble.[283] However, the process of bringing them to justice is unnecessarily lengthy, fraught with tension and has been a source of instability within the country. The general feeling of many survivors towards the Anglican Church was one of very strong misunderstanding and mistrust. Repeatedly, in the course of investigating the massacres, I saw survivors and witnesses who were horrified that God's own servants could have been a part of this betrayal of humanity. It was even common knowledge that some Hutu priests who dared to speak up against injustice were

---

[281]Ibid.
[282]Ibid.
[283]African Rights, Rwanda: Death, Despair and Defiance 2nd edition.

something of an embarrassment to others. The main concern for people now is the circumstance in which several Tutsi priests met their deaths.

For example, the witnesses say that soldiers took the three priests; Fr. Irene Nyamwasa, Fr. Canisius Murinzi and Fr. Aloys Musoni who had looked for sanctuary at the Butare Bishopric, They were imprisoned in Butare, now Huye district and then transferred to Gikongoro prison where they were killed in mid May 1993. According to witnesses, a few days prior to the priests' removal, Jean Kambanda the prefect of Gikongoro and Laurent Bukibaruta together with military officers, well known Interahamwe and Bishop Misago did not volunteer to protest against the arrests. The criticisms were that they neither to prevent it nor raised the alarm in the weeks between the arrest of the priests and their murders.[284]

According to respondents, Jean Kambanda had the courage to accept responsibility for the genocide after the massacre.[285] Another Hutu priest, who sought help from Bishop Misago, was Fr. Joseph Niyomugabo of the parish of Cyanika. He tried to escape the massacre at his parish on 21 April 1994, by hiding at Cyanika Health Centre. He telephoned the Bishop several times and sent an emissary, but the Bishop replied that he should defend himself. A few days later some Benebikira sisters travelled from Cyaninka to Butare. The Bishop told them that; 'Niyomugabo was enough of an adult and should remain indoors.'[286]

On 24 April the priest was discovered murdered.[287] It has been reported by survivors that throughout the genocide, Bishop Misago was to be seen in the company of the men responsible for the killings in Gikongoro. These men included the Prefect, Laurent Bukibaruta and military

---

[284] African Rights; Witness to Genocide, No. 3, May 1996.
[285] Ibid.
[286] Interviews at Cyaninka with local residents, July 1998.
[287] Ibid.

officers. According to survivors, Bishop Misango participated in all the major security meetings organised by the Prefect and the army. It was also alleged that after the genocide Bishop Misago's diocese had become a safe haven for killers and that several of these later became employees of the Caritas office of the diocese, which was run at the time by Madeleine Raffin.

Those using the 'safe haven' included Camille Rutahintare, a former Member of Parliament, who himself made it clear that all Tutsi must be killed in the genocide in his commune of Runyinya, Butare. Although he did not intervene to rescue priests from his diocese when their lives were endangered, Bishop Misago did all he could to save priests who were deeply implicated in the genocide. It was also alleged that he met frequently with some of the priests who are accused of having taken an active part in the killings. These include Fr. Thaddee Rusingizandekwe and Fr. Robert Nyandwi of the parish Kaduha in Gikongoro, as well as Fr. Anaclet Sebahinde, Fr. Hormisdas Nsengimana and Fr. Martin Kabalira.[288]

During his visit to Rwanda in June 1984, Bishop Misago had been heard to ask Cardinal Roger Etchegarary to enquire whether or not 'the Pope will find a place for Tutsi priests because the Rwandans do not want them anymore.'[289] The question arises here; who is Rwandan and who is not? What about the Tutsi priests? Were they not Rwandan like the Hutu? In this case, it suggests that anyone who was not a Hutu in the view of the Church leadership was not a Rwandan. In the view of Bishop Misango, this suggests that the Catholic Church and other Church denominations in Rwanda had decided to exclude Tutsi and supported the regime's policy of keeping them out of Rwanda.

---

[288] Interviews at Gikongoro, July 1997.
[289] African Rights; Witness to Genocide, No.3, May 1996

Survivors still hoped that the commission established by the French National Assembly to examine French policy in Rwanda, would have occasion to interview the Bishop, survivors and those French soldiers who just ignored the victims. The present Archbishop Thaddee Ntihinyurwa was Bishop of the Catholic diocese of Cyangugu during the genocide. The Bishop was anxious to safeguard the buildings, so with the exception of some clergy and a few acquaintances, he refused to allow Tutsi refugees to seek sanctuary in the cathedral. He did this with the assistance of the notorious prefect of Cyangugu, Emmanuel Bagambaki; the man who massacred Tutsi in Bugesera in 1992. On the way to the stadium where they were to be killed, the refugees sang funeral songs, knowing the fate that awaited them. Bagambaki stated publicly that three copies of the list of their names had been made: one copy for him, one copy for the prefect and the third for the gendarmerie.[290]

After a few weeks, the list was used to facilitate the abduction of Tutsi men and boys from the stadium, particularly selecting educated people and businessmen, who were later killed. Before their deaths, the Bishop visited them on the 13 and 14 May 1993, while well armed militiamen and villagers surrounded the parish. Sensing that their deaths were imminent, the Bishop gave them Holy Communion and departed. He took no other action, not even an attempt to save the people whom he had entrusted to Bagambaki and who remained at the stadium. Between 15th and 17th April 1994, several thousand refugees were massacred at the parish of Nyamasaheke in killings sanctioned by Bagambaki. The Bishop did not visit them again throughout April, May or June 1994. Bagambaki organised and participated in further massacres of Tutsi who were sheltering in Catholic parishes that belonged to the Bishop's diocese.

---

[290] African Rights; Witness to Genocide, No.3, May 1996.

Bagambaki was seen elsewhere, but the Archbishop remained silent.[291] Alain Destexhe seems to have been right to suggest that the Anglican Church's 'refusal to admit the reality of this first case of genocide would represent a huge obstacle to the Anglican Church's role in reconciliation' (added emphasis).[292] The Tutsi priests staying at the Bishopric, while fearing for their lives, accuse the Archbishop of having prevented them leaving for the safety of the Republic of Congo. The Archbishop had ordered that all priests sign a document undertaking not to flee, telling those who refused his order to sort themselves out as well as their finances, knowing that they needed his permission to obtain money from the diocese. In addition, the Archbishop wrote letters to dioceses in the Congo asking them not to receive any Tutsi priests.

Later Fr. Alphonse Mbuguje was murdered after being taken for interrogation from the Cyangugu Bishopric. The Bishop was seen talking with Father Mbuguje's abductors during their initial visit and then personally asked his watchman to open the gates for their vehicles when they returned. The Bishop could have helped Fr. Mbuguje to escape across the border to the Republic of Congo before the soldiers returned but he did not. African Rights reports stated that, 'the Bishop's watchman accused him of turning away his uncle, who was deaf and dumb. The Bishop insisted that his uncle must leave the Bishopric and he was subsequently killed'.[293]

Although the Bishop had refused to help priests to leave Rwanda, even though they feared for their lives, he later used the diocesan vehicles to assist those fleeing to the Congo in July 1993. Amongst others, he gave a minibus

---

[291] Ibid.
[292] Destexhe, Alain; Shawcross, William. Translated by Marschner, Alison. (1996), Rwanda and Genocide in the Twentieth Century, New York: New York University Press, p. 3.
[293] African Rights, Witness to Genocide, No.3, May 1996.

that belonged to the parish of Nyamasheke to the military Chaplain, Fr. Emmanuel Munyakazi. Also, a Deputy Governor of Kikongoro was able to evacuate his family using the gift of a minibus that was owned by the health centre in the parish of Harika.

After the genocide, Bishop Ntihinyurwa again made his priorities clear. When Fr. Dieudonne Rwakabayiza was ordained in April 1995, the Bishop thanked the Christians of the parish of Mwenzi for having protected parish properties during the genocide. However, he said nothing about the Christians who were murdered there in April 1994 at the Parish and Commune office. According to African Rights, a positive eyewitness said that 'The genocide in Mwenzi was so successfully planned that when human rights organisations visited the area in early 1995, they were unable even to locate a single survivor, despite a search that lasted a week'.[294] Confident that the evidence was concealed, the Bishop criticised the destruction of houses in Mibilizi, but nowhere in his speech did he mention the series of massacres that had devastated the Parish of Mibilizi and claimed among its victims Fr. Joseph Boneza, the parish priest. It was left to a layman, the father of the priest being ordained, to condemn the assassins for murdering innocent people and for making many members of the parish widows and orphans. Not long after the genocide and despite survivors openly condemning Bishop Ntihinyurwa's behaviour, he was appointed Archbishop.[295]

The Rwandan public stressed the need for the prosecution of those participating in the 1994 genocide, at both national and international levels. They felt this was an important condition in order to achieve peace and reconciliation. Priests and nuns denounced for their role in the genocide are now living in European countries. Two

---

[294]Ibid.
[295]African Rights, Witness to Genocide, No.3, May 1996.

Benedictine nuns, Mother Superior Gertrude Mukangango and Sr. Juliene Kizito, were evacuated to Belgium and are accused of helping in the murder of Tutsi and the allegations implicating Sr. Juliene Kizito can be viewed in the Rwandan genocide documentary, which was recorded in Rwanda by British television's Channel Four.[296]

Those murdered included the relatives of their fellow nuns and even their own staff who had taken refuge in their monastery in Sovu, Butare.[297] Father Wenceslas Munyeshaaka of the parish of St. Famille in Kigali has been accused of having collaborated with the Interahamwe. It was alleged by respondents that he had raped Tutsi women, withheld food and water from refugees and that he had prevented those most at risk from being evacuated by UNAMIR.[298] Father Munyeshaaka will now stand trial in France after a four-year struggle to bring the prosecution. Other Anglican Church leaders who have been identified among the perpetrators of the genocide have been transferred to parishes outside Rwanda and to elsewhere in Africa or to Europe. The latest Catholic World News and the BBC both indicate that several priests and Bishop Samuel Musabyimana (44) formerly bishop of the Anglican diocese have been arrested and charged with participation in the genocide. Two nuns, Gertrude Mukagango and Kizito Mukabutera were sentenced in a Belgian court on 8th June 2001.[299]

Throughout the genocide, many of these men and women were notorious for their close ties with extremist

---

[296] See Appendix: IV Rwandan genocide documentary.
[297] African Rights, Witness to Genocide, No.3, May 1996; Appendix: IV Rwandan genocide documentary.
[298] Ibid.
[299] See http:www.catholicculture.org/news/features/indexcfm?recrum=47719 Catholic World News (CWN) and BBC 11th June 2001 and Rwandan Documentary appendix IV.

politicians, their anti-Tutsi sentiment and their open involvement in politics. The report by African Rights argues that the Catholic Church showed a remarkable lack of concern. For example, Fr. Emmanuel Rukundo had been dismissed from the minor Seminary of Kabgayi in 1973 because of his participation in anti-Tutsi violence. He went on to the church schools in the parish of Nyumba in Butare where a White Father, John Pristil, became his mentor. Rukundo gained his position as a seminary student, graduating from the Major Seminary of Nyakibanda.[300] After the war broke out in October 1990, a committee was formed at the Grand Seminary of Nyakibanda, the primary aim of which was to collect money in support of the former army, FAR. The committee members included Fr. Rukundo and Fr. Athanase Seromba. The initiative had the support of the rector of the Grand Seminary who was, at the time, Bishop Augustine Misago.[301]

It is often a dangerous thing to speak out but, eventually, someone will do it. In this case the voice that was raised belonged to Bishop Thaddee, a Catholic Bishop who wrote an open letter on December 1, 1991. In his letter he stated that 'the Catholic Church is sick.' He concluded this because of the Catholic Church's close relationship to government, its silence on ethnic discrimination and its unwillingness to negotiate a settlement of the war, begun a year earlier by the RPF.[302] However, church history is littered with records of martyrs and sadly Bishop Thaddee Nsengiyunva, Vicent Nsengiyunva, the Archbishop of Kigali and a few other outspoken parish priests were among

---

[300] African Rights, Witness to Genocide, No.3, May 1996; Appendix: IV Rwandan genocide documentary.
[301] African Rights Appeal to the World Council of Churches contains a copy of the Bishop's Report, December 1999, p. 2.
[302] McCullum, Hugh, (1995). The Angels Have Left Us. The Rwanda Tragedy and the Anglican Churches, with a foreword by Desmond Tutu, Geneva: World Council of Anglican Churches, p. 79.

the first to be killed.[303] Interpretation of what was happening in Rwanda became an issue of whose interpretation you were listening to.[304] Sometimes during interviews this concern was expressed about the way the conflict was portrayed and is the reason why some of the outsiders objected to describing it as 'genocide.'[305]

The Rwandan view, however, still stressed that its concern about certain interpretations, which were often linked to the discrimination, was a subjective notion and that it was a particular form of conduct stigmatised in Belgian policies. On the other hand, the reason could be a combination of factors: for example, a lack of real facts as to what had happened, or simply carelessness. The same verdict could be levelled at foreign journalism, in that it reflects a conscious effort to avoid acknowledging the heart of the conflict and the suffering that journalists chose to ignore. A great deal of what has been written about the ethnic conflict in Rwanda is significantly different from what local people say. Little has been written, for example, to acknowledge that the conflict might be seen as 'genocide'.

Furthermore, John Penned and Barry Crawford of Africa Direct cast doubt on the appropriateness of the term 'genocide', choosing instead to call it 'attempted genocide'.[306] However, Lemarchand described the scale of the killing in Rwanda, as a 'synonym for abyssal violence, a name that will go down in history as the epitome of an Africa Holocaust'.[307] Also, the evidence presented by

---

[303]Ibid. p. 80.
[304]Radio Muhabura was at the time the official RPF-run radio station.
[305]Interviews in Kigali and Butare July 1998.
[306]Hastings, A., 'The Tribal Contest behind Africa's Bloodbath' The Tablet, 5 September 1998, p.1152
[307]Lemarchand, Rene, (1994). Managing Transition Anarchies: Rwanda, Burundi and South Africa in Comparative Perspective, The Journal of Modern African Studies, 32, 4, Cambridge: University Press, p. 582.

human rights organisations such as Amnesty International, Africa Rights and other agencies, as well as the UN commander for 'Mission for Rwanda', Brigadier General Romeo Dallaire confirms it as 'genocide'.[308]

According to the Geneva Convention, the Genocide Act 1969 gave effect to the Genocide Convention, Article 11. It is an offence under this Act to commit any of the acts falling within the definition of genocide in Article 11. Under the Geneva Convention, genocide is described as acts committed with intent to destroy in whole or in part, a national, ethnic, racial or religious group. This includes the killing of members of the group or causing serious bodily or mental harm to members of the group.[309]

A thorough analysis by the UN and other sources concluded that genocide took place in Rwanda in 1994.[310] Harris also agrees that 'Of course, the revelations only confirm what experts have long suggested: that the world's nations knowingly did nothing about the slaughter of one million Tutsi and moderate Hutu'.[311] As this evidence emerges, Harris highlights the fact that 'African lives don't matter a tinker's curse to the West if oil, diamonds or gold aren't involved'.[312] McCullum argued that, internationally, the wider church was either unable or unwilling to provide

---

[308]Cfr. African Rights, 1984, Who is killing; Who is dying; What is to be done? May 1994, 49 pages, Rwanda: Death, Despair and Defence (new expanded edition) 1995, 1243 pages, Rwanda-Killing the Evidence: Murder, Attacks, Arrests and Intimidation of Survivors and Witnesses, April 1996, pages 105; Human Rights Watch, UN Human Rights Commission of 11th November 1994.
[309]Cfr. Smith, J. C. and Hogan Brian, (1992). Criminal Law, Seventh Edition, London: Butterworths, p. 396.
[310]Briggs, S. M. & Chen, L.C., (Eds.), (1999). Humanitarian Crises, The Medical and Public Health Response, London: Harvard University Press, p. 236.
[311]Harris, D., in the Anglican Times, Anglican of England Newspaper, 31 August 2001, p. 7.
[312]Ibid.

anything comparable with the unquestioning support and solidarity it gave for more than twenty-five years to the victims of apartheid in South Africa.[313]

It seems, as a matter of tragic fact, that this lack of action was a sign of all Christian Churches' failure in Rwanda and a judgement on the international community in its failure to defend the unprotected and those exposed to danger in society. I wish to argue that this is a weakness causing powerful nations to view human rights violations in poor countries through a distorted lens. In a way, it suggests that this failure mirrors the Belgian theories that speak of an unconscious racism, just as the stereotyping of Rwandans hints at exploitation. Ironically, it is this situation that allows corrupt regimes to remain in power because they are serving Western interests.[314]

4.3 The State of Security after Genocide

Everywhere one went in the country, only demolished buildings in trading centres could be seen, while in Anglican Church compounds children played on the sites of numerous mass graves. During interviews, it was reported that bodies were discovered every day in Anglican Churches and bushes. Also, despite the Rwandan Patriotic Army's defeats of Habyarimana's forces, the killing continued and caused the greatest challenge to security in the country. It required tougher new powers and action in the long term, so that the guns could not succeed. It was also necessary to trace infiltrators who had deserted the insurgents and had been granted clemency before being integrated into the national army. The task was to discover

---

[313]McCullum, Hugh, (1995). The Angels Have Left Us. The Rwanda Tragedy and the Anglican Churches, with a foreword by Desmond Tutu, Geneva: World Council of Anglican Churches, p. 65.
[314]Amnesty International, Index: AFR 47/17/, Report, November 1994.

what happened. This took me to the people involved and to the places where events took place. I interviewed ex-infiltrators to hear their side of the story.

It was possible to interview some of them, but only by assuring them of their anonymity. Names, therefore, cannot be revealed. It was important to assess whether testimonies were trustworthy as there remained a confrontation between insurgents and the army that had led to the deaths of thousands of people. The killings increased between 1997 and 1998. These insurgents were known as 'infiltrators' although most of them lived inside Rwanda. The killings began very shortly after exiles returned and were one of the methods of preparation to attack local communities from inside the country.

On the issue of ambiguous relationships, Laurent Mbanda was careful to point out that it was these past ideas, developed and used by politicians and militias as propaganda to attack Tutsi before and during genocide, which made it clear to their victims that these infiltrators intended to wipe out the Tutsi survivors of the 1994 genocide.[315] Not only did they succeed in killing many people, but they also drove others from their homes in fear. Some fled to neighbouring countries such as Tanzania and to Goma and still others to the capital city Kigali to escape the violence. The victims included not only Tutsi (who were perceived by their attackers as a 'fifth column' of the RPF) but anyone 'educated', anyone 'affluent', those who supported human rights or those with a political opinion that did not conform to the ideology of the Hutu extremists.[316]

Infiltrators also killed anyone suspected as hostile to their agenda, even murdering the Hutu families of those described as traitors. Local government officials were

---

[315]Mbanda, L., (1998). Committed to Conflict, The Destruction of the Anglican Church in Rwanda, London: SPCK, pp. 9-13.
[316]Amnesty International, Index: AFR 47/17/94.

especially vulnerable and many of them were killed because of their commitment to peace in their areas. As is so often the case in guerrilla warfare, the local people were the backbone of the insurgency. Hutu local people were the fertile ground for rekindling a hard line ideology known as Hutu extremism. Equally important is the extent to which the insurgents received help from both outside and inside the Congolese army under Joseph Kabila. Seninga Habinshuti indicates that the 'deep-rooted spirit of corruption' which existed in the army had played a role in ensuring a measure of support, along with fear.[317]

For Habinshuti, the overwhelming majority of the insurgents' support came from the countryside. These insurgents were supported in the villages, particularly since so many of the leaders and fighters had families and friends who lived in the countryside. Local supporters fed and financed the insurgency with regular donations. There was a well-organised network of supporters known as 'resistance members', operating from within the civilian population, fundraising for the cause and supplying food to insurgents. They also acted as informants, messengers and reinforcements during operations, providing shelters to infiltrators and being used as human shields for infiltrators fleeing or hiding from the RPA. The supporters even assisted in distributing leaflets designed to incite hatred and create fear to win support in the countryside and beyond. The texts called for a popular uprising of the Hutu against the Tutsi 'oppressors'.

In addition to the loss of human life, the economic and social consequences of the conflict had been disastrous. The infiltrators used the language of extremism as a rallying cry with the intention of making the country ungovernable. They ambushed vehicles and murdered

---

[317] African Rights, Rwanda, the Insurgency in the Northwest, September 1998, p. 41.

passengers, killed school children, burned down administrative offices and freed genocide suspects and common prisoners. The main reason for joining the infiltrators was that those who were alleged to have taken part in the genocide dared not return to their communities of origin where they could be identified and arrested. The study of infiltrators' resistance reveals two vital reasons as to why those who were still carrying guns had not given up the fight. Firstly, there was misleading information from the high command suggesting that victory was close and that there was no need to give up. Secondly, for others it was fear of justice that prevented them from claiming their new identity card in order to re-integrate with their communities.

The infiltrators were prepared to fight to the death rather than be brought to justice. Infiltrator respondents stressed that above all else, fear of improvement and trial drove them to continue the attack.[318] Whereas in (table 3) 55% respondents argued that people are scared of one another; even infiltrators were scared of being punished for their actions during the genocide. The reasons given were believable since most of the men and women participating in genocide were known to people and were wanted for trial. The insurgents were well-organised armed groups with ambitions to recapture Rwanda for the previous political regime that instigated the genocide. They are known in the country as 'infiltrators' and were people who entered the country disguised as returning refugees. According to respondents, most of these 'infiltrators' were inside the country. They consisted of ex army officers and Interahamwe 'militia' refugees, who from their position of exile in neighbouring countries, especially the DRC, had sustained a campaign to destabilise the country. In an effort

---

[318]Interviews with former infiltrators August 1998; Cfr. African Rights, Issue 7: "Antoine Sebomana and His Supporters: Burying the Truth in the name of Human Rights", September 1997.

to halt the violence, the government response was to deploy RPA troops to enforce security.

Some RPA soldiers behaved brutally, particularly during search operations and the army was held responsible for a series of attacks in which civilians were killed. According to human rights groups such as African Rights, Red Cross, Oxfam and Amnesty International who were reporters on the conflict, abuses committed by the Rwanda Patriotic Front in operations sometimes exceeded abuses perpetrated by the infiltrators.[319]

What follows next is an attempt to put all the findings together and to analyse how the situation got out of control. The analysis of this conflict is based on evidence gathered in interviews from written literature and from personal observation. From examination and analysis a picture can be painted, illustrating how Rwandans understand the concept of 'reconciliation' and the Anglican Church's involvement in it. This is important as it may help to understand how the Anglican Church can prepare to tackle problems that exist today. Despite categorical denial by local voices, the Anglican Church must help to clarify and assert the underlying fact that are no fundamental differences between peoples and that, where any difference is found, it is so small as to refute past hatred.

The supporting evidence for this is the shared values such as language and culture found in all ethnic groups continuing to live among traditional settings. The broad meaning of the term culture is 'way of life'. It refers to the system of belief and norms of behaviour within a particular community and to conventions regarding manners and language. In essence, it was these culture values that determined what was normal within the community and what was expected from members of that community. It

---

[319]See AI Rwanda: Reports of killings and abductions by the Rwandese Patriotic Army, April-August 1994.

follows that this explanation is one that stresses the importance of the failure of foreign writers to ask critical questions about both the wider ethnic conflict concerns of behavioural influence and also the resulting strains that underlay the events of the conflict. This is the kind of context used routinely in the media to describe natural hatred.

Another important issue is that local views are never heard; therefore, the whole situation was regarded as a kind of 'conspiracy theory' to use ethnic hatred to conceal the Belgian legacy. As a result, the issues of poverty and Belgium are overshadowed by simplistic interpretations of the conflict, as if the conflict was a result of only 'natural hatred'. This study will try to present the local voices that are often conspicuously absent from one-sided foreign interpretations that concentrate on symptoms, rather than look back at the origins and causes. The crucial point here, however, is to have a good analysis of local interpretations that offers an approach to the conflict while considering the historical social breakdown.

It is this analytical approach that may serve to explain some of the apparent inconsistencies in the interpretations that distinguish hatred and the use of ideological propaganda. It is an approach that also considers the economic crisis, stressed by local people and the few foreign voices who agreed that conditions of poverty added to the political crisis. All of these factors will be considered with regard to the part each played.

A different dynamic role correlates with the cover up of Belgian policies that had influenced the onset of the political crisis. In fact, respondents argued that it was wrong to rule out the impact of the ideological politics of ethnicity. This is an ideology that has been played out for so long by politicians and that is to do with economic factors or something that is based more on ideological ethnic policies. Respondents argued that if the Anglican

Church took spiritual and material needs equally seriously, then contextual reconciliation theology is justified in pushing the point home. It is therefore not possible to point to a single conclusive explanation, but the political ideology of ethnic distinction appears to be a mechanism by which the politics of conflict were reinforced. Indeed, this is most Rwandans' interpretation of the causes of the genocide today.

All these were important factors in the cause of conflict, demanding an understanding of the situation that may provide a meaning for the ideology of ethnic conflict. This was achieved through interviews with various groups, whose past and present experiences contributed valuable information in this attempt to build a picture of the consequences and to lay bare the political and social context that has made the situation so intractable. Overall, the central issue of concern to all respondents interviewed was security and development. At this period there was still a general feeling from respondents that the RPF should put effort into restoring security and stability for sustainable development, since education, that forms the foundation for national recovery, was to be at the forefront. The central issue of concern to all the people that were interviewed was security.

It is important to argue that, security - or the lack of it - has also a multiplier effect that permeates all other sectors of national recovery. Security is one of the important issues that was stressed and, apart from the safety of individuals, security was to be the key to economic recovery. Freedom of movement, for example, would allow children to attend educational activities. These were normal responses from people wanting to lead normal lives. Those recalling the past lamented that, from the beginning, evil acts had negative consequences, just as good acts had positive consequences. They argued that these were chains of cause and effect that had been forged down the centuries through the exercise of people's free will. Even in the middle of conflict, goodness was generally approved of by society, but evil acts were disapproved of and respondents wondered 'How could anyone do this'?[320]

The country suffered from acute shortages of food and, in a country without an industrial sector, the result was widespread hunger. After the genocide, the country was left in ruins; the agricultural sector, the mainstay of over 90% of the population was badly ravaged by the war. Individual production that had formerly produced 80% to 90% of food requirements had declined by 4.5% per year since 1984.[321]

Respondents stressed that insecurity had made farming difficult and thousands of people in the countryside were displaced far from their farms and fields.[322] The main source of food was the World Food Programme and other humanitarian food donor organisations, although there were complaints in most camps about the quality and quantity of food supplied. It was evident that in each camp visited, people were struggling to survive and desperate for food. Male peasants interviewed in camps said hunger forced them to send their wives and children to abandoned gardens in search of food, despite the imminent potential danger. Demands by the Interahamwe (militia) for food and money depleted the population's meagre supplies and resources, while the continuing violence, in turn, forced international aid organisations to leave some parts of the country. Social disintegration had reached such a point in some areas that residents were afraid to go out or to let others in. Many people were living in fear, without freedom and with a sense of powerlessness and despair.

Genocide left Rwanda with a legacy of lingering mistrust and division among Rwandans who were afraid of

---

[320] Interviews at Gatuna, Nyamatimba and Gahini Mission, July 1989.
[321] United Nations consolidated Inter-Agency Appeal for persons Affected by the crisis in Rwanda January – December 1995 Vol. 1 p. 9.
[322] Cfr. http://www.jhuccp.org.puhs/sp/19/English/19.pdf./21/9/07

neighbours, to the extent that they could not even greet each other. Even ten years later, the powerlessness felt was evident on many of the respondents' faces. Fear and mistrust still continued to create feelings of anxiety as if they remained in the areas where infiltrators had influence. During the daytime people moved freely, though cautiously, within the town, but as soon as it was dark everybody retreated to their homes for fear of encountering the militia. A large number of villagers I interviewed were not happy about the ineffectiveness of local leadership. Even the most optimistic elderly villagers and other local people interviewed said that 'Peace and development needed economic solution and determination of the government officials in charge of the villages.'[323]

The absence of a forceful leadership and a capable civilian administration was still detrimental to the security of the population. At the time of the interviews, people were still asking the government to establish strong national structures that could help to prevent human rights abuses. They wanted the government to monitor the situation and to respond in good time to the reported abuses.

The people wanted respect for human rights to be institutionalised and they agreed that security depends to a considerable degree on the ability and willingness of civilians to establish a good working relationship with their military counterparts. In an attempt to improve good relationships between the RPA and civilians it was agreed that local leaders would mobilise the population to discuss security. Respondents also noted that where leadership was weak or supported the militia, the infiltrators could be certain that some members of the population would help them, either willingly or by coercion. Both Tutsi and Hutu

---

[323]Interviews at Kigali, Mutara, Gisenyi, Butare and Nyamata between July and September 1998.

sides were afraid. Another important point that was observed by respondents was the way the RPF's discourse differed from that of Habyarimana's regime. RPF's focus was to unite the country without acknowledging that belonging to a given ethnic group had any meaning.

At this time, the playing down of ethnic differences by the RPF had a dramatic impact on the populations who had thought the organisation was against the Hutu: something that has not yet been proven. Also, the belief that the RPF was committing crimes against people at this time was mistaken as both Hutu and Tutsi were equally worried about the lack of peace and security. The overriding priority of residents in the camps for displaced persons was the pursuit of security and economic survival; while the most urgent concern for the government was the pursuit of infiltrators.[324] By far the most common view was that if the right policies were implemented, any eventual return of the infiltrators would not seriously destabilise the country.[325]

4.4 Infiltrators' Loss of Local Support

This section describes the loss of support by infiltrator forces opposed to the RPF government. It was understood in the early days of the RPF that under extremely difficult conditions it would be unrealistic to expect the population to support a government without worthwhile leadership experience. People's experience of war, the unbearable conditions they had endured when they fled the country and the cruelty of the infiltrators towards civilians were the main reasons for not supporting them. In addition, people in camps and villages said that without substantial local assistance, infiltrators could not sustain guerrilla warfare.[326]

---

[324] Interviewing Government officials at Kigali, July 1998.
[325] Interviews, Gisenyi, Nyamatimba, Nyamata camps, August 1998.
[326] Ibid.

In Rwerere, in table 3, 43% agreed with the local people's argument concerning how to end the war that, if collectively the population, local officials and the army cooperated and if security measures were implemented in accordance with the wishes of the local population, the infiltrators would be defeated.[327] As noted earlier, the amnesty policy for insurgency contributed significantly to breaking and winning those who were tired and weakening, with less hope of winning the struggle. This idea had great strength because when it was eventually implemented, it was shown to weaken the power of the infiltrators.[328] From another point of view, the Anglican Church had a critical role to play in allaying people's fears and in promoting mutual understanding and confidence not only between different communities, but also between the civilian population and the RPF army.

44% who blamed Interahamwe agreed with the explanation that defeating the Interahamwe, who were leading the insurgency, would be of limited value unless something was done to make the country less receptive to their message of hatred.[329] There were eyewitness accounts and stories told by severely traumatised survivors revealing that the torture and the suffering they had endured was too much bear unless it changed more than just their personal views and feelings. Nevertheless, some Hutu Anglican Church leaders had been exemplary in their courage and commitment to the protection of their Tutsi neighbours, despite the serious risks they took. Some lost their own lives in an effort to shield refugees from danger; among them was the only Tutsi Anglican Bishop saved by his fellow Hutu Bishop. The whole train of events shows the

---

[327]McKinnley Jr., International Herald Tribune 16 December 1998.
[328]Cfr. African Rights, Briefing Paper on the Northwest Region of Rwanda, January 1999, p.9.
[329]Interviews in Rwerere, Kamana and Mutara refugee camps, July 1998.

Anglican Church caught up in the middle of conflict and struggling with the wider issues of faith both outside and particularly inside itself. This meant division where one section of the Anglican Church was still in exile, while the new leadership demanded that those who were perpetrators of genocide should be brought to justice.

Conclusion

The essential conclusion emerging from the interpretations of the ethnic conflict in Rwanda is that weakened and poisoned trust created fear and, subsequently, people were driven by ideological political propaganda that enshrined policies of ethnic distinction. By working with local eye-witnesses, the study has attempted to discover the source of the conflict and to identify reasons why people become killers. The views expressed here are representative of many local voices that suggested that a change in human relationships exacerbated the political ideology of the ethnic conflict crisis. It has argued that 'erroneous interpretations' were the result of the foreign writers' failure to acknowledge the part played by Belgian ideological policies and economic structures. It was either ideologically or politically expedient for these writers to choose to ignore the damage caused by the past Belgian legacy. Finally, today as then, we have much to learn about the processes through which political propaganda can generate the circumstances in which infringement of social codes is accepted as 'normal behaviour' and generates an expected response from people.

The next chapter will assess a 'way out' of this many sided crisis, a crisis that has defied and continues to defy the mission and pastoral role of the Anglican Church in Rwanda. It is now a view held by many people in Rwanda that this is a grave and fundamental political problem that cannot be resolved by military means alone. It is apparent that the use of military force has so far failed to offer a lasting solution.

Chapter Five

Challenges Facing the Anglican Church in Rwanda

5.0 Introduction

Moving from a mainly interpretive to mainly descriptive chapter, the objective of this chapter is to draw together some of the threads left open at earlier stages and to delineate the recovery of the Rwandan Anglican Church on which the reconciliation argument is based. The Anglican Church in Rwanda, like every other stratum of society, suffered much through the genocide. It was especially important to identify the Church in question and how it recovered in the aftermath of genocide. For three years the Anglican Church of the Province of Rwanda functioned without clergy in the places where many of the Anglican Church leaders had died or were in exile. After the genocide, parishes were without clergy and local congregations without leadership. This was a major concern of Anglican Church members. In addition to the physical destruction of property, the people's faith in the Anglican Church leadership had been affected as well. Since then, many changes have occurred in the country; and it is the purpose of this chapter to try to bring the Anglican Church record up to date.

The study seeks to highlight any significant changes over the past years and the likely challenges implied for the future of the Anglican Church in Rwanda during the reconciliation process, a process that is needed for society to function properly. The first task of the study was to assess some of the ways in which people see how the Anglican Church could once again function in Rwanda and to examine whether the Anglican Church was still needed by society there. It is mainly concerned with discovering how people describe the Anglican Church in Rwanda and hearing their views on the rights and wrongs of the Anglican Church, in order to see whether Rwandans can forget and can trust the Anglican Church again. At the time of this research the Anglican Church in Rwanda was still full of questions about the wider issues of life and faith, but, more particularly, with questions about itself. In the whole of the Anglican Church in Rwanda, these questions were high on the agenda.

Not only were people in wider society asking specific questions, but questions were also being asked within the Anglican Church itself: why, for example, was the Anglican Church silent? Outside the capital some Anglican Church members around the city of Kigali felt that there was a hidden potential and openness to Christian outreach. For some, new ways of thinking were opened up as their congregations were drawn from a wider area. In other areas, there was already some degree of cooperation in ecumenical worship and other activities. It is for this reason that it is appropriate to examine the Anglican Church to see how the process of recovery developed, how it restored its credibility in the country and how it was engaged in the reconciliation process. One of the main areas of enquiry focuses on the ways in which the Anglican Church became involved in the political conflict. These questions were evidence of how public opinion was not happy with Anglican Church leaders. Many questions asked much the same thing: how did the political conflict invade and receive acceptance in the Anglican Church?

The Bishop's morality was questioned by 62% of Tutsi Anglican Church members. They questioned how the Bishop could claim that ethnic cleansing was done on divine authority or, as one Anglican Bishop said, 'in the name of God. Many saw this as the greatest perversion of religious belief.[1] In many respondents' opinion, to suggest that God sanctions such evil acts is to clothe divinity with the attributes of the demonic.[2] These questions were sometimes posed in very general terms, for example, 'Why does God let bad things happen?' 'Does God intend life to be this way?' or 'Why should I believe when the world is the way it is?'[3] Mario Aguilar was right to ask: 'Can Christians in Rwanda really trust one another after what happened?'[4]

5.1 Église Épiscopale au Rwanda (EER)

Rwanda is divided into twelve administrative areas known as Prefectures and follows the Belgian system. The Anglican Church has a presence in each of these prefectures. Kigali has two prefectures, one urban and one rural, but is one diocese. The Anglican Church in Rwanda consists of nine dioceses with the See of the Archbishop in the diocese of Kigali. The Anglican Church in Rwanda is made up of all ethnic groups. To test the Église Épiscopale au Rwanda who supported the Anglican presence, I put forward five statements and one question to assess how much the Church was supported countywide. This section also examines those who do not attend the Anglican Church in order to explore different views of supporters and non-supporters of the Anglican Church's presence in Rwanda. Therefore, the next table represents responses to a question about the presence of the Église Épiscopale au Rwanda for comparison, to assess those who miss the Anglican

---

[1] African Rights Appeal to the World Council of Churches contains a copy of the Bishop's Report 1999, p.6.
[2] Interviews in Byumba, July 1997.
[3] Interviews in Kigali, Gahini and Byumba, July 1997.
[4] Aguilar, M. I., (1996). The Rwanda Genocide and the Call to Deepen Christianity in Africa, Uganda: AMECEA GABA Publications Spearhead Nos. 148 – 150, p.VI.

Church's presence, those who disagreed and those who were not sure.

Table 4: The Question of Église Épiscopale au Rwanda's Presence

	Agree %	Disagree %	Uncertain %
I support the Anglican Church's presence in Rwanda	61	32	07
Despite the genocide, the Anglican Church is still relevant to life	49	46	05
Would you miss the Anglican Church if it was not restored?	72	22	06
Do you think the Anglican Church is united?	36	62	02
Do you receive any help from the Anglican Church?	32	63	05
Was the Anglican Church involved in genocide?	34	60	06
Does the Church for spiritual and social needs?	43	54	03
Do you fear your neighbours or going to Church buildings alone?	75	21	04
Is the Anglican Church's presence important to you?	56	43	01

Statistics show both 61% and 49% agreed with the Anglican Church's relevancy to life. From this presentation of figures, it is quite clear that Anglican Church attendees were more likely than non Anglican Church member attendees to feel disappointed by the way the Anglican Church leaders involved themselves in ethnic cleansing. At the same time, they still want the presence of the Anglican Church.

Of the three questions asked about the Anglican Church's presence, it is shown that Anglican Church attendance makes a difference. Responses from those who want the presence of the Anglican Church revealed the extent to which Anglican Church attendance altered survivors' perception of the Anglican Church. Not surprisingly, 75% of Anglican Church members had concerns as to fear of neighbours or going to buildings alone. This reflected the depth of these fears, since only 21% respondents would not mind being alone in a Church. 56% supported the Anglican Church's presence in Rwanda and agreed this was important, too, for 'spiritual guidance' Two different groups expressed this in that 43% and 49% of respondents respectively attended Anglican Church worship occasionally and attended nearly every week. While 4% of Anglican Church members (assumed not to be regular attendees) remained unconvinced, the interviews show that active Anglican members are more likely to want a place to turn to for spiritual guidance and they find this guidance by attending Anglican Church worship.

In more detail, the figures show that 56% agreed that people need a place where they can meet for reflection and share their thoughts, needs and experiences with others, provided that there is a willingness to be open to each other's thoughts. However, they acknowledged the need for God and saw the Anglican Church as a place to pray and for spiritual reflection.[5] The question of Anglican Church involvement in genocide does not seem to be significantly related to Anglican Church attendance. This is the reason why 60% of Anglican respondents disagreed with the opinion that the Church leadership was involved in genocide, while the first 61% agreed with the Anglican

---

[5]Questionnaires and interviews in Mutara camps, August 1998.

Church's presence and express how they would miss the Anglican Church. The questionnaires completed in the nine dioceses showed that the majority of 72% and those questioned at Kigali expressed how they would miss it if it were not there, but they were unclear about ways in which the Anglican Church could get involved in reconciliation issues.[6] This general response reflects an acknowledgement of the need for God, but also a lack of clear understanding as to how the Anglican Church relates to their everyday life and situation.

This survey reveals a predicament: people felt the need to go somewhere (in the Anglican Church) but at the same time they could not fully trust it. It is remarkable that even survivors who had witnessed the involvement of Church leaders during genocide do not support the absence of the Anglican Church in the country after what happened. It is fascinating that, during interviews, one survivor at Kigali compared the Anglican Church to a mother and went on to argue that 'The Anglican Church has been our mother and if a mother offends you does she cease to be your mother?'[7] Therefore, if the Anglican Church helps people to reclaim these values, the process may help to soften the impact of ethnic differences in the country.

According to the responses, people often need time and space to work through their troubles without being catapulted unwillingly into the system.[8] They need a place to speak out and receive spiritual guidance and to be given control over the process of making choices about what happens to them. Therefore, the next task here will be to describe how the Anglican Church in Rwanda recovered from destruction to rebuild itself from the ashes of the genocide. The description shows diocesan appointments for the new leadership and how the Anglican Church was

---

[6] Interviews at the Cathedral, Kigali, August 2004.
[7] Interviewing a choir member of the Cathedral at Kigali, August 2004.
[8] Interviews at Kigali diocesan Office; Questionnaire analysis.

preparing to engage in the process of reconciliation. It also allows openings for the Église Épiscopale to take up its role as a mediating institution, most Churches accepting it as a venue for meetings about issues affecting communities and as an enabler of change. The Église Épiscopale au Rwanda consists of nine dioceses with about two hundred parishes and with about twenty-one parishes in each diocese. There were two hundred and ten clergy at the time of this research in the whole province of the Anglican Church in Rwanda, most of whom had been ordained outside the country.

The ordained clergy returned from Uganda and Burundi and a few returned from the Democratic Republic of Congo (formerly Zaire); these included the new Archbishop Emmanuel Kolini who had been ordained in Uganda before he was transferred to the Anglican province of Congo. Among the clergy, forty had passed retirement age but were still actively in service. The first task for the Anglican Church was to reorganise the leadership, following the genocide and losses by either death or exile. Though some failed to return to Rwanda, it was not until October 1996 that their Sees and that of the Archbishop were deemed vacant and new leaders appointed.

The Anglican Church in Rwanda was virtually paralysed by the lack of Anglican Church leaders and by the conflict between the Anglican Church leadership and surviving members. A particular crisis emerged in the diocese of Kigali with the reappointment of Bishop Jonathan Ruhumuliza as the diocesan Bishop where before he was coadjutor Bishop in 1994. The tensions were mainly triggered by Tutsi clergy and lay people who opposed Bishop Ruhumiliza's appointment and who forced the new Anglican Church leadership to confront him with allegations concerning his conduct during the genocide.[9]

---

[9]Interview, Kigali Diocese, July 1997.

Widely divergent negative views were expressed towards the previous Anglican Church leadership. These opinions emerged in Kigali diocese and were expressed in the Anglican Church in Rwanda as a whole. Though only 34% lacked trust in the Anglican Church leadership, its past involvement in ethnic cleansing raised tensions in the Anglican Church congregations in Rwanda regarding the lack of trust and credibility and the moral authority of the leadership.[10] A report by African Rights shows: 'The failure of the Anglican Churches to take a collective stand against the genocide and the overwhelming evidence of the direct participation of many clergy in the massacres is one of the most disturbing aspects of what is universally considered to have been among the worst crimes against humanity of the 20th Century.[11]

The problem here is not only to establish the failure of the Anglican Church in Rwanda, but also to examine critically the explanations that are being put forward from different sources. Initially the approach of the Anglican Communion worldwide was to try to calm the situation, smoothing over rather than addressing the allegations. This had done little for the survivors who believed that there was no place in the Anglican Church for those who they alleged had been involved in the genocide.[12] Bishop Jonathan Ruhumuliza returned to Rwanda on 5 August 1994. Immediately after the genocide Bishop Adonia Sebununguri, the former Bishop of the diocese of Kigali, appointed Ruhumuliza as his successor. The Archbishop of Canterbury also approved his appointment.[13] But there was a great deal of hostility towards him in Kigali, both from

---

[10] http://www.jhuccp.org.pubs/sp/19/Enlish/19.pdf/19/9/07.
[11] African Rights Appeal to the World Council of Churches contains a copy of the Bishop's Report, December 1999, p.1.
[12] Ibid, pp. 9 – 11.
[13] Affidavit of Nicholas Martin Cavender, 9 The Precincts, Canterbury, Kent England.

pastors and other members of his own Anglican Church who alleged his active role in the genocide. His presence as Bishop of Kigali soon turned the diocese into a battleground between his supporters and a group of clergy and Christians who rejected him entirely.[14]

They questioned why the Anglican Church wanted to walk quietly away from what happened in the genocide.[15] The Reverend Schonecke, speaking about the Anglican Church's failure to protect people, said that the Anglican Church hierarchy remained 'too closely linked with the ruling regime' and that this was the reason why the Anglican Church failed to be a credible voice of protest'. He also said: 'Their many declarations during the genocide were insignificant and inadequate. Reaction was too late and too little.'[16] Again, the Rt. Reverend David Birney, the Archbishop's envoy to the Anglican Church in Rwanda, in 1996 spoke of the Anglican Church's surrender in the face of the genocide. Some of the clergy of the Anglican Church were believed to be implicated in the planning and execution of the genocide.[17] It was not until 13 May 1994, five weeks after the start of the genocide, by which time the Anglican Church leadership had begun to respond after Hutu had been killed, that the Catholic and Protestant Anglican Churches issued a joint public statement calling for calm and peace.[18]

There was no mention of the genocide and no reference to the government's central responsibility for the slaughter.

---

[14]African Rights Appeal to the World Council of Churches contains a copy of the Bishop's Report, December 1999, p.11.
[15]Branson, Roy, 'Never Again', Spectrum, Vol. 25, No. 4, June 1996.
[16]Schonecke, AMECEA, Report, (1994), No. 423.
[17]Rosenthal, James, M. and Currie, Nicola, (1997) Being Anglican Church, compiled by James M. Rosenthal and Nicola Currie, Anglican Church Consultative Council X, Panama City, p.138; Doyle, Mark, BBC News, 26 March 2004.
[18]African Rights Appeal to the World Council of Churches contains a copy of the Bishop's Report Rights, December 1999, p.11

Instead, the statement focused on the war between the government and the Rwandan Patriotic Front. The statement did not mention the massacres, the desecration of Anglican churches or the murder of priests and Anglican Church workers.[19] While 34% of respondents argued that had the Anglican Church leaders shown the necessary determination to resolve the conflict, they could then have played an instrumental role in halting, or at least limiting, the genocide. The mistake made was in being too close to those in power and this must never be repeated. The Anglican Church should praise and support the government when it does what is right and challenge it fearlessly when it departs from the justice and righteousness that God requires.[20] Similarly, the former Secretary-General of the United Nations, Kofi Annan, was right when he said that 'Religious leaders have not always spoken out when their voices could have helped combat hatred and persecution, or could have roused people from indifference'.[21]

Furthermore, Eugene Bayingana argued that Anglican Church leaders could have shown more courage at the time.[22] However, to be a credible voice of protest, these leaders would have had to disengage themselves from close links with the ruling party and regime. Furthermore, some failed to see any need for reconciliation to attain Ubumwe (a Kinyarwanda word meaning national unity). Instead, Bishop Aaron Ruhumuliza, in his capacity as legal representative of the Council of Protestant Churches in Rwanda (CPR), went to Nairobi after the genocide in July 1995 to release a report entitled 'The Point of View of the Protestant Churches on the Rwandan Crisis'. The thirty-seven-page document was almost entirely dedicated to

---

[19] Ibid.
[20] Interviews at Butare, Gahini and Kigali August 1998.
[21] Kofi Annan, Fellowship, April 2001, Vol. 6, No. 2.
[22] Bayingana, Ng. E., Art., (1994). 'Reconciliation: Foundation for Reconstructing a New Rwanda', Nairobi: Evangel Press, pp.1-5.

minimising the genocide; it described the Tutsi as 'foreign invaders who had, since the 16th century, governed Rwanda only by dictatorship and terrorism'.[23] However, according to Mark Huband: 'The Anglican Church leaders were asked [by a group of journalists] if they had condemned the murderers who had filled Rwanda's Anglican churches with bodies. They refused to answer. They dodged questions, became agitated, their voices reaching an even higher pitch, [as] the core of Rwanda's crisis was laid bare. Even the most senior members of the Anglican Church were acting as errand boys for political masters who have preached murder and filled the rivers with blood.'[24]

Christians dismissed the report as simply a response to the criticisms levelled at them by people who had suffered under them and their fellows.[25] McCullum summed up the extent to which the Anglican Church has been discredited in Rwanda when he said: 'For this silent acquiescence and lack of courage, the Anglican Church as an institution paid dearly. They will continue to live under a cloud of suspicion for years to come'.[26] Repeatedly, the matter of Bishop Ruhumuliza's letter and his press conference in Nairobi, where he failed to condemn the genocide that was taking place in Rwanda, created tension throughout this period. In addition, his betrayal of colleagues and their families during the genocide was raised, along with questions about the irregularities of his appointment.

The first protest against the appointment of Bishop Ruhumuliza occurred on 15 January 1995 when two

---

[23] African Rights, Rwanda: Death, Despair and Defiance (new expanded edition) 1995, pp.3-21.
[24] Huband, Mark, 'Anglican of the Holy Slaughter', The Observer, 5 June 1994.
[25] African Rights Appeal to the World Council of Churches contains a copy of the Bishop's Report 1999, p.21.
[26] McCullum, Hugh, (1995). The Angels Have Left Us. The Rwanda Tragedy and the Anglican Churches, with a foreword by Desmond Tutu, Geneva: World Council of Anglican Churches, p.3.

representatives of the Council of Anglican Church Provinces of Africa (CAPA) arrived in Rwanda. After their visit they described the protest as 'an attempt to humiliate Bishop Jonathan' and that 'throughout this period Bishop Ruhumuliza remained calm and composed'.[27] However, in the eyes of victims of genocide, the representatives of CAPA were viewed as having failed to have seen the significance of Bishop Ruhumuliza's self-imposed exile and that of other Anglican leaders. Their protests, written and verbal, reached the ears of many members of the Anglican Church both within and outside Rwanda.

The criticism, although genuinely felt, was not taken seriously by the Anglican Church. Instead, the report of their visit considered Bishop Ruhumuliza's return to Rwanda to have been an act of courage. Concerning his conduct during the genocide they said that, despite his shortcomings at the time of war, he had been recognised as a brave young Bishop. However, they noted the joint public statement on 13 May 1993. In May 1995 the Archbishop of Canterbury visited Rwanda. This resulted in a further outpouring of emotion and anger. During the five-day visit he was confronted on several occasions by demonstrators waving placards denouncing several of Rwanda's Anglican Church clergy. The Archbishop, however, showed unwavering support to Bishop Ruhumuliza. In his letter to the government of 14 November 1995 he wrote, 'I know personally of his profound commitment to the development of democracy in Rwanda'.[28]

After this, several other leaders of the Anglican Church, from Australia, Canada, Uganda, Kenya and South Africa visited Rwanda. All expressed their deepest sorrow at the genocide of 1994, but according to respondents none

---

[27] Rosenthal, James, M. and Currie, Nicola, (1997) Being Anglican Church, compiled by James M. Rosenthal and Nicola Currie, Anglican Church Consultative Council X, Panama City, pp.137-38.
[28] Ibid.

has demanded an investigation into the part played by Rwandans in the genocide. According to an African Rights report which was submitted to the World Council of Churches and views from respondents during interviews, several respondents expressed their disappointment and concern that none of Anglican leadership had volunteered to accept any responsibility for the part they had played in the genocide and that none of the foreigners dared to ask any questions about their role.[29] The Bishops chose to support Bishop Ruhumuliza, thus allowing the situation to spiral out of control and clouding the issue of his responsibility.

Respondents also criticised the Anglican hierarchy for perceiving Bishop Ruhumiliza as a victim. Moreover, his critics tended to be dismissed as 'dissidents' with personal ambition. Bishop Ruhumuliza's legal right to occupy the position of Bishop of Kigali was challenged by protesters over a period of months. However, the entire Anglican Church in Rwanda was in turmoil, with most of its former leaders in exile and these same leaders would, in any case, have supported Bishop Ruhumuliza.[30] Without an Archbishop of Rwanda to appeal to, Anglican Church members either boycotted Bishop Ruhumuliza's services or confronted him directly and sought help from Anglican Church authorities outside Rwanda. The situation deteriorated to the extent that each side became involved in physical assaults upon the other.

Six months later, the situation in the diocese of Kigali remained unsettled. Soon after, Robert Shropshire of the Anglican Church of Canada Primate's World Relief and development Fund (PWRDF) made a visit to Rwanda. Shropshire was aware both of the details of the accusations against Bishop Ruhumuliza and the chaos and violence

---

[29] African Rights Appeal to the World Council of Churches contains a copy of the Bishop's Report 1999, p.9.
[30] Ibid. Interviews at Kigali Cathedral August 1997.

within the Diocese. His report, however, still sympathised with the Bishop.

By May 1997, Bishop Jonathan Ruhumuliza was experiencing an increasingly difficult time in Kigali, where he was accused by Anglican Church members of supporting the regime responsible for the killings in 1993 - 1994. The Provincial Standing Committee had said that for the sake of the Church, the Bishop should resign. Bishop Rwaje as the Dean of the Province of Rwanda at the meeting of the Primates of the Anglican Communion at St George's College, Jerusalem reported that, 'the Diocese of Kigali was in a particular state of crisis. There had been fighting in the Cathedral in an effort to evict the Bishop'.[31]

In reply, the Archbishop of Canterbury said that he 'wished to express deep admiration of Bishop Rwaje and the role he was playing. He added that the situation of the Bishop of Kigali was quite untenable, but there was a problem in finding a suitable ministry for him outside of Rwanda'.[32] Eventually, Bishop Ruhumiliza was forced to resign and left the country with his family. He was later offered a post in the diocese of Montreal, Canada, but later moved to the UK.

5.2 Église Épiscopale au Rwanda - New Leadership

Église Épiscopale au Rwanda, after receiving the approval of the Bishops in Congo, saw the House of Bishops in Rwanda endorse the decision to elect Bishop Mbona Kolini as the new Bishop of Kigali. He was then duly nominated to be the next Archbishop of Rwanda.[33] At the diocese of Kigali on the 3 August 1997, Bishop Kolini

---

[31] A report, Meeting of the Primates of the Anglican Communion and the Moderators of the United Churches St George's College, Jerusalem 10-17 March 1997.
[32] Ibid.
[33] Interviewing the new Archbishop of Rwanda August 1998

was enthroned as the Bishop of the Diocese of Kigali and the new Archbishop of the Anglican Church Province of Rwanda at a ceremony in the large stadium in Kigali. In his inaugural speech, he asked the people of Rwanda for their forgiveness for the genocide, even though he had not been in the country at the time. He now has the task of uniting the people of Rwanda after all the years of turmoil. The first task was to organise elections, especially in areas where Church leaders had gone into exile and were unable to return and a new Anglican Church leadership needed to be appointed.

The next task for reconstruction was in the diocese of Shyira that has three prefectures: Ruhengeri in the north, Gisenyi and Kibuye in the west. Shyira Diocese is situated in the mountains and was one of the first 'mission stations' of the Rwanda Mission (CMS) with the typical 'three legged stool' of hospital, school and Anglican Church. It was the second diocese to be separated from Kigali and the first Bishop, the Right Reverend Augustine Nshamihigo, was consecrated there in 1983. However, after the genocide, he was still in exile in Kenya. The present Bishop of Shyira, the Right Reverend John Kabango Rucyahana, was consecrated on 8 June 1997 in Ruhengeri. Bishop Rucyahana was brought up in Uganda, although originally from Ruhengeri. Before that, he served as Archdeacon of Bunyoro Kitara diocese in Uganda, where he was much loved by the people.

A hundred Ugandan Christians made the journey across the border to Bishop Rucyahana's consecration. He now works in Gisenyi which, according to respondents, was a very difficult part of the country where many refugees who had supported the previous regime returned.[34]

---

[34] Interviewing archbishop Kolini at St. James the Great, Hackney, London July 1998

Then appointments followed in the diocese of Butare which is situated in the south, in the University town, eighty miles south of Kigali. The Anglican Church Cathedral and diocesan centre is situated between a large Catholic centre and the Butare National University campus. The former Bishop of Butare, the Right Reverend Justin Ndandali, was studying in California when he was called to become the first Bishop of the diocese in Rwanda in 1982. Bishop Ndandali was the only Anglican Church Bishop to stay in the country throughout the 1994 genocide. He became very ill suddenly in December of that year and died in hospital in Nairobi, Kenya. He was also the second and last Archbishop of the Francophone Province of Burundi, Rwanda and Zaire from 1981 to 1992. The present Bishop, the Right Reverend Venuste Mutiganda, was studying in France during the genocide and afterwards returned to the diocese where he had been elected as Coadjutor Bishop in 1991. He was consecrated in Butare Cathedral on 27 April 1997.

The diocese of Shyogwe is quite a large one, with its official headquarters built on a site given to the Anglican Church by the Belgian government for a boys' secondary boarding school. Previously, the only secondary school education was at Butare (Astrida as it was then called). Along with the school at Shyogwe, houses were built for the staff and a missionary who set up trade schools in Rwanda, Mr Ted Sisley, started building an Anglican Church. Later, other institutions were added; a Bible School for the then Butare diocese, a training centre for Sunday school work and a rural development centre. In 1991, when Shyogwe became a separate diocese, Christians from Germany financed the completion of Mr Sisley's Anglican Church as the diocesan Cathedral. The first Bishop of this diocese, the Right Reverend Samuel Musabyimana, went into exile during the troubles in 1994 and has never returned.

The diocesan Synod declared the seat vacant and elected the Right Reverend Jered Karimba as the new Bishop. Bishop Karimba lived in Rwanda throughout the political troubles and was elected to continue the diocesan duties because of his knowledge of the area and his ministry experience. He was consecrated in an open air 'Cathedral' service near the school on 15 June 1997. The Vice-President, the Prime Minister and leaders of all the major denominations attended the service.

Kigeme diocese was another one of the first 'mission stations' in the 1930s and has the Anglican Churches, a school and a hospital that have been built on three hills at an altitude of 7,000 feet. The girls' secondary school is the twin of the school at Shyogwe and has educated many of the leading women in the country today. The hospital has two hundred beds and used to care for sick people from as far away as Cyangugu prefecture (south-western Rwanda) which is about fifty miles away. The soil is poor in this region and there is severe malnutrition.

The Reverend Norman Kayumba was elected the first Bishop of Kigeme when it was created out of Butare in 1991. The Right Reverend Kayumba was there during the first months of the 1994 genocide, when thousands of people, who were registered as Tutsi on their identity cards, were rounded up and taken to be massacred. 'Unfortunately,' reported Amnesty International, 'every Rwandan citizen is required by law to carry identity cards stating their ethnic group (their ethnic group is determined by their father's).'[35]

Alexis Bilindabagabo, the only Tutsi Bishop of the former House of Bishops at that time, has been moved from being diocesan Bishop of Cyangugu to being Assistant Bishop of Kigeme. For months the militia had tried to kill him and his family but they were helped by Bishop Norman

---

[35] Amnesty International, Rwanda, Index: AFR 47/17/94, p.11.

Kayumba and survived. Bishop Bilindabagabo has since been consecrated elsewhere. There was also evidence that a large number of Church members who had left the country during the 1994 genocide had returned. However, due to the shortage of Anglican clergy in the diocese Bishop Kayumba had set up a local system of continual training for clergy. He had also built new offices for the diocese and a new guesthouse.

The diocese of Gahini is a new diocese created in the east of the country by the Anglican Church after the genocide, due to the creation of the new Prefecture of Umutara by the government. Alexis Bilindbagabo was elected the first Bishop and later consecrated in a colourful service on 25 May 1997. The preacher was the Bishop from the Eastern Ankole diocese in Uganda, from where many of the people in the congregation had returned after years of exile following the killings of 1959 and the 1960s. Having had his own life constantly threatened, the Bishop had escaped across the border into Bukavu. When the present army, the Rwandan Patriotic Army (RPF), took over the country - and the government - on 4th July 1994, Bishop Bilindbagabo came back to find that many of his family had been massacred.

He was moved by the plight of the 300,000 orphans left by the genocide and appealed for help. For the first two years after returning from exile, Bishop Bilindbagabo built up an organisation for the support of orphans. The organisation, called the 'Balakabaho Foundation,' is now looking after many orphaned children and a number of women who were raped during the genocide.[36] His second task was to repair damaged and neglected Anglican Church buildings in preparation for a large convention in

---

[36]International Alert in Rwanda: Justice and Reconciliation – Gacaca Process, 28 August 2006, p.12.

September 1997, the aim of which was for reconciliation in the new diocese.

This large conference drew people from many places to where the great Eastern African Revival in the 1930s had begun its mission in Rwanda. The theme of the reconciliation message was 'Walking with Jesus in the first love'. All speakers on this occasion stressed that 'the country and people of Rwanda need a great measure of love, primarily the love of God, but also the love of other Christians around the world, in order to heal the deep wounds inflicted by the massive slaughter of innocent and unarmed men, women and children'.[37] Bishop Bilindabagabo has also built a restaurant and guesthouse by the lakeside at Muhazi and the money raised supports both the project and diocesan work.[38]

Kibungo diocese is situated in the east, towards the Tanzanian border, where the huge exodus of refugees took place. The previous Bishop fled across the border in 1994 and spent two years as pastor to refugees in the massive camps in Tanzania. When he received the ultimatum to return within three months he resigned his See, saying that he was looking after the people with whom he fled. Those who visited the camps all commended his work of pastoral care. Since then he has returned with a large number of refugees and is now settled in the country; but on his return he did not go back to his diocesan duties because there were still accusations against the Bishop that he was involved in the genocide.

These allegations dragged on until the Church members demanded a Bishop because the diocese without leadership was losing its members, who were converting to new independent Churches. Finally, the new Bishop was elected by the Electoral College (as it is known) in March

---

[37]Interviewing Bishop Alexis Birindabagabo at Gahini Diocese July 1998.
[38]Ibid.

and was consecrated on 29 June 1997. Bishop Prudence Ngarambe had lived in exile in Tanzania and Kenya. The Archbishop of Kenya, David Gitari, who was invited to preach at his consecration, ordained him. The service was held in the open, next to one of his parishes, as there was at that time no cathedral. Before his election as a Bishop, Ngarambe was working as Development Officer in the Provincial Office in Kigali. Bishop Ngarambe has the huge task of development of this diocese, which has lost an essential centre to the new diocese of Gahini.

In Byumba diocese, Bishop Onesphore Rwaje was elected Dean of the Province of Rwanda in July 1995 and was Acting Primate when there was no other. He had to steer and lead the Anglican Church single-handed, through some difficult times, to a point where it can now move forward. Like all Primates before him, he had to look after his own diocese in the Northeast while attending to the affairs of the province within the country and abroad. He represented Rwanda at the Primates' Conference in Jerusalem and at other meetings in preparation for the Lambeth Conference. His diocese of Byumba was badly hit in the war from 1991 when the RPF moved in from Uganda on its northern border. Bishop Rwaje has had many homeless and bereaved people to look after and has received grants from a number of bodies in the Anglican Church communion. All these things illustrate an Anglican Church re-building its caring base and preparing for a future where reconciliation has to be a major part of its concern.

From the above Anglican Church leadership appointments and structural reorganisation, it seems that all nine dioceses had begun to engage in community issues, under their respective leaders from all groups. The training centres were also getting busy recruiting new Anglican Church leaders, this time without discrimination against other groups; previously Tutsi were not considered for higher office in the Anglican Church. From the pulpit the message is about forgiveness, reconciliation and rebuilding the country. Anglican Church clergy are daily sharing the love of God with thousands of people whose lives have been shattered; with orphans and with broken-hearted and traumatised individuals. Many clergy from local congregations have a wide range of skills to help refugee returnees and all those in need.

5.3 The New Leadership and the Composition of Anglican Church Congregations

From the outside, the Anglican Church appears to be cosmopolitan with all ethnic groups represented in the congregation. However, in table 4, with reference to fear of neighbours, 75% of respondents at the time of interview, both Hutu and Tutsi Anglican Church members, were still afraid and suspicious of one another.[39] The Church congregations are very friendly and welcoming, but seem to be made up of several groups with very weak links between them. Conversations and observations showed that congregations were made up of those who wanted change and those who did not. Anglican Church teaching and the style of worship that I observed seemed to adequately reflect and involve a variety of people in the congregation. Though, there is some mileage in the suggestion that a pastoral care must be of the type through which all ethnic groups might reach their potential. Nevertheless, some groups are trying to get involved and become influential in the life of the Anglican Church as a whole.

In addition, Anglican Church leaders are getting more involved in local and national issues; the evidence for this being in the appointments of bishops based on a balance of ethnic representation. The evidence for this broad-based

---

[39]Interviews at Kigali, Byumba, Butare, Gahini Cathedrals July 1998.

representation was that five Bishops were Hutu, four Tutsi and one English. In the case of the Église Épiscopale au Rwanda, the parish fellowship is well placed to act as a micro-barometer for the National Anglican Church. Regarding local representation from village, sub-parish, parish, archdeaconry, diocese to the Archbishopric, all these offices are occupied by both Hutu and Tutsi as employees of Église Épiscopale au Rwanda. Kigali, Shyira and Kibungo were the only dioceses with Bishops ordained outside Rwanda. Six Hutu Bishops and one Tutsi Bishop were ordained and consecrated in Rwanda.

At one Anglican Church Cathedral at Gahini, 56% represented in table 4 thought that the Anglican Church was united and very friendly and appreciated the fact that there was a lot of openness and welcoming of others among Anglican Church members. Also, in Kigali at the Anglican Church Cathedral, the most commonly mentioned good thing was the mix of people from all ethnic groups.[40] In some places, it was a very encouraging and positive sign that the Anglican Church was working as hard as possible to promote a spirit of openness.

This new openness and welcoming spirit was widely stressed during interviews by survivors who believed that the Anglican Church should work for reconciliation, whilst knowing full well that justice has to be established first before the reconciliation process can happen in the country. Though, survivors stressed that it was important for the reconciliation process to reach 'beneath the surface'. The comments of some respondents showed that there would need to be to a structural basis that would enable Hutu and Tutsi Anglican members to be open with each other, so that they cared and could show and could bring to the surface any bad feelings or fears which still existed. 36% of Anglican Church respondents in table 4 agreed for unity

---

[40]Interviews with survivors in Kigali, July 1997.

across ethnic differences and also saw Anglican Church leaders as having a special role in bringing communities together.

5.4 Pastoral Ministry

Almost all of the Anglican Churches are energetically serving and responding on a vast scale to the daily pastoral needs of society; family tensions, caring for orphans attending Anglican Church schools, poor health and mental illness. But each diocese tackled social needs in different ways; the valuable asset is that right across the Anglican Church, the leadership was busy assessing both theoretical and practical ways forward to reconciliation, preaching the importance of the practice of repentance and forgiveness in this process.

Some rely on prayers and faith, but each diocese is approaching these social needs in different ways. Some Anglican Church leaders are using a social work caring approach and others apply a combination of both spiritual renewal and pastoral care; Anglican Churches normally care for people in need as part of their pastoral ministry. They also preach God as the Parent of all without any discrimination and that human beings are His children regardless of sex, ethnic group or social status. Some rely on prayers and faith, but other Anglican Churches try to combine these approaches and almost all care for people in need with a good measure of Christian compassion. To look at different kinds of experience is to recognise the value of different groups and of different communities that exist side by side. On the other hand, much depends on finance and unless we learn as Christians to be generous with our gifts and resources and learn to share them for the benefit of others, the Anglican Church on the ground will be limited in the social care it can and should be providing and encouraging.

The study has looked at the pattern of warfare and ethnic cleansing and how it affected people in society. The greatest problem after the genocide was how to handle the mess created by the conflict. Interviews accumulated considerable evidence showing how social and economic difficulties still posed problems in many areas. Anglican Church leaders will, on occasion, have to face the issues squarely by demanding that the politicians remove the political and economic obstacles that stand in the way of fulfilling ordinary people's needs. The government, for example, changed policy to spend less of the national revenue on military defence.

However, this could not apply directly after the genocide, but only after some time had elapsed when the insurgents have been dealt with. National resources should be invested in the thousands of refugees who are living in camps in poverty and who require food, medicine and clothing. As with any armed conflicts such as this, there is a huge increase in the number of refugees, major disruptions and interruptions in the production and supply of food for the population and an increase in poverty and disease. It is argued that despite the Anglican Church's having failed in the past, it still has a chance to reverse its past behaviour and persuade the government to spend money on people's needs, especially on water projects and agricultural schemes in villages to improve farming.

Although this does not improve the country's economy, it would give refugees in camps and in villages' confidence and self-respect rather than being the annual beneficiaries of handouts. As part of the response to people's needs the Anglican Church has to assist those trapped in destitute conditions. The practical way in which the Rwandan Anglican Church is approaching the need for reconciliation is through the organisation of seminars to address the search for peace issues. The first seminar was held from 25 to 28 March 1998 at St. Joseph's Anglican

Church Centre, Kibungo Prefecture, where Anglican Church Leaders gathered to discuss how to respond to the crisis in the aftermath of the genocide. The title of the seminar was 'Reconciliation in Rwanda'. It was organised by REACH, which is a local interdenominational organisation based in Kigali and sponsored by friends from the United Kingdom to deal with four main objectives:

- Evangelism
- Social action
- Care and counselling
- Partnership in mission.[41]

Building on exchanges between the participants, the seminar explored theoretical and methodological trends in the study of reconciliation, theology and their relevancy to the Anglican Church in terms of the best way forward and which might be the best model to apply in the case of Rwanda. The seminar began by asking: what could be a permanent solution to the conflict in the country? The seminar then focused on historical legacies, as well as contemporary developments. Suggestions were made for how Rwandan traditional cultural 'wisdom', within the interplay of traditional culture and society in general, could be realised and valued in Rwanda. It asks questions about the nature of 'church' and how our relationship with Christ enables us to be 'overcomers', both in the sphere of collective action related to reconciliation issues and in other ways to benefit the Church family as a whole.

---

[41] African Rights Appeal to the World Council of Churches contains a copy of the Bishop's Report 1999, p.1.

5.5 A Silent and Compromised Anglican Church

The seminar participants asked: what could have the Anglican Church have done when the country was at war? The response from seminar members was that when the Anglican Church was most needed by the country for a prophetic voice, it opted for silence. This section examines the accusation regarding the Anglican Church's lack of response. The refusal to recognise what happened was interpreted not only as an insult to the members, parishioners, families and friends of those who perished, but a betrayal of those priests who died protecting their flock. Respondents remarked: 'What comment can we make on such silence?' 'Was it their tacit wish that their followers should be killed? If not, was it, then, fear that forced them not to criticise the government?' It is therefore vital to ensure that the nature of the accusations made against the Anglican Church and individuals within it are explored.

If investigations show that those in positions of pastoral responsibility ignored their role, then these church leaders should be brought to answer for their neglect and, if found guilty and unrepentant, dismissed. In this world where the Anglican Church has considerable influence and where it is looked to for setting an example of love, care and even 'suffering' (2 Tim.4:5) this denial of responsibility is clearly unacceptable.

As one could see from the way Rwandan people lived in a close community, in the majority of cases the perpetrators of the cleansing policy were close neighbours of the victims, who were known and can be identified by the survivors. Throughout the interviews, refusal was generally seen as failure because during the genocide people knew each other and the failure of the Anglican Church to investigate its role in the genocide not only created mistrust in the leadership, it also disturbed many of the faithful.[42] In the aftermath of the genocide, Tutsi Anglican clergy and lay leadership who survived the genocide increasingly 'questioned whether they have a place in an institution that refuses to recognise the enormity of the genocide, its consequences and its own contribution'.[43]

Gerloff Roswith added that 'The truth hurts, but silence kills'.[44] Survivors wondered if Anglican Church leaders were silent collaborators who did not like to expose themselves to danger or whether they were merely ignorant of the nature and extent of the conflict.[45] Whatever the case may be, they had a duty to condemn the killers and defend those who were in danger of being killed, since it was their responsibility to teach and preach the truth. It is argued that, by the failure of the Anglican Church to hold on to Christian principles, it was abdicating its spiritual leadership responsibility to society. This situation complicated the positions of Anglican Church leaders who had previously served the Anglican Church, as they were to be seen as suspects and possible sympathisers of insurgence in the country. Again, after the genocide, it was noted that some Anglican Churches used the service from the pulpit as an opportunity to discourage the faithful from accusing the perpetrators of the genocide.

There was a concern that potential witnesses (who survived the genocide) might be killed in order to remove the evidence and proofs of genocide. The massacres in

---

[42] Being Anglican (1997), compiled by James, M. Rosenthal. and N. Currie, Anglican Consultative Council X, Panama City, p. 138.

[43] Interviews with Diocesan Synod members, Kigali, August 1998.

[44] Gerloff, R, (1998). Truth, a new Society and Reconciliation: the Truth and Reconciliation Commission in South Africa: a German Perspective, Leeds: University Press, p. 17.

[45] Interviewing Anglican members at Byumba, Butare, Gahini and Kigali, July 1997.

Kibuye and Gisenyi schools are examples of this.[46] For both legal and ethical reasons, I was unable to record the denomination and the location of these incidents. However, according to a government report, Southern province has the largest number of killings and violence against genocide survivors and Gacaca witnesses. The report on genocide related killings and violence prepared between 1995 and 2008 indicates that a total of 176 survivors and witnesses were killed countrywide of which 105 of the killings occurred in the south. Muhanga and Nyamagabe districts had the leading numbers, with 12 residents killed especially during the April genocide commemoration month.[47]

It was suggested that the Anglican Church was slowly realising the extent of its failures in general terms, but that it had avoided singling out individuals whose conduct was the subject of inquiries. At some Anglican Churches people are still asking how they can trust Anglican Church leaders after what happened. There are many people who need pastoral care who are still scared and hurt and others who are still traumatised and need support, but wonder whether the Anglican Church leaders are the right people to turn to for help. Adrian Hastings states that Mbanda was right to insist that many clergy were deeply involved in this truly appalling crime.[48]

The accounts of the genocide raise the question as to why the Anglican Church failed to express both concern and Christian responsibility to speak out against the atrocities committed against fellow believers and neighbours. African Rights has done well in documenting

---

[46]African Rights, Issue 7: 'Antoine Sebomana and His Supporters: Burying the Truth in the name of Human Rights', September 1997.
[47]The Times Rwanda, Tuesday, 30th September 2008
[48]Hastings, A., "The Tribal Contest behind Africa's Bloodbath" in the Catholic Tablet, 5 September 1998, p.1152.

the priests and pastors who killed or encouraged killings.[49] According to McCullum there were two Anglican Churches and many denominations – the official Anglican Church, almost all of whose leaders were close to government and another Anglican Church which is now the surviving Anglican Church.[50]

The political position of Archbishop Augustin Nshamihigo had been made clear, even before the genocide. A former government soldier and army chaplain, he was often with President Habyarimana.[51] His closeness to politicians was bound to create implications for him and, even in exile in Nairobi, he continued to be a close associate of the politicians, army officers and businessmen who were the chief architects of the genocide. There was a reluctance to return because of a justified fear of reprisals, without recognising that it was largely prompted by a fear of justice. Respondents criticised Archbishop Carey's comment, 'I know of one significant leader who is afraid of going back, but I am sure that he is innocent'.[52] In the view of many survivors in Rwanda, all clergy who participated should acknowledge their involvement in the genocide and humbly ask forgiveness for the sake of justice and reconciliation and to make a new start.

After the genocide, there was a public call for the Anglican Church hierarchy to search its conscience and many members of the Anglican Church have expressed regret for its whole failure to speak out against the killings from 1990 to 1994.[53] A memorandum from a group of

---

[49]Mbanda, L., (1997). Committed to Conflict, The Destruction of the Anglican Church in Rwanda, London: SPCK, p.91.
[50]McCullum, Hugh, (1995). The Angels Have Left Us. The Rwanda Tragedy and the Anglican Churches, with a foreword by Desmond Tutu, Geneva: World Council of Anglican Churches, p.74.
[51]African Rights Appeal to the World Council of Churches contains a copy of the Bishop's Report 1999, p.11.
[52]Ibid.
[53]Anglican Communion News Service, 16 February 1996.

Rwandan Christians addressed to the Western Anglican Church leaders in 1996 asked, amongst other things, that the Anglican Church leaders adopt measures to ensure that the Anglican Church confessed and ended its errors of the past. It criticised the Anglican Church leadership in general for its support of bishops in exile whose politics were linked with ethnic conflict. Bishops in exile have been able to find new roles within the Anglican Church.[54]

Robert Shropshire of the Anglican Church of Canada's Primate's World Relief and Development Fund (PWRDF) made several practical suggestions for a resolution to the conflict. What this meant in practice, with regard to the position of leaders of the Anglican Church in Rwanda, was that only a court of justice could decide on the guilt or innocence of the Anglican Church leaders.[55] In Shropshire's opinion, an ecclesiastical court could be responsible for hearing pleas in this matter, since the questions raised were leaning equally on the laws of the Anglican Church. It was the right option at a time when it was difficult for the Anglican Church to come under scrutiny for such collusion. It is argued that prosecution before the ecclesiastical judiciary could have enhanced the legitimacy of all those who were suspected, but were proved not guilty before the ecclesiastical court of law. We must remember that the principal function of the ecclesiastical court is to support the restoration of the rule of law.

The large number of survivors stressed that this was not a matter for recrimination. They criticised the Anglican Bishops for not allowing the judicial institutions to perform the task they were created to perform and had performed

---

[54] Cfr. McCullum, Hugh, (1995). The Angels Have Left Us. The Rwanda Tragedy and the Anglican Churches, with a foreword by Desmond Tutu, Geneva: World Council of Anglican Churches, p. 73.
[55] African Rights Appeal to the World Council of Churches contains a copy of the Bishop's Report 1999, p.2.

for centuries. The problem was in finding these Bishops, who proved to be elusive. Despite using a variety of techniques by approaching them, telephoning and so forth, I was unable to make contact, especially with Bishop Ruhumuliza. This remains a significant lacuna in this study, since it would have been of benefit to hear his viewpoint in seeking to understand the problem.

Jonathan Randall asserted that the ways in which the Anglican Church had failed to respond to the accusations against their members shows how ill equipped they were to handle crises on the scale of this genocide.[56] The major concern for many is the failure of the Anglican Church's leadership to respond to the allegations of its role in the massacre and this same failure also betrays the memories of the clergy who were killed in the genocide.

This failure to respond to allegations also undermines the many priests, lay leaders and Anglican Church workers who took no part in the killings, but who were regarded as suspects. Some Anglican Church leaders showed a lack of sensitivity by simply dismissing local communities, described by them as a bunch of politically oriented activists whose intention was to destabilise the Anglican Church. 61% of the respondents interviewed thought it ill of the Anglican Church leadership to ignore the public outcry. Especially after what had taken place, this refusal to respond justified the criticisms levelled against the Anglican Church. It is argued that the Anglican Church leadership, under these circumstances, should have been more transparent and willing to be called to account, so that the judicial system could hold those responsible to answer for their crimes and thereby restore the rule of law as an alternative to vigilante justice.

---

[56]Cfr. Jonathan Randall, Washington Post, 29 June 1994; African Rights, Report No.3, May 1996.

There is an alternative viewpoint that Anglican Church leaders did not commit crimes on the same scale as the Interahamwe, ministers, army officers and local administrators who were named by the RPF government as the leading perpetrators of the genocide. Failure to bring to justice the perpetrators also, in turn, obscured those Hutu who made heroic efforts to hide Tutsi, in order to save lives and to comfort the bereaved. Those thus rescued included both Rwandan clergy and foreign missionaries.[57]

Accusations against the Anglican Church may vary in strength and consistency. However, there was still a strong perception amongst survivors that there had been no concerted international effort to encourage Anglican Church leaders to express regret for what they did and what they failed to do. As a result of this, almost a million Tutsi and many of the Hutus were killed together with their families. Moreover, the effect of delays, notably for victims awaiting action against perpetrators and in those clear-cut cases where both evidence and witnesses were available, was stressed by respondents as a sign of failure on the part of the local and the Anglican Church.

There is every reason to examine allegations of their role in the genocide in order to clear the cloud of doubt surrounding them. African Rights argued that the friendship and influence of foreign Anglican Churches and the support and protection of suspects, makes it harder to bring those same suspects to justice, because of the lengthy procedure and the political controversies involved in it.[58]

The United Nations Criminal Tribunal for Rwanda has indicted most of them and the indictment shows that Anglican Church leaders belonging to every denomination are wanted for the crime of genocide. A few cases have

---

[57] African Rights, Rwanda: Death, Despair and Defiance (new expanded edition) (1995), p.329.
[58] African Rights Appeal to the World Council of Churches contains a copy of the Bishop's Report 1999, p.22.

been heard in European courts and over 2,500, who include Anglican clergy suspects, have been tried and sentenced in Rwanda (ICTR)[59]. However, Anglican respondents interviewed at the Cathedral in Kigali, argued that the real danger is that, as a consequence of the delays, witnesses will be less willing to cooperate with the courts in the helpful way they do at present.[60] The question of delay was linked with foreign influence and support and, in addition, it is where so far ICTR has only tried and sentenced eight suspects.[61] At the present time, many victims of genocide see the delay as a failure on the part of the international community to bring several Category One suspects who remain at large around the world to trial. The Rwandan government argues that those wanted are the planners, organisers, instigators, supervisors and leaders of the genocide, numbering in total two thousand one hundred and thirty-three, to be tried by International Tribunal in Arusha.[62]

The government of Rwanda is still keen to apprehend suspects and bring them to trial.[63] When considering the views of respondents, this highlights an alarming lack of accountability within the Anglican Church. For instance, a journalist asked an Anglican Church leader whether the Anglican Church had made any official statement about the Ntakuritimana's case. His reply was that 'There should be a point where we just say what is gone is gone. Let's begin afresh'.[64] There is overwhelming evidence to show that Anglican Church leaders not only failed in their duties, being a silent and compromised witness to the killings, but

---

[59] http://www.skepfiles.org/moretext/genocide.htm/10/11/08).
[60] Interviewing Diocesan staff members at the Cathedral, Kigali August 1998.
[61] Cfr. http://www.ambarwanda.org.uk/genocide/index.htm.
[62] http://www.ambarwanda.org.uk/genocide/index.htm
[63] Ibíd.
[64] Byrd, Alita, Spectrum, Vol. 25, No.4, June 1996.

that they violated Christian principles. What is important here is that consequently the Rwandan Anglican Church leadership will remain affected by these problems from which they cannot easily be free.

Following a visit to Rwanda in May 1995, the Archbishop of Canterbury was critical of the Anglican Church in all its dioceses, stating that 'the Anglican Church in Rwanda lost an opportunity to be prophetic during the genocide'.[65] He said that 'The Anglican Church should have been calling out for justice. It should have been pointing out some of the atrocities that were done, but, by and large, its voice was silent'.[66]

The killings in Rwanda began in 1959 and no one condemned them. A further dimension to this problem was that in the First Republic the government was killing slowly, but no one from the Anglican Church spoke out. In the Second Republic there were more killings and more people tortured, more rapes and disappearances and even then, out of either fear or complacency, the Anglican Church did not speak out.

The Rwandan government decided to scrap the death penalty in order to encourage the transfer of suspects for justice; they argued that if that were done there would be no reason for the Anglican Church not to 'come clean'. The process for Rwanda to make the death penalty illegal was published in the Official Gazette on 25 July 2006.[67] In Kigali on 17 Nov 2006, (IRIN) a military tribunal found a priest, Wenceslas Munyeshaka, resident in France, guilty of rape and involvement in the 1994 genocide.[68] As with this case, it is important that all submitted evidence be

---

[65] Ecumenical News International, 16 May 1996.
[66] Ibid.
[67] http://www.rwandagateway.org/article.php3?id_article=6743/6/07
[68] http://www.irinnews.org/report.asp?ReportID=56408&SelectRegion=Great_Lakes/18/9/07.

substantiated where allegations against Anglican Church leaders are concerned. Nearly all the responses analysed referred to further demands that all denominations in Rwanda should investigate allegations made against the clergy and that conclusions should be made public. As part of a preliminary investigation, the investigators should make a thorough investigation into allegations made by survivors against any denominational Church leaders.

Opportunities for investigating the genocide should be expanded considerably now that refugees have returned from exile since late 1996. This should not only be regarded as a sign of respect for the rule of law, but as the restoration of Anglican Church credibility in society. Many of the refugees include former militiamen, some of whom would be willing to provide detailed testimonies. The Anglican Church leadership has shown no sign yet of taking the necessary initiatives to assist the public in finding out the truth about the Anglican Church leaders accused of involvement in the genocide.

Theo Tschury states that: 'The Anglican Church is challenged constantly and critically to search the scriptures as it seeks to understand the seriousness of accusations made to open itself to new insights and honesty, acknowledging where it has abused scriptures to justify its own understanding of ethnicity and nationalism. In searching the scriptures and seeking to live as the body of Christ, the Anglican Church leaders were called to repent and to walk the path of Christian discipleship, which is always under the shadow of the cross and may often lead to the cross.[69]

Survivors still feel that the efforts made by the Anglican Church on behalf of those accused of genocide have not been matched by efforts on behalf of the victims

---

[69]Tschury, Theo, (1997), Ethnic Conflict and Religion, Challenge to the Churches, Geneva: WCC Publications, p 154.

of that genocide. Bayingana said that 'Even to talk about reconciliation in this country sounds hollow unless basic issues of justice are addressed'.[70] In my view, most crucially, if the search for justice is genuine, it will allow people who are involved to come to their own understanding of what justice means, not only in the enlightenment sense of the punishment of perpetrators, but in finding a way forward for the future. There is a need to identify and to bring to justice all suspects of ethnic cleansing and to discipline them as an example to others never to repeat the same. To prevent this happening again, there is a great need in Rwandan society to put right the structural system, so that it can operate as a mechanism for justice in society.

5.6 Survivors Felt Neglected by the Anglican Church

This section assesses another accusation made against the Anglican Church; that it had failed to offer support and care during and after the genocide. The question of Anglican pastoral care was seriously challenged by information gathered in the following ways: observation made of the areas visited, interviews with various Anglican Church members, an interview with the Rwandan Archbishop and interviews with residents of Mutara, Nyamata and Gisenyi.

The following are views and needs to be taken in the light of those interviews. The interviews revealed that, in May 2004 at Nyamata and Gisenyi Anglican parish churches, the Anglican Church neglected elderly survivors. Survivor support in any real sense of the term was nearly nonexistent.[71] One type of support needed by survivors was

---

[70]Bayingana, Ng. E., Art., (1994). 'Reconciliation: Foundation for Reconstructing a New Rwanda', Nairobi: Evangel Press, p. 23-26.
[71] Interviews in Nyamata, Mutara and Gisenyi, May 2004.

more to do with material need and another offered protection from neighbours who threatened to kill witnesses, in order to prevent them giving evidence of their involvement in the genocide. Their fear was justified as most of those witnesses in the Nyamata, Bugesera and Gisenyi in Shyira dioceses have, since then, been killed (Gisenyi).[72]

My argument here is that the Anglican Church must look at the size of the problem to meet the challenges; it cannot walk away from its responsibilities of caring for and supporting its members. It has also been argued that Anglican Church leaders from different theological persuasions develop a reconciliation model. It is seen as the Anglican Church's responsibility to reflect as closely as possible the socio-economic needs of the society in which the Rwandan Anglican Church is called to be faithful to the gospel. Therefore, this reconciliation has to be inclusive in its process of advocacy for economic justice, because the reconciliation role of the Anglican Church among the poor is vital.

At this present time, survivors interviewed in August 1997 in Mutara and Gisenyi felt isolation, abandonment and a lack of support, practical or spiritual, from the Anglican Church. Nevertheless, there was a large group of survivors, 63% of respondents in table 4, brought together in deliberations over this period. These particular survivors say they have not received support from the Anglican Church. Considering that the extent and quality of support varied from area to area, respondents did not find the Anglican Church helpful, particularly in rural areas, Therefore, the 63% figure suggested alienation of significant numbers of people in these areas. In some rural locations like Nyamatimba and Gatuna, survivor support, in any sense of the term, was virtually non-existent. This

---

[72]Ibid.

situation was extremely frustrating and discouraging; the elderly people in particular were isolated and found the situation very difficult. Nevertheless, the vast majority (63%) of survivors were clearly not satisfied by the minimalist approach taken by the Anglican Church to support them. On the other hand, from what I witnessed, I wish to argue that for the Anglican Church to implement this obligation immediately after the genocide was no easy task. Survivors, however, argued that the Anglican Church's extensive network and resource of charitable structures in Rwanda had not been used to a significant extent to help them.[73]

Overall, it was a situation where both Anglican Church lay respondents and priests in the aftermath of the genocide had been affected, where every individual in the country had been left with orphans to look after, most being small children or disabled survivors. Effectively, the aftermath of genocide had changed normal social boundaries and stretched the people to breaking point. In some instances, the elderly or adult disabled at Byumba were the only surviving members of the family, adding to the great difficulties they already faced.[74]

At this time after the genocide, even the Anglican Church could not fill that void and the little help survivors had received had been at the insistence of a few priests' search for help from donor agencies. Nevertheless, help was essential because, when survivors lost their relatives, they not only lost the people they loved, they also lost the (welfare) support of the extended family that in the past had characterised Rwandan culture and served as a 'safety net' for coping with life's problems. As is the way in poor countries, it had been their only form of social security and protection.

---

[73]Interviews in Mutara and Gisenyi, August 1997.
[74]Interviews at Byumba, August 1997.

It should be made clear that community or ethnic support within a group is not to be condemned. Ethnic affiliation as an extended family system is a great asset in nation building, especially when acting as a moral restraining influence upon and means of security for its members.

Conclusion

What has been learnt from this chapter is the discovery of a catalogue of (human) violence suffered by the Rwandans and the extent of the failure of society at large to deal with it and survive. The chapter has also assessed the Anglican Church's failures and the strength it has gathered in the midst of criticism in its struggle to restore its credibility in society. However, the people's wish is for the Anglican Church to confess its involvement in genocide. Certainly, considering 62% of respondents did not believe that the Anglican Church was united and that 63% did not find any pastoral care, it was a major concern for those who were interviewed. Nine dioceses were also of the same opinion that the Anglican Church needed to inspire more confidence in the people and to be a service provider. They needed to be transparent and to give clear direction. Interviewees stressed the need for somewhere to turn for advice, spiritual guidance, support and protection.[75] Furthermore, Bible college staff members at Butare unanimously agreed that 'Those involved in reconciliation should focus on how to achieve unity'.[76]

I will conclude by stressing that the Anglican Church leadership took unity seriously and recognises that ethnic groups are a very strong foundation upon which a lasting bond can be built. To do this effectively, it is necessary to

---

[75]Interview, Kigali, Butare, Gahini, August 1997.
[76]Interviews, Butare Bible College, August 1998.

apply Christian values to daily living in order to reconcile. It is argued that Christian values can achieve reconciliation among people, but that the Anglican Church in Rwanda would have to be aware of its boundaries in order to act effectively in an advisory capacity. It must not, however, repeat the past mistake of being too intimate with the government.

The next chapter will make an attempt to assess the question of reconciliation in Rwanda and explore the strategies the Anglican Church has put in place, or is proposing in order to liberate the mass of poor Rwandans trapped in refugee camps.

Chapter Six

Part II:
Theological Reflection and Analysis

The Nature of Division in the Post-Genocide Anglican Church

6.0 Introduction

This chapter examines a paradoxical question suggesting that the Anglican Church in Rwanda should have been at the centre of nurturing Christian values, engaging Christians in social development and influencing people's behaviour rather than involving itself in ethnic distinction politics. Previous chapters have stressed the necessity for the Anglican Church to restore its spiritual teaching and to take a role in the process of reconciliation.

The following two chapters will discuss the type of theology that is needed for the Rwandan Anglican leadership to be able to engage the Church in this reconciliation process. In effect, after listening to what was expressed by Anglican Church leaders and respondents from different occupations, I selected men and women from all ethnic groups to represent nine Anglican dioceses in Rwanda. Next, I took one step further to assess what Anglican Church leaders and Church members had to express as being the best way forward for the Anglican Church and how it could help the country towards reconciliation.

A number of theologies are dealt with and a combination of approaches (contextual and revivalist theologies of sin) was discussed. Recommendations were made for spiritual renewal and for contextual language in an effective search for peace. In addition, the mode of reconciliation that was suggested during interviews with Church leaders particularly concerned the 'palaver' mode, which will be discussed in the next chapter.

The main objective here is to examine the Anglican missionaries (Revivalist Heritage) in Rwanda and the changes made in the name of Christian conversion, to see whether they had played any role in the theory of exclusion. The purpose here is to assess the work of Anglican missionaries for any discrimination policy that can be seen as fuelled by social changes in Rwanda, changes characterised by the historical exclusion of Tutsi people from many areas of achievement and the implicit stereotyping of Tutsis on which ethnic distinction ideology rested.

This chapter argues that the theology of the Anglican Church can be made more relevant to the local communities, in order to strengthen commitment to the Christian faith and to make it possible for people to see the need for reconciliation. For this to happen, the Anglican Church needs to develop a contextual theology in order to reverse the impression of abandoning traditional culture to become a Christian.

This chapter will argue for the Anglican Church in Rwanda to develop relevant theology. If it is to provide authentic gospel meaning for a new generation it must analyse the criticisms of present day Anglican Church theology. The purpose of this is to assess whether it was the missionaries' failure to effectively ground converts in the Christian faith or the missionaries leaving the Church in the hands of Rwandan leadership that created misunderstandings surrounding religion and politics. A further aim is to establish whether there is any connection with the later political conflict. It will examine the reasons why there were no signs of any Christian resistance among Anglican Church members during the genocide in Rwanda and will try to explain the reason why the missionaries' converts were not able to learn to express their faith in action or to develop an interpretation of Rwandan theology. I will also debate how the missionaries' teaching was misunderstood, in order to highlight the kind of Christianity that was introduced to Rwanda.

6.1 The Revival Heritage

The former Ruanda Mission, founded in 1921, established its first station at Gahini in 1925. Two lay missionary doctors, Joe Church and Stanley Smith, collaborated with some Ugandans and Rwandans (who had been converted in Uganda) to inaugurate the Anglican Church in Gahini. This was a period of revivalism in East Africa. The Mission extended its ministry throughout the country, with the resulting Anglican Church growing both numerically and spiritually during the time of revival in the 1930s and 1940s, as claimed by respondents.[77]

Barrette observes that, 'By 1920, the Anglican Church already had five indigenous priests and by 1952 there were 100 priests and the first Rwandan Bishop'.[78] The Rwanda (Revival Heritage) Mission, missionaries spoke in a way that ordinary people understood. They offered an emotional experience of conversion that cleared people's minds of repressed emotions and feelings of guilt.

This conversion experience made possible a revolution in their personal experiences and moral lives. Revivalists believed that, in a very particular sense, they were 'saved by the blood of Christ'.[79] The Revivalist missionaries and their converts, known as 'Abalokole', lived a strictly disciplined life of daily devotion. Its members were able to

---

[77]Osborn, H. H., (1995). Revival – A precious heritage, London: SPCK, pp. 17-21; Interviews at Gahini, July 1998.
[78]Welbourn, F. B., (1965). East African Christian, London: Oxford University Press, pp. 37-38.
[79] Ibid.

quote the exact date of their conversion to give testimony to their faith. Revivalist converts bear witness to the power of 'Jesus on the cross', where they were freed from their sins to walk in light. The movement definitely touched individuals in all churches, but seemingly did not reach society as a whole, because it broke cultural taboos.[80] Indeed, the Revival Heritage teaching had influence that spread throughout the country and the first Rwandan Anglican Bishop was appointed in 1965.

After that, the autonomous Église Épiscopale au Rwanda grew, creating nine dioceses throughout Rwanda. Before the genocide, each diocese had up to forty parishes, which in turn comprised fifteen to twenty scattered congregations. The parishes were under the care of an ordained clergy, with local lay leaders looking after the congregations. Rwanda is a very small country and thus the Anglican Church forms a third of the Rwandan population. During the 1930s, more than one thousand people were being baptised each week.[81] Christianity was easily established because it had the support of Rwandans.

On the other hand, it is notable how the Anglican Revivalist Church was never the church of the Tutsi from the early days. This was partly because King Musinga and his chiefs were already converted to Catholicism, but the King did not see the Anglican Church as a threat because they had not interfered in the politics of the country and according Mbanda, King Musinga often described them as exemplary. Gahini became the favourite mission station of King Musinga who, in appreciation, donated to the mission a drum called Rwamu.[82] In fact, the rapid conversion of the

---

[80]Kolini, Emmanuel, (1995). 'Towards Reconciliation in Rwanda', Transformation, Vol. 12, No2, April/June, p. 13
[81]Cfr. Osborn, H. H., (1995), Revival-A precious heritage, London: SPCK , pp. 94-99
[82]Mbanda, L., (1998). Committed to Conflict, The Destruction of the Anglican Church in Rwanda, London: SPCK, p. 24

social class of the chiefs in the 1930s meant that the Anglican Church was almost entirely excluded from making converts among the elite. The success of the Revivalist mission was with lower status Tutsi and with the Hutu majority. On the other hand, Revivalist missionaries saw their task as involving more than just converting Rwandans to Christianity.

The aim of the Rwanda (Revivalist Heritage) mission was about bringing a full Christian culture to fight the social evils of poverty, ignorance and disease. Apart from converting people to the Christian faith, Anglican missionaries saw the need to get involved in development projects such as the building of schools, hospitals and health centres throughout the country,[83] all of which were available to Rwandans. Almost all of the earliest educated people in Rwanda were educated in Church schools.

In order to answer some of the issues that surfaced in these conversations, I explored the teaching of the Revival Heritage (Anglican Church) missionaries in Rwanda. To supplement questionnaires, I put questions to interviewees, asking them to make comments on the relevance of the Bible to them, how far lay people were involved in teaching and preaching and the role of the Anglican Church missionaries in the Belgian period in Rwanda.

Elderly Anglican Church members were asked about the relationship between missionaries and converts and to comment on the attitude of missionaries towards Rwandan culture. They were also asked to comment on the teaching of the Anglican Church before and after independence.

---

[83]Gatwa, Tharcisse, "The Anglican in Rwanda", *Transformation*, Vol. 12, No. 2, April/June 1995, pp. 4–5, 17.

Table 5: Anglican Missionary Teaching of Christianity in Rwanda

Agree %	Disagree %	Uncertain %
Are the Bible and Anglican Church teachings still relevant to life today?		
49	46	05
Are lay people involved in your ministry teaching/preaching?		
46	53	01
Does the Anglican Church in Rwanda need contextual teaching?		
48	47	05
Was Revival heritage teaching to blame for weak commitment?		
69	27	04

Not surprisingly, Bible relevancy in Table 5 is a chief concern for Anglican Church leaders and this is followed by literacy. The distinction between respondents is substantially confirmed by the 46% who disagreed with Bible relevance, suggesting the obstacle faced by Anglican Church members to fully understanding Anglican doctrine. This agrees with those who identify one of the serious problems as the high level of illiteracy among the Balokole.

As far as Christian commitment is concerned, only 27% disagreed that missionary teaching was to blame and attributed the lack of commitment to personal choice. A small group of 4% were uncertain on the matter. 53% disagreed that lay people were involved in ministry and interviewees stated that active Anglican Church members are able only to memorise hymns and Bible verses that are frequently used in Anglican Church services. Otherwise, a huge majority 69% agree with Revival Heritage teaching as the main area of criticism and argued that it was a combination of lack of ability to read the Bible and to understand the Christian message fully that hindered converts from developing their faith from conversional level to grounded Christian knowledge.

This section considers some criticism of the Revival Heritage teaching that led its converts to the lack of Christian commitment argued in this chapter. Evidence for the weakness in Revivalist teaching was even confessed during the missionary period. In July 1938, Dr Algie Stanley wrote: 'I didn't give the Cross the place it should [have had] in my teaching and generally gave 'soft soap' to people instead of reproving them of sin and warning them to free [them] from the wrath to come.[84]

It is right, however, to give credit where it is due. As mentioned earlier, the interventions by Revival Heritage in favour of Rwandan people's interests, for example, in crucial issues such as the introduction of identity cards was appreciated. This was because Anglican missionaries in general had sensed that the issue of identity cards was eventually going to affect people's relationships. Among the Revival Heritage missionaries, a weakness often pointed out by respondents was its lack of solid Christian teaching and taking on board cultural issues. This was seen as the reason why the leadership of the Église Épiscopale au Rwanda was unable to resist the temptation to challenge the political leadership during the crisis.[85]

In addition, various sources show the lack of contextual Christian teaching in the Anglican Church as a fair point for criticism in Rwanda. This teaching was described by Archbishop Kolini as the kind of 'softly-softly' approach. Mbanda argues that missionaries in Rwanda could have laid the foundation of the Christian faith starting from a people's point of view. From an Asian point of view, the missionaries brought not only the seed of

---

[84]Osborn, H. H., (1995), Revival-A precious heritage, London: SPCK, pp. 94-99.
[85]Cfr. Prunier, Gerard. (1995). The Rwanda Crisis: History of a Genocide, New York: Columbia University Press, pp. 130 - 31.

the gospel, but also the 'soil', the 'flower' and the 'flowerpot'.[86] I wish to add that as the gospel seed grew on local soil in Rwanda, it was necessary to use the Rwandan concepts of cultural expression, in order that the Christian faith might be related to ways in which Rwandans understood God. Banda argues that it is important to use cultural language to convey the message in a relevant way to the people it is aimed at and to explain its abiding principles as interpreted in their culture.[87]

Kolini and Mbanda pointed out that from the early teaching of the Anglican Church the Bible was not focused upon in terms of its relevance to the people's culture. Similarly, while 46% of respondents disagreed about the relevance of the Bible and some respondents criticised the Biblical message. In this relation to this, Mbanda is right to criticise early Christian teaching as 'shallow'. Kolini is very definite when he refers to it as 'inadequate teaching to consolidate people's conversion and equip them for leadership, particularly in the midst of political turmoil'.[88] We might ponder on the cultural presuppositions we bring to the Bible as well as the value of seeing it through the eyes of other people and through their own culture.

Much has been said about Christianity being introduced by Revival Heritage to Rwanda as the religious dimension of Western civilisation, concerned not only with saving souls, but also with changing society for the better. Nevertheless, the change must be characterised by the relevant factors that take into consideration the possibility

---

[86]Cfr. Lewin, Hugh, Compiled, (1987). A Community of Clowns, Testimonies of People in Urban Rural Mission, WCC Publications: Geneva, p.296
[87]Mbanda, L., (1998). Committed to Conflict, The Destruction of the Anglican Church in Rwanda, London: SPCK, back covers.
[88]Kolini, Emmanuel, (1995). 'Towards Reconciliation in Rwanda', Transformation, Vol. 12, No2, April/June, p.13.

of better knowledge and methods with which to improve their lives.

One other significant feature of the Brethren fellowship relationship is that most interviewees acknowledged that the 'Revival Brethren' in Rwanda was the only Church that went far beyond ethnic barriers. It was stressed that Revivalists were actively involved in the defence of justice and truth that was both a liberating and an example of powerful Christian witness; the only weakness identified being a lack of deep Christian teaching. What is obvious is that one should not overlook the significant contribution that Anglican Church missionaries brought to Rwanda, especially in education.

It is not over-simplifying the Revival Heritage work in Rwanda to suggest that converts were not ready for the rigours of life in society and the process of political change. Thus, at this time, the Anglican Church leadership had little knowledge of both political manipulation and political ideologies. To put it another way, 51% in the first table confirm that when the power struggle started in the country, i.e. when the Revivalist movement was most needed, the revival failed. However, it is equally important to identify some of the reasons why their teaching did not sufficiently penetrate the life of the society of the time, as is evidenced by the undervaluing of people's culture and a specific focus on long-term needs. Mbanda saw it as a 'low view of the Rwandan culture, combined with a heavy dose of Western theology'.[89]

In interview, the new Archbishop Kolini, Bishop Alexis Birindabagabo and Bishop John Rucyahana blamed the Anglican leadership its lack of Christian commitment to its responsibility to challenge and to act and guide Church members as Christians in a political world and to discern

---

[89]Mbanda, L., (1998). Committed to Conflict, The Destruction of the Anglican Church in Rwanda, London: SPCK, p.16.

between the true and false. Anglican leadership failed to resist political manipulation. Archbishop Kolini argued that when the Church leaders and members were faced with enormous challenges, there was no Christian resistance to say 'no' to injustice and 'yes' to life. M.I. Aguilar argues that it was unsurprising that, after independence, Church leaders who had been intellectually stimulated by different theologies, applied different pastoral, social and political modes to create a Christian society in Rwanda.[90] All these issues demanded answers from the people that the Anglican Church mission had not prepared them to give.[91]

Of course, this is not to deny that, after independence, the Anglican Church leadership did not go any further to address the problem of deeper teaching. Given the state of the Église Épiscopale au Rwanda after independence, it is necessary to recognise three other factors that might have contributed to this lack of deeper teaching. Firstly, after independence the Anglican Church in Rwanda was caught up with political developments, so that, at this period, it was still in its infancy. Secondly, the Église Épiscopale leadership too quickly made close relationships with politicians, the aim of which David Rawson described as being to enhance their own power within the Church hierarchy.[92] Thirdly, at this period the Église Épiscopale au Rwanda administratively was still under the province of the Church of Uganda, Rwanda, Burundi and Boga-Zaire and this created language barriers to the extent where the English speakers at the provincial headquarters in Kampala, could not provide the necessary pastoral support to the

---

[90]Aguilar, M. I., (1996). The Rwanda Genocide and the Call to Deepen Christianity in Africa, Uganda: AMECEA GABA Publications Spearhead Nos. 148 – 150, p. 3.
[91]Kolini, Emmanuel, (1995). 'Towards Reconciliation in Rwanda', Transformation, Vol. 12, No2, April/June,
[92]RAWSON, David 1995. Rwanda: analysis by the US ambassador. Evangelical Missions Quarterly 31(3):p.:322.

young Church a hundred miles away. The point Kolini argued was that the lack of Christian commitment was attributed to most of the Anglican clergy not being properly trained for the ministry, since training emphasis was only put on religious behaviour; for example that, they should keep away from politics.[93] The major weakness of the Revival Heritage teaching lay in what Mbanda observed as missionaries' emphasis not to discuss politics but instead to pray.[94]

However, this emphasis on prayer could, in one sense, be thought of as denying converts a sense of personal adequacy and I will add that prayer means little without action – like the priest who finds a man in need and passes by the other side, praying that someone else will come along and deal with it (Luke 10:30-31). Thus, the Christian argument is that when human lives are endangered and when human dignity is in jeopardy, differences and sensitivities become irrelevant.[95]

Anglican Church leaders run the risk of being accused of hypocrisy when they echo the slogan that politics and religion do not mix. On the other hand, converts were told that if they stopped smoking and drinking, it would lead them to the Kingdom of God. Rogers Bowen noted that the teaching of the Anglican Church in Rwanda usually focused on a limited range of personal moral questions such as lying, stealing, adultery and drunkenness.[96] Of course this teaching did change, because, no sooner had they obtained independence, then both clergy and Church members found themselves face to face with the problems

---

[93]Interviewing the new Archbishop of Rwanda August 1998.
[94]Mbanda, L., (1998). Committed to Conflict, The Destruction of the Anglican Church in Rwanda, London: SPCK, pp. 23-25
[95]Wiesel, Elie, Speech while receiving Nobel Peace Prize, 1986 Evangelical Missions Quarterly, Vol. 33, No. 4, October.
[96]Bowen, R., (1995). "Rwanda, Missionary Reflections on a Catastrophe", London: SPCK, pp. 33 – 47

of power struggle, corruption and a drift back to ethnic conflict. When their Tutsi followers and even Tutsi clergy were killed, they kept quiet as if nothing was taking place.[97] Also, elderly respondents at Gahini observed that the Anglican Church was always slow in giving the guidance that people need in order to work out national issues.[98]

The obstacle faced by the Anglican Church leadership in either taking the ethnic side or moral responsibility for spiritual care was seen by respondents as resulting from Revival teaching, which emphasised care for the soul; it had nothing to do with the social life of the people and to mention politics was a sin of the first order. On the other hand, exploring the relationship between Christian commitment and attitudes towards politics, the findings show the shift of the Anglican Church leaders' spiritual perspective changed dramatically due to the influence of school friends or neighbours who had become government officials and others who were cabinet ministers. At this period, Anglican Church leaders also enjoyed friendship with politicians and began to enjoy a luxurious standard of living and lives with personal gain.

David Rawson and Gary Scheer both observed that, at this time, a young man who wanted to 'climb', to get ahead, would go to Bible school. Pastors have prestige and influence. They gain access to foreign money and government officials and this influence underlines the Anglican Church leadership shift where it was not possible to tell who was a committed Christian and who was not.[99]

---

[97] Ibid, p.39.
[98] Interviewing Anglican clergies at Gahini and Kigali at the provincial headquarters, July 1998
[99] RAWSON, David 1995. Rwanda: analysis by the US ambassador. Evangelical Missions Quarterly 31(3):320-323: Cfr. SCHEER, Gary 1995. Rwanda: where was the church? Evangelical Missions Quarterly 31(3): 324- 328.

This negates the Revival Heritage lack of interest in politics while, equally, the Rwandan way of life did not help converts in differentiating between the reality of Christianity and the reality of the world of politics.

Here is a clear example of the point made earlier that things which cannot be explained in the common sense world, may require interpretive explanations placed upon them through cultural realities. If this is true, cultural apparatus is the lens through which people see; the medium by which they interpret and understand. On the other hand, if the Anglican Church leaders had received adequate training this would have allowed them to investigate how politics functions in order to advance or defend national interests by non-violent means. It is not an exaggeration to suggest that Christianity, not only in Rwanda, but also across the whole continent of Africa, has recently been undergoing a crisis which is not yet resolved and may, in fact, be irresolvable.

Hinga observes that the difficulties in the conversion process were often associated with the missionaries' exclusivist mentality about African culture, language and attitudes that were entirely ignored in Church teachings.[100]

It is also argued by A. J. Hughes that the so-called creator of liberation was the very agent that moved the country steadily into an ideological agenda that involved Belgian administrators making exploitative divisions among Rwandans at the expense of their claimed development in the colonies, rather than securing future liberation for them.[101]

On the other hand, for the sake of better communication and good intentions, it was essential for

---

[100]Hinga, Teresa, (1994). "Jesus Christ and the Liberation of Women in Africa", in King (Ed.) Feminist Theology from the Third World, Maryknoll: Orbis, p. 262.

[101]Hughes, A. J., (1963). East Africa: The Search for Unity, New York: Penguin Books, pp. 28 – 29.

Revival Heritage missionaries to study Rwandan anthropology in order to best understand the people to whom they wished to address themselves.

In the Rwandan context, culture is the way things are done. It is important to realise the impact of these changes and the damage they caused. Edward Sapir's hypothesis states that people perceive the world through a cultural lens.[102] Rwandan culture provided a directness, togetherness, humour and earthiness that were jointly expressed in the family as a concept or theme.

Rwandan religious experience and therefore its customs and institutions, were all manifested through culture and the logic of the struggle for independence was also a struggle for these rights. The critic of the missionary approach argues that learning the Rwandan way of life was necessary. Criticism is also levelled at the training of the clergy and at the theology that was developed in the Anglican Church. These critics argue that it was important for Anglican Church teaching to articulate the Christian faith in the experience of their everyday lives.

Farmer argues for a fresh approach, whereby the Anglican Church in Rwanda can reach a better understanding when people recognise that God meets them in a saving encounter at the deepest interpersonal level.[103] He also further argues that there was arrogance in the work of missionaries, many of whom exhibited little respect for the beliefs of the people they sought to convert.[104] The fact that people's ability to organise comes from their own experience of collective life and the life of their society was often not considered. Some of these weaknesses were

---

[102]Sapir, Edward, (1949). Selected Writings of Edward Sapir in Language, Culture and Personality, David G. Mandelbaum, Ed. Berkeley, USA: University of California Press, p. 162.
[103]Cfr. Farmer, H. H. (1935). The World and God, London: Nisbet, pp. 107 – 27.
[104]Ibid.

criticised widely by respondents from all the Anglican Church leaders and members, who stated that the problem was that the teaching of the Church lacked and still lacks relevance to daily living. For example, Church teaching spends a lot of time explaining heavenly life, while the worries of Church members are for their survival in conditions of poverty and for security in their communities.

This lack of Christian relevance in Rwandan society is often identified with the historical exclusion of Rwandans from many arenas of achievement and the assumptions on which that exclusion is based. Looking back to the past, it is argued that ethnographically documenting Rwandan perspectives could have provided a context in which local culture might have added a cultural dimension in which the Anglican Church could convey meaningful messages.[105] Archbishop David Gitari, Anscar Chupungco, Elisha Mbonigaba and Solomon Amusan, Professor of Liturgy at Immanuel College, Ibadan, Nigeria all agree that: 'The struggle of the colonised countries is aimed at human liberation, not only at the social, political and economic levels, but especially at the religious level of life. Full liberation based on biblical teachings has a more comprehensive character than political liberation because it also involves spiritual freedom. This is why we now speak of indigenisation, contextualisation, inculturation and liberation of liturgy.[106]

Elisha Mbonigaba and Anscar Chupungco agree that, 'The Church must incarnate herself in every race as Christ

---

[105]Cfr. Russell, B., (2002). Research Methods in Anthropology: Qualitative and Quantitative Methods, Walmit Greek: Altamira Press. pp. 3 – 9.
[106]Gitari, D., "The Kanamai Statement", in Anglican Liturgical Inculturation in African, ed. David Gitari, Grove Books Limited, Bramcote, Nottingham, 1994, pp.37-48

incarnated himself in the Jewish race'.[107] Victor, R., Atta-Bafoe and Philip Tovey defined inculturation as, 'The incarnation of the Christian life and message in a particular cultural context in such a way that not only do local Christians find expression for their faith through elements proper to their culture, but also that faith and worship animate, direct and unify the culture.[108]

The above observation is very important for the Rwanda Anglican Church to be able express gospel, for it is only when cultural context has been considered through an anthropological input that it could have highlighted the existence of local or indigenous knowledge or practices of Rwandans, ensuring that missionaries' strategies were culturally compatible with the local context in which they were applied.

Revivalist teaching overlooked many of these issues, yet understanding gleaned from experience often provided a form of equilibrium. The missionaries held to the assumption that they represented a higher culture and that no civilisation existed in Rwanda. These experiences, described as 'fellowships' between missionaries and Rwandans at Gahini, did not look beyond the mission to discover what was happening externally. Converts were faced daily with the harsh reality of struggling to survive. Daily experience, however, contains seeds of conflict, since to live a godly life in such an environment can lead to contradictions to missionary teaching. Among the objectives was the establishment of some 'centres of Christianity and civilisation', for the promotion of true religion, agriculture and lawful commerce. Arguing from

---

[107] Mbonigaba, Elisha, "Indigenization of the Liturgy" in A Kingdom of Priests: Liturgical Formation of the People of God, ed. Thomas J. Talley, Grove Books, Bramcote, Nottingham, 1988, p.41

[108] Atta-Bafoe, Victor, R. and Tovey Philip, "What does inculturation mean", in Liturgical Inculturation in the Anglican Communion, ed. David R. Holeton, Grove Books, Nottingham, 1990, p. 14

the point of civilisation, it is said that, if missionaries had not excluded the existing cultural values, they could have complemented and facilitated the impact of Christian influence in society.

The African Catholic priest, Meinrad Hegba, argues out of his conviction that 'the Christian Church must share in our efforts to rationalise and modernise people's culture but not to abolish their tradition'.[109] Another Catholic African Priest, Thiam, asserts that 'The work of spreading the gospel should have as its pivot the values that are characteristic of the soul of the black man and should not disorganise the established order'.[110]

It is argued that the message of Christianity will only become a fact when the Church adopts the African contribution to civilisation and culture. It was a necessary feature that civilisation must, in the first place, be judged by the possibilities it offers for people to live and grow correctly in the conditions and societal settings in which it finds itself. It should, moreover, be judged by the same means that it offers, to make this same people live and grow in unity, promoting the Christian faith from where they are. A civilisation should not nurture forms of intolerance as in the case of Rwanda, where converts lived among deeply ingrained attitudes, the removal of which required a great work of grace.

The key to this people's society, although this is referred to elsewhere, may perhaps offer the explanation as to why Rwandan culture and customs were not considered by Catholic missionaries. Tina Beattie writes about worrying developments, describing a situation in which the missionaries saw people who lived in poor and basic conditions as being 'primitive' and unable to understand

---

[109]Hegba, M. Article "un Concile a l'Heure de l'Afrique" in "Personnalité Africaine et Catholicisme", Paris, 1962, p.14 :

[110]Thiam, J. Article, "Tribal Clan And Christian Community" in "Des Pretres Noirs s'interrogent", p.49

the difference between right and wrong. She observes that missionaries harboured an attitude of deep mistrust informed by pseudo-ethnology, which created 'the ideology of the blackness and despising them'.[111] Beattie further argues that the missionaries had a mind-set clothed in a 'sense of racial and cultural superiority, underpinned by the evolutionary theories which were fashionable at the time,'[112] and this situation 'sometimes lent arrogance to their work and many of them exhibited little respect for the beliefs of the people they sought to convert'.[113]

It is important to analyse questions of good and evil, right and wrong, obligation and prohibition as they arise in a social context. Yoder observes that even before there could be a Moses and a people to hear him, there had to be an oppressed community affirming its identity by talking about the fathers and the God of the fathers.[114] So far, in Rwanda, the Anglican Church was still taking serious consideration of the people's culture and values, pondering how to restore and preserve the cultural authenticity that had united communities in the past.

Again 48% of respondents agreed with a change in Anglican Church teaching both in rural and urban areas showing that the inculturation of the Christian message was long overdue and urgently needed. In a way inculturation is a dialogue between the gospel and culture. This is the reason why some Anglican Church leaders were eager to find the answer to these demands for cultural identity. It suggests that there were misunderstandings between people trying to relate the Christian faith to their own needs and

---

[111]Beattie, Tina, (1994). Dominant Discourse and Silent Rebellions: Christianity, Culture and Liberation in the lives of African Women, Dissertation Presented to the University of Bristol towards a BA Degree, May 1994, p. 11.
[112]Ibid. p. 10.
[113]Ibid.
[114]Yoder, J. H. Article, Pretoria 2, 1, 1974, pp. 29-41.

their understanding of God. Missionaries often saw Rwandan cultural values in society as a return to the past, somehow not valuing diversity. The promotion of obedience to authority, without question, as in the past, tended to exclude people from decisions that affected their lives.

I will argue that if, after independence, the Anglican Church had concentrated on interpreting its biblical teaching to emphasise that all Rwandans were equal in the eyes of God, the fellowship of the Anglican Church might have become grounded in a Christianity that would have resisted divisive politics. This is why there is a need for valuing culture within a theological approach. We need to find out what God has to say about ethnicity and diversity, based, not on the tolerance of difference, but on the acceptance and affirmation of diversity and difference.

This approach to the investigation of the conversion experience provides a rich depth of insight into what might have been the weaker side of the Anglican Mission in Rwanda. Respondents argued that if converts demonstrated an inquiring mind, they were in most cases regarded as having misunderstood the missionaries and their teaching. Louise Pirouet adds that the type of ethnocentric European Christianity and education introduced in Rwanda had little basic orientation towards an education offered to people; it was a trip 'out of Africa'.[115] Today, an emerging belief is held in Rwanda that if there had been an attempt to understand its education and traditional systems, it would be in terms of European belief in its superiority, demonstrated in a disrespect of local culture and values.[116]

This is one way of seeing things faith-wise, but it is argued that it would have been easier to refer to God

---

[115] Cfr. Pirouet, L., (1989). Christianity Worldwide, Anglican Church History 4: AD1800 Onwards, London: SPCK, p. 160.
[116] Cfr. Osborn, H. H., (1995). Revival – A precious heritage, London: SPCK, p.96

through traditional concepts, in a formal way known by Rwandans.

Max Gluckman argues that such thinking highlights the fact that missionaries did not take the performance of rituals seriously; indeed, where they tried, rituals were interpreted in terms of the symbolism of the West.[117] More significantly, Neckebrouck argues that no faith harmonises itself to people's situations and requirements. However good it may be, it must be explicitly imposed upon people and an unwilling society.[118] Evidence from local and scholarly sources has suggested that a lack of relevance in the Anglican Church's teaching was, in most cases, a serious problem; one of the basic causes for the growth of the Anglican Church schism.

As an example, the Aladura movement in Nigeria and Ghana happened at a time when Christians were confronted with a spiritual need and a challenge to the Anglican Church.[119] In the same way, Christ was proclaimed to the Rwandans and elsewhere in Africa by European missionaries with their particular faith agenda. However, when an Anglican Church member was in the middle of spiritual crisis and confusion, he/she would turn to familiar traditional ways to meet needs for which the Anglican Church could not provide the answer.

All suggested that the situation needed the Anglican Church missionaries to find a realistic discourse capable of

---

[117]Cfr. Gluckman, Seven Year Research Plan of the Rhodes – Livingstone Institute: Human Problems in British Central Africa: The Rhodes – Livingstone Journal, No. 4, December 1945, p. 224.

[118]Cfr. Neckebrouck, V. (1971), "Afrique Noire et la Crise Religieuse de I' Occident." T.M.P., Book Department. Tabora: Tanzania, p. 241; Harris, E. H. (1968), A Ministry Renewed, London: SCM Press Ltd, p. 99.

[119]Cfr. Turner, Harold, W., (1969). The Place of Independence Religious Movements in the Modernisation of Africa: Journal of Religion in Africa, 2, p.43 – 63.

engaging Church members with their history. It was essential to use the experiences of people to address their fears and to provide a better understanding of the current debates in Rwandan communities that proliferated, notwithstanding there being a culture of neglect. The recent indirect reaction in Rwanda encapsulates many of the issues surrounding complex cultures of resistance among converts. The fact that many members of the Pentecostal (independent) Churches in Rwanda today had attended mission schools and even catechism classes without ever seeking full membership of the Anglican Churches, also points to dissatisfaction with the Church's teaching.

The real attraction of independent Churches for young members derived from their original, creative attempts to relate the good news of the gospel in a meaningful and symbolically intelligible way to the innermost needs of an African. I have argued that, anthropologically, the Anglican Church did not go deep enough. However, the independent Churches are in the process of reaching a high percentage of young people and have already been very successful. Another area of importance is that of ritual theory, which has many functions both at the level of the individual and of groups in society, through which these groups can channel and express emotions, guide and reinforce forms of behaviour, support or subvert the status quo, bring about change or restore harmony and balance. The Anglican Churches are not primarily designed to provide service and spiritual guidance to young people, but go further to provide the scope for forming friendships and a ground on which to unite.

The ability to create friendship was also important at this time of ethnic division and alienation when there was a great need for an intimate circle of friends and where the individuals could receive recognition and feel at home. This is a necessary component of relationships in independent Churches. Individuals are encouraged to regard one another as 'brothers and sisters in the Lord', which breeds a sense of solidarity and gives rise to a new type of extended family. At this juncture, it is fair to draw a comparison between the independent Churches (Pentecostals) and missionary Anglican Churches. This is not to imply that everything in the independent Churches was satisfactory. There is also a negative side that continues to be noticed to the present day. Rivalry was the order of the day for some pioneering groups and there were leadership struggles from the very day they began. Individual leaders' struggles for status and control of the finances occasionally caused disputes in some independent Churches; in most cases they promoted the birth of numerous other independent Churches.

Though the Anglican Church's missionary approach, adopted throughout the Belgian rule in Rwanda, reflected a conscious effort to understand the people, according to informed respondents, in many instances its attitude appeared to have little concern for the real world during the days of the missionaries. Respondents argued that Anglican missionaries did not do enough to explain how to live as Christians. Instead, their emphasis was placed on conversion and public confession for 'those who are on fire', the 'Abaka'.[120] This was interpreted as a failure by Anglican missionaries to distance themselves from Belgian administrators, which, at times, left Anglican Church members silently angry about the lack of guidance in aspects of the Christian daily life. On the other hand, this was not always the case because there is evidence of Revivalists engaging in political developments in Rwanda. The history of the Revivalist mission shows that the Revivalist Heritage strategy was based mainly on

---

[120]Cfr. Osborn, H. H., (1995). Revival – A precious heritage, London: SPCK, p. 99

evangelising and on enthusiastic conversion, being 'born again', so as to save perishing souls.

6.2 The Strains of Conversion

In the beginning, the Anglican Revivalist missionaries seemed to have had clear intentions to recruit catechists and train them for their responsibilities in serving the Anglican Church in a theological, contextual way. However, many respondents wondered why missionaries did not encourage catechists and priests to translate the gospel into Rwandan ways of understanding and why they did not use local methods of communication. Another criticism raised by respondents was that the approach used in conversion to Christianity in Rwanda did not take into account people's background or their experience. They felt that people's culture, experience and knowledge, that they considered were vitally important, should not have been summarily dismissed in the light of any preconceived theory. In fact, conversion to Christianity involved a degree of stress, both for the converts and for the communities to which they belonged.

If they were members of a community they were liable to be treated as 'traitors', whose alien manners must, once and for all, be rejected. While the change of hearts and minds was essential, it did perhaps cause problems for what Father Hillman referred to as 'Black Europeans', a new anthropological category devised by Julius Nyerere.[121] As a respondent at Butare National University commented, 'Religious behaviour is distinctly cultural and traditional, passed on deliberately through communication and imitation, generation after generation'. Rwandan observers did not see anything to suggest any danger.

---

[121]Hillman, E., (1975). Polygamy Reconsidered, African Plural Marriage and the Christian Anglican Churches, New York: Orbis Books, p. 14.

It is argued that one concern, during this period of Revivalist conversion, was that conversion is not about how converts should behave, but rather about the basis upon which the newly acquired faith is practised in society. The pressure that Rwandans experienced in this period, either to remain traditional or to become 'modern' was powerful. Festo Kivengeri once said that changes would change you even if you did not want to change.[122] After years of Belgian rule, Rwandans looked for new kinds of spiritual guidance. They turned to the missionaries, but elderly respondents say they often found that these missionaries were also part of a European system, preaching submission and obedience to those in authority.[123] In their view, this meant submitting to the Belgians' authority.[124]

However, the pressing problem for the Anglican Church in Rwanda today is not the quantity, size of Anglican Church membership, but its quality. It is this very point that dominated comments from respondents, who attributed the problem to the shallow quality of the teaching from Revivalist missionaries. Respondents said that there was a mixture of very good and very bad missionary teachings that had had a negative impact on Rwandans.[125] Respondents described vividly and genuinely the Revivalists' warmth and their loving spirit of true Christian fellowship, but the weakness in the teachings that they referred to was their short-term vision.

The efforts of Revivalist missionaries were only put into conversion; after conversion they did not continue to educate converts in how to apply the Christian faith in daily living. Scheer observes that 'Rwandan spiritual development rarely advanced much past the initial point of

---

[122]Kivengeri, Festo, in his speech at Bishop Tucker Theological, Mukono 1975.
[123]Interviewing elderly Anglican members at Cyangugu, August 1998.
[124]Ibid.
[125]Ibid.., July 1998.

conversion. The saved were called to be saved, on Sunday after Sunday.'[126] On the other hand, Revivalist missionaries left aside systematic teaching and focused on personal salvation. In this view, not a great deal is expected of the world and in the realm of sin, any affect will be brought about by personal example or through God's direct intervention, if He so desires.[127] For example, in November 1983, Joe Church wrote: 'There is a large and growing number of Christians on every station, called sometimes the "Abaka"; these men and women have had a definite experience and often go off at once to witness to their friends. Two hundred went off from Gahini last August and it was three of this great band that got as far as Buhiga and was the cause of the trouble there, or rather the devil was!'[128]

The use of passages from the New Testament created the impression that the experience of conversion was something that occurs once and for all, as a sudden and complete affair, which is similar to thinking that everything that was previously dark is now illuminated. This impression created a misunderstanding in the process of conversion, as if it was an immediate action of passing from death to life. It is argued that the word 'conversion' is problematic, since it conveyed more than just a change in outward appearance and rather implied a change of internal and spiritual character. The ambiguity of the missionary approach of the Anglican Church seems to have left converts at a transitional level in their rite of passage. For example: 'One of those for whom this issue was very distressing was Dr Algie Stanley Smith. He saw that unity was essential for a clear witness to Jesus Christ and His

---

[126] Scheer, Gray, (1995). Rwanda, Where was the Anglican Church, Evangelical Missions Quarterly, Vol. 31, No.3, July, p. 326.
[127] Interviews at Gahini Mission July 1997.
[128] Osborn, H. H., (1995). Revival – A precious heritage, Apologia Publications, p.100

saving Gospel. Because of this he refused to be associated with the Abaka, despite the great sympathy he had with their stand for truth and openness and their evangelistic zeal'.[129]

Of course, Dr Stanley Smith's objection had a sound basis; one can't entrust the responsibility to convert others without imparting experience and skill. Despite this, especially in Rwanda, Revivalist converts are sometimes heard referring to St Paul's conversion. It is often forgotten that St Paul was well educated and trained before he embarked on his mission (Acts 22:6-16; 26:12-18). Alison Des Forges goes further, stressing that from the start it was important for the Anglican Church to take cultural training into account, along with the mode of thinking and the mentality of the people involved.[130] It is argued that the mission starts with people, so they must be deeply sensitive to the cultural reality in which their existence is rooted. Given the social nature of Rwandans, the failure to respect their cultural reality was a failure to respect them as people.

A similar view was echoed by the Catholic priest Thiam, who wrote that the work of spreading the gospel has held as its pivot the values that are characteristic of the soul of the black African.[131] The crucial point here is that one missionary approach might consider becoming a Christian to be rooted in a psychological and geographical present. However, in almost all of these religious issues, people needed careful explanation and persuasion in order for them to abandon their traditional ways of life and beliefs, which raised a number of sociological and psychological questions. Furthermore, Alison Des Forges argues that when customs were not taken into consideration, it was, at

---

[129]Ibid. p.102

[130]Des Forges, Alison, (1999). Leave None to Tell the Story: Genocide in Rwanda, New York: Federation for Human Rights Leagues, p. 58.

[131]Thiam, J. An article, (1986), "Tribal Clan and Christian Community" Des Prestress Noirs' Interrogent, pp. 48–49.

the least, imprudent, in choosing the surest way of producing apostles.[132] The argument here is that the Anglican Church mission either overlooked or failed to recognise that Rwandan society had been built on the idea of each taking responsibility for the others' survival, based on the community's continual development and inspired by communicating life experience.[133]

Rwandans knew that they existed because of others, the 'vital force' of their elders and ancestors that were passed on through procreation. This belief was conditioned by survival, wherein people depended upon the collective analysis of knowledge and information acquired as a group. It is argued that the question of change and survival and the search for knowledge demanded an answer. As pointed out previously, these were long-term concerns.

To rebuild the foundations of the Anglican Church is a major task. First and foremost, it is important to create an atmosphere within which the Anglican Church is integrated into society. In Anglican Church worship, members should feel at home worshipping God and seeking solutions, although not from the 'foreign' God, obscured by foreign liturgical tradition and theological context, with no relevance to local needs. The basis of this argument for developing authentic theology is related to culture and experience within the particular context of a society. It is an argument for a theology that can shape people's lives and which has led to very many different forms of equally valid Christian theology.

The idea is to dispel the impression that the Anglican Church seems to have only one God-given theology from outside Rwanda. It is argued that faith can speak to faith, both inside and outside the designated household of faith.

---

[132] Ibid.
[133] Cf. A report of the three days Anglican leaders' seminar on reconciliation organised and sponsored by REACH from 25th to 28th March 1998 held at St. Joseph Centre, Kibungo Prefecture.

However, turning to the context of what is brought forth, the enquirer must ask what is meant by 'Christianity' and what is not. Christianity is not simply a belief in Christ, although Christ is central. For some who are active in the Anglican Church and for others who are not, the part played by Christ as a living contemporary is personally important.

On the grounds of faith, for example, similarity to the traditional concept of God's company is probably central to the devotion of a considerable number of farmers. In Rwanda and elsewhere in Africa, farmers are often heard saying that they talk to God while 'working on the gardens'.[134] However, when they describe their faith, most of these farmers say with honesty that they believe in God rather than in Christ.[135]

These conditions argue that genuine faith turns upon an personal encounter with Christ as the 'Word of God'. Even if the Anglican Church were to be successful in achieving its goals, it would actually be a hindrance to a full Christian commitment, since the neglected past conceals rather than discloses the activity of Christ. Rutiba's perceptive observation is that people make their own history, but do not make it just as they please; they make it under circumstances directly encountered and transmitted from the past.[136] Paul Tillich makes the position quite explicit when he says: 'The foundation of Christian belief is not the history of Jesus, but the biblical picture of Christ. The criterion of human thought and action is the constantly changing and artificial product of the historical happenings,

---

[134]Interviews at Gahini and Mutara July 1998
[135]Cfr. Shorter, A., (1975). Prayer in the Religious Traditions of Africa, Nairobi: Uzima Press., pp. 3-7.
[136]Interviewing Rutiba at Makerere University, Kampala, Uganda, July 1998.

but the product of Christ as it is rooted in ecclesiastical belief and human experience'.[137]

If this is to be the keynote of Rwandan theology, then the missionaries' narrow theological views about human experience have to be explained. Over the range of the religious experience in Rwanda, elderly Anglican Church members assert that long before any of these political conflicts, men and women had encountered mysteries for which they could find no words.[138] Peter C, Hodgson and Robert H. King in an editorial of Martin Luther show how there is a twofold knowledge of God: the general and the particular. 'So it is that people know naturally that there is a God, but they do not know what He wants and what He does not want. For it is written (Rom.3:11): 'No one understands God' and elsewhere (John 1:18): 'No one has ever seen God, that is, no one knows what the will of God is'.[139] It is in this soil of unknowing that the seeds of all religions first take root.

This mystery is the pattern for which the Christian revelation is seen to be strikingly relevant. Thus, the door is open to constructive theological reflection, freed from the past inhibitions that have been in danger of turning it into a meaningless enterprise. The unknown mystery, as it is made available by human means of transmission from one group to another, is in this way made expressible, whether verbal, symbolic, or ritual. Without expression, no community of faith can come into being.[140]

These arguments seemed to be vindicated by the fact that, such expression is necessary for the full flowering and

---

[137]Tillich, P., (1954). The Interpretation of History, New York: Scribner, p. 34.
[138]Interviews at Gahini and Mutara July 1998
[139]Hodgson, P. C. and H. King (Ed), (1988). Readings in Christian Theology, Fortress Press Philadelphia, p.92.
[140]Cfr. Ilongu, E., (1973).Journal of Asian and African Studies, XIV, 1-2, 121-128.

fruiting of spiritual growth. In terms of the necessary biblical interpretation of Rwandan contextual theology, Ryangombe's historicity is comparable to that of Israelis (Yahweh): He is of cultural rather than cosmic significance. His title is a respectful surname (as in the Old Testament); therefore it is argued that Yahweh of the Jews was very much a God of Gihanga character. Yahweh was interested in the welfare of the Israelites, took their side against other nations and expected certain behaviour from His people if they were to retain His favour. The other argument is that of Old Testament sacrifices, which have their origins in paganism's attempts to keep the tribal gods content (Genesis 22:1–14).

Yahweh called the Israelites out from the familiar security of family, clan and household gods, to the insecurity of a desert journey (Genesis 12:1–16). Likewise, Gihanga is a god who plays a part in Rwandans' daily affairs and in the living faith. To some, including those that have little or nothing to do with active membership of the Anglican Church, He is real, His presence is near and His care is certain.

A belief in Christianity is not a belief in the Anglican Church. Yet the Anglican Church is an important vehicle for Christian worship and service that is believed in and is said still to be trusted. However, it is never identified with Christianity; it is 'only human'. If the Anglican Church is believed in, it is as a vehicle of Christianity, supporting followers of Christ's 'Way' as witnesses to Christianity, teaching its virtues and appealing to believers.

Richard Gray called it 'a problem of historical perspective' asking In order to become a Christian must the African cease to be African?'[141] Moreover, this did not mean that the disappearance of traditional belief was

---

[141] Gray, R. A paper originally submitted to the conference on 'The Anglican in a Changing Society' held in August 1977 to mark the quincentenary of Uppsala University.

imminent; rather that converts adopted the culture of the missionaries, at least on the surface, to become 'Black Europeans' rather than Christians. All of this could have contributed to the state of confusion surrounding the meaning of Christianity. This meant that to be a Christian involved a number of things, including the abandonment of traditional culture and preaching of the gospel, which they had been taught in a foreign context.

It was even stated by a respondent at Gahini Mission that converts were encouraged by revivalist missionaries to despise the old ways, which created a crisis among converts. A respondent at Butare National University commented: 'Among humans however, religious behaviour is distinctly cultural and traditional, passed on deliberately through communication and imitation generation after generation. Rwandan observers did not see anything suggesting of any danger'.

This crisis led to the fact that converts were expected, based on the demands of their new faith, to be detached from the local community. The whole network of informal interpersonal relationships ceased to play a determining role in the systems of mutual aid, welfare, recreation and economic production and distribution. They were manifestly detached from positions of functional relevance to society and decisions about the communities they had belonged to. At the same time, the method of evangelism had some incentives to attract needy people to conversion. The emphasis in conversion was put on charitable work. To improve the social welfare of converts, they were rewarded with benefits such as handouts of clothing, salt, soft pins and other imported objects.

It is argued that in a way, this charitable service attracted ordinary Rwandans who frequently visited missions and were eventually persuaded to convert to Christianity. Thus, the methods used could have contributed to later developments and led to a weaker commitment to the Christian faith. The fact that those who had access to missionaries meant that they also had access to such benefits. This created a 'relationship' between religion and material products.

The Rwandans were used to the belief that wealth brought with it certain obligations, as well as the opportunity for status, prestige and approval by providing feasts and demonstrating personal generosity. In fact, I do agree in particular with an argument of Richard Harris, that these were contradictions that caused confusion in the minds of many converts. The implication here is that when converts tried to relate their new belief to their traditional concepts, wealth and success were naturally seen as signs of the blessings of God or of the ancestors. In other words, it was their way of making sense of conversion.[142]

It is argued that under these contradictions, converts reasoned that by accumulating wealth beyond personal need, as the Europeans did, they could then acquire prestige through the re-distribution of this excess wealth. However, the converts continued to see missionaries living with what they saw as unimaginable wealth, preaching the message of Christian charity and love for one's neighbour, yet giving away very little. The question of 'Who is my neighbour?' challenged missionaries to share the common life in Christ.

In this respect, many elderly respondents stressed that such practices were often connected with conversion and others saw this move as dangerous and deluded. It appeared to them that the new order of life was altering the very institutions that had created real worlds for them.[143]

Popper asserts that an individual's perception of what they can do is largely formulated upon an abstract sense of the prevailing situation. Therefore, if the missionaries' good intentions were to be understood by converts, the

---

[142]Harris, Richard, (Ed.), (1975). The Political Economy of Africa, Cambridge, Mass: Schenkman, p. 99
[143]Interviews at Gahini mission, July 1998.

latter clearly had to be given enough time for both the actions and the message to be digested. Mario Aguilar argues that it was also essential for missionaries to have considered the importance of identifying what was necessary for change, through considering the implications that might involve converts. Where the converts' ways of living had had to change as a sign of moving on from the past, respondents argued that, at the same time, missionaries used messages which were often misunderstood by converts.[144] One criticism of this procedure is that to insist on change was not necessary. Harris agreed that the missionaries' role must have seemed rather confusing to converts.[145]

It is true that under such conditions, converts faced startling differences between what they observed and what they were told. The situation can only be understood through what Southall observes as the Christian missions being forerunners of those that were Belgian.[146] Fieldhouse added that, during the period when most political philosophers began to defend the principles of universalism and equality, the same individuals were still defending the legitimacy of colonialism and of imperialism.[147]

One way of silencing those apparently opposed to the principle was to use the argument known as the 'civilising mission', which suggested that a temporary period of Rwandan dependence or tutelage was necessary in order for the 'uncivilised' society to advance to the point where they

---

[144]Aguilar, M. I., (1996). The Rwanda Genocide and the Call to Deepen Christianity in Africa, Uganda: AMECEA GABA Publications Spearhead Nos. 148 – 150, p. xii.
[145]Harris, Richard, (Ed.), (1975). The Political Economy of Africa, Cambridge, Mass: Schenkman, p. 100.
[146]Southall, A., (1961). Social Change in Modern Africa, London: Oxford University Press, p. 3.
[147]Fieldhouse, D. K., (1961). "Imperialism; an Historiographical Revision"; Economic History Review, X1V, 2, p. 80.

were capable of sustaining liberal institutions and self-governance.[148]

Whilst the situation brought great insight and greater sensitivity to the philosophy of universalism, by treating people equally, it had its own limits specifically to do with a European cultural influence affecting the deepest level of the local culture. To render this argument powerful, we could assert that, in the first instance, universal equality was a Christian obligation, concerned with equality for all people everywhere. However, despite the positive sound of universalism, it was taught and developed in Europe and, obscured by a poor approach to local needs and the aspirations of people in the colonies, it was rendered ineffective.

Nevertheless, from the Rwandan perspective of self-determination, this argument made sense of this linking of the structure of society and the structure of thought. It suggests that people should learn ideals of value and forms of morality from their society. In fact, this dilemma presents a significant difficulty at the heart of any effort aimed at defining morality by reference to an external authority. I will quickly add that, in a way, the notion was a sociological solution to the problem of the Western forms of value and morality that are often seen as outdated, because new forms could be developed as society developed. So, at any one time in modern society, the morality implied in the nature of that society is open to debate. On the other hand, it is also important to note that universalism has nothing to do with Christian spirituality, even though some might have it was treated it as such.

Furthermore, I mentioned that respondents felt that missionaries brought not only the seed of the gospel, but also the soil, the flower and the flowerpot.[149] It was these

---

[148]http://www.seo.leeds.ac.uk/entries/colonialism/11/9/07
[149] Interviews with elderly Anglican Church members at Gahini Mission, July 1998.

aspects of missionary zeal that showed a lack of awareness of local beliefs and thought and implied a 'universal culture'. Since there was no completely universal perspective of policies, all human thoughts and beliefs were limited by structural bounds. It is argued that recognition of universalism at the time could have encouraged openness in the Anglican Church mission and in Belgian dealings with Rwandans. In assuming a level of communication but knowing that the provision of adequate information is not a guarantee of successful communication, the question is really whether or not the message is relevant and transparent to the receiver.

I wish to argue that the messengers of the gospel paid more attention to their values and the message than they paid to the receiver. In other words, thinking and acting in context involves valuing other people more than us and our cherished methods or culture, regardless of the recipients' perceived backwardness or lack of development. Here, I recognise the significant role, during the early period of development. Universalism could have helped the Rwandans in making rational decisions, enabling them to formulate well-developed strategies that would function in a reasonably integrated fashion. This is argued as the right universal revelation, which raises the issue of finite human understanding, through which God's love and self-disclosure were visible.

However, respondents who asked about change were of C.R. Burdon's opinion that it was necessary for Anglican Church teaching to help link common experience, that it has a legitimate place in the context of the theological scene and that there are signs that such approaches must be taken seriously in the contemporary wider Anglican Church as well as in Rwanda.[150] However, I wish to argue that,

---

[150]Burdon, C.R., 1964, "Theological Expository Times", February Issue, p. 12.

while the Anglican Church in Rwanda was still searching for a way forward towards reconciliation, the idea of contextual theology could have developed from the practical experience of the people, not only derived from volumes of books, but also lived out through the lives of individuals. It suggests that taking such contextual experience into consideration is a vital basis for reconciliation theology and is a process whereby Anglican Church members may find a way forward to choose to seek the mind of Christ (1 Corinthians 2:16) and be faithful to Him.

At this stage, the Anglican Church had to be clear on what kind of theology should be involved in the process of reconciliation. Another group of respondents argued that for the Anglican Church to communicate the meaning of reconciliation and be understood by the people, its theology had to be adapted to cultural contexts. They saw this as important for the Anglican Church and as a requirement of its participation in the process of national reconciliation. Burden argues that, 'theology is about the nature and will of God for humanity; the Bible encourages us to look at our present experiences in the light of the nature of God and His will for community'.[151] Hinga notes that the image of Christ that prevailed was the presentation of Christ as the conqueror, a warrior King 'in whose name and banner (the cross) new territories, both physical and spiritual, would be fought for, annexed and subjugated'.[152]

It is the observation of these influences that underlines the need to dispel misconceptions created in the missionary conversion. Here the form of conversion that involved further teaching and discipleship is argued for, as opposed to the narrow mission of saving and protecting souls. In

---

[151]Ibid.
[152]Hinga, Teresa, (1994). "Jesus Christ and the Liberation of Women in Africa", in King (Ed.) Feminist Theology from the Third World, Maryknoll: Orbis, p. 263.

general, missionaries from denominations that interfered with the social arrangements of Rwandan society lessened the bonds in which that society functioned. Furthermore, Rwandan communities were held together, in the past, by a solidarity that had a well-developed division of responsibilities as part of the people's customary duty. These responsibilities were divisions of labour or bonds that had united people and existed for the common cause. They were treasured by those involved as the glue that held the Tutsis and Hutus together. Considering that, over the years, there have been changes in Rwanda, I wish to argue that by laying the Anglican Church's foundations upon those values that held Rwandans together in the past and then insisting upon changes, they were undermining the very bonds that united people and creating the conditions for conflict.

On the other hand, it is argued that cultural values had a functioning role in community activities that brought together Hutu and Tutsi in a friendship based on different qualities. The differences involved in the division of labour also brought them together to create a feeling of solidarity. This point resonates with the observation that missionaries needed to recognise the difficulties associated with changes, where people needed to be given the opportunity to decide what might be the most appropriate and realistic path they should (or must) take. Perhaps most crucially, with reference to the theory of exclusion, when making changes it is important to remember the local people's cultural experience. In this case, the historical structure of the society that was known to people was important to them. Missionaries needed to recognise and value these social arrangements.

Thus, it is argued that these arrangements had created bonds that embodied Rwandan society until outside influences reversed that order. Communities had a common experience with a communal way of life at their heart. On the other hand, a valid argument was that it was simply common sense that the division of labour such as 'Uburetwa' was had economic advantages. In relation to the values and objectives of this way of life, it is also argued that both missionaries and Belgian administrators were obliged to consider service to society as a whole and not just to their own interests. This may also mean that their joint failure was a lack of recognition of this society's value and purpose, a blindness for which their mission was criticised.

For that matter, the approach to society by missionaries in Rwanda was seen to be influenced by their determination that Rwandan society and people had to change, as a sign of their conversion to Christianity and through collaboration with Belgian administrators. In short, this insistence meant that missionaries not only saw their role as being to achieve conversion and to save souls, but also to change social life and its organisation. The inevitable result of missionary success, no matter which faith is being taught, requires that the society in which that success is achieved be irrevocably changed for better or for worse and often in ways that are quite destructive and possibly unforeseen. However, the logic of reciprocity can also work the other way round, such that destructive local behaviour points, not to Rwandan past immorality, but to questionable changes of human conduct. It is important to add that Christian moral duty required tolerance and competence in handling the process of change.

According to Alexandere Kimenyi, Rwandans had characteristically seen Christian teaching about God as referring to their familiar 'Supreme Being' and so drew freely on such ideas in the process of explaining their conception of this Supreme Being.[153] It was as justification

---

[153] Kimenyi, A., (1989). Kinyarwanda and Kirundi Names, The Edwin Millen Press, pp. 47-48

for people's belief in God that they had so many words to describe His existence. These names are symbolic and represent God as He is seen or felt in the real circumstances of their daily living. Examples of these names are 'Ryangombe', 'Gihanga', 'The eternal God', 'Imana', 'Supreme Being', 'Nyagasani', 'Indeza', 'The One who is powerful and good' and 'Rulema' from the Ukulema-to form.[154]

These names were used while praying to the Supreme Being during times of worry and need. Christians still use them, especially when making supplications for the health of someone who is ill. Beliefs that lasted rested on how traditionally valuable they were and still are, especially at celebrations. Regarding this issue there has been a steady increase in the use of such names as Nsengimana (I pray to God), Nsengeyunva (I pray to the one who listens), Habimana (God exists),[155] and Ryangombe, which is a 'praise-name' of the ruler of everything that is. From names like these and from proverbs and other sayings, we may conclude that Rwandans had a concept of a personal, invisible and living Supreme Being, from whom all life comes.

6. 3 The Anglican Church in Independent Rwanda

This section attempts to explain what made the Anglican Church in Rwanda drift into ethnic politics. It might provide insight into how, after independence, the Anglican Church's leadership was entangled in party politics and seen as failing to offer a prophetic voice during the political crisis. Perhaps the shift occurred when the leadership failed to separate issues surrounding the

---

[154]Nothomb, D., (1965). "Un Humanism African", Editions Lumen Vitae, Bruxelles, p. 88.
[155]Kimenyi, A., (1989). Kinyarwanda and Kirundi Names, The Edwin Millen Press, pp. 47 – 51.

application of the Christian faith and failed to challenge the crisis created by ethnic conflict. This might be viewed as a weakness in its teaching. For various reasons, Christianity had not penetrated deeply enough into society to form the basis for a national conscience, providing the Anglican Church with moral leadership.

It was argued repeatedly by respondents that, when party politics intensified in the country, Anglican Church members developed mixed conceptions about religion and politics. The political climate was such that the Anglican Church was seen by elderly respondents to be seeking success. It became harder for some to maintain the traditional values of the gentle mother or father taking the nurturing role in the home. In terms of Rwandan social conduct, good and evil are not particular individual moral agents residing in specific decisions and actions, but are rather found in traditional institutions, social arrangements and all family ritualistic celebrations.

A significant number of responses pointed out that when Rwandans turned towards Western ways, they gradually became less and less effective in communal activities. Stanley Diamond observed that: 'Custom is obeyed because it is intimately intertwined with a vast living network of interrelations, arranged in a meticulous and ordered manner. Thus custom is very much part of the social reality, the shared commonsensical, taken for granted, everyday world which it is even difficult to talk about because it is so ordinary that the thought of disagreement does not arise.'[156]

In connection with contextual teaching, 48% in table 5 agreed that, inevitably, people began to experience cultural degradation and pressured for a change from what was often referred to in the missionary teachings as 'abandoning

---

[156] Diamond, S. (1971), "The Rule of Law versus the Order of Custom", 38 Social Research 42.

the old way'.[157] Rwandans lived a communal life, where individuals supported each other and freely lent out instruments to neighbours and family friends. Modernisation led to an exaggerated emphasis upon the autonomous individual over and against the community's values. A common view of elderly Anglican Church members at Gahini Mission expressed that religious conversion had made people become disengaged from social activities in their community. According to Rwandan tradition, life had previously revolved around the community, difficulties were shared and the community made collective decisions.[158]

Critics of change saw the failure of the Anglican missionary Church to be a lack of recognition and support of the function of these values in Rwandan society; a lack of respect argued by respondents as being both un-social and un-cultural behaviour on the part of godly people. It should also be noted that the Anglican Church Mission came to Rwanda with the purpose of converting people, but did not show them the Christian way of operating in the political world on a daily basis. For instance, to teach converts how to eradicate injustice and bad behaviour in society, Revivalist Heritage chose to engage in the relatively narrow areas of friendship within fellowships and evangelistic outreach, without worrying about the issues surrounding the social problems converts had to face. This did not mean simply providing them with material things, but also offering the protection of traditional values, which had previously acted as restraints upon indiscipline in society.

In the view of many respondents, this revealed how contextual theology is vitally important if the Anglican Church in Rwanda is to play the necessary roles of

---

[157]Interviews at Gahini Mission and Kigali Diocesan Office, July 1998
[158]Interviews at Gahini Mission and Kigali Diocesan Office, July 1998

conciliator and liberator. This contextual theology includes within its scope an awareness of the Anglican missionaries' neglect of Rwandan culture, in its requirement to rehabilitate weakened moral conduct in society. Contextual thinking aims at inclusion and recognition of the traditional ways forbidden by missionaries or disregarded by converts in their haste to acquire European culture. Respondents at Butare University argued that it was not only a mistake but disrespect to ignore people's values, traditional structures and the community arrangements which established bonds between these communities.[159] Based on the respondents' criticism, the weakness of the Revival Heritage's teaching in Rwanda is in its lack of appeal to the people's conscience for social justice by addressing the issue of ethnic differential and by challenging all kinds of social injustice formed by colonial policies.

In fact, during the reconciliation seminars at St. Joseph's Centre Kibungo, Anglican Church members even suggested that the Anglican clergy needed re-training, since their theology was irrelevant to today's Church needs. As agents of change and an influence upon society, the Anglican Church clergy faced a very challenging situation with regard to both political and economic influences. This became even more problematic for the Church due to the intense pressure applied by many organised political groups.[160] As explained above, the method of conversion and the European cultural life styles created other influences during this period; the idea of the accumulation of wealth as an end in itself. This might have influenced Christians to become weaker in their Christian commitment. Church respondents saw a connection

---

[159] Interviewing lecturers at Butare National University of Rwanda, July 1997.
[160] Interviews at Gahini Mission and Kigali Diocesan Office, July 1998

between promoting differences among members and the unequal acquisition of wealth. 169

The Anglican Church and campaigns of Habyarimana's Government constantly repeated the rhetoric of ethnic hatred. One regime after another manipulated people to act without questioning what they had been asked to do.[161] This explains how the Anglican Church blindly accepted political propaganda to treat Tutsis as enemies and to become mutually suspicious of them. At the same time, the Anglican Church in Rwanda was faced with ethnic tensions of its own. Apparently, for many years the Anglican Church had been seen as one place where Tutsis were welcomed to train as clergy, but most leaders were Hutu and it was difficult for Tutsi clergy to be promoted to senior positions.[162] It is argued that in the upheavals of 1960, 1963, 1967, 1973 and 1990, Anglican Church leaders were usually spared, except for the occasional revenge killing or accidental fatality.

In March 1992, the extremist Hutu party, CDR (Coalition pour la Defence de la Republique) was set up, having close connections with RTLM radio station and Kangura magazine.[163] The Anglican Church was close to politicians and the intention of this was to involve the Church and as many Hutus as possible, to create an ethnic crisis and to make it look as if they were defending themselves from the rise of the Tutsi enemies. Anglican respondents, at this time, saw the Anglican Church as playing a role in the genocide. It appears that there was a drive for the total mobilisation of all Hutus to get involved

---

[161] Aguilar, M. I., (1996). The Rwanda Genocide and the Call to Deepen Christianity in Africa, Uganda: AMECEA GABA Publications Spearhead Nos. 148 – 150, p. xii.
[162] Mbanda, L., (1998). Committed to Conflict, The Destruction of the Anglican Church in Rwanda, London: SPCK, pp.70-71.
[163] Cfr. Prunier, G., (1995). The Rwanda Crisis: History of a genocide, New York: Columbia University Press, pp.130-31.

in 'ethnic cleansing' as a response to extremist politicians. The latter might have led even the Anglican Church to have closer ties with the regime. 71% in table 1 agreed with the view that the Anglican Church had a commitment to work with all people. Others believed that the Anglican Church was naïve in its failure to realise that their moral authority was being undermined and that they should have been aware of the intentions of those who organised the genocide.

These findings underline the viewpoint that political developments in Rwanda continued to cultivate differences even after independence and demonstrated the extent to which the mentality of the general population had been manipulated by Habyarimana's regime.[164] They also highlight how deliberately it was set up to create the type of 'fear-mongering' that continued throughout the presidencies of both Kayibanda and Habyarimana. The systematic use of propaganda and misinformation was aimed at people who already lived in poverty, who were less informed about politics and who lived in fear. This led many to respond to the propaganda by instigating and executing acts of genocide.[165]

It was claimed by respondents that others acted out of fear in that, if they did not do what they were asked, Government supporters would punish them. In this case, it was also a necessity for the Anglican Church in Rwanda to realise that politics is a 'power game'. For the Anglican Church in Rwanda to become involved in such a game was not only a risk, but also went against its calling as a servant of the people. The argument is that the Anglican Church's teaching in Rwanda must state clearly and precisely that all

---

[164]Goose, S. and Smyth, D., (1994). "Arming Genocide in Rwanda" Foreign Affairs 73 (5), pp. 86–96.
[165]Chrétien, J. P. (1991), 'Presse libre' et Propagande raciste au Rwanda : Kangura et 'Les 10 Commandements du Hutu', Politique Africaine 42, pp. 109 – 120.

people are equal in the eyes of God. In the Church's teaching, emphasis must be placed firmly on unity, whereby faith in God can help Christians to understand what is good and what is bad for living out the Christian life. In attempting to analyse the past through these historical events, one can trace the reason why Anglican Church members misunderstood vital Christian principles and values. The Anglican Church has to walk the tightrope between political involvement and retaining the freedom of its calling. The practice of divisive methods was seen as the Anglican Church's mistake. It encouraged Anglican Church members to believe that there was the possibility of danger and that the enemies were the Tutsi. As a result of the fear it had created, its members were led down a path that finished with ethnic cleansing. In a sense it was a misuse of the power of both Church leadership and the media that created fear in the population under the Habyarimana regime that justified a tough approach to anyone who did not support the Government.

Respondents stressed that one regime after another had manipulated people into acting without question on whatever they were asked to do. Indeed, 'fear of the enemy' had important implications. 34% of respondents in table 4 agreed that the Anglican Church's tacit involvement in the genocide that witnessed the killing of Tutsis and moderate Hutus was connected to and influenced by a propaganda of hatred. 42% disagreed with the view that Rwandans acted out of fear that if they did not do what they were asked, then they would be punished by Government supporters.

This suggests that not all people acted freely and willingly in the genocide. To an extent, it means that people who were acting under fear and political pressure were eventually turned into political objects, doing what the Government wanted them to do. Also to an extent, as claimed by some respondents, the majority acted in the belief that it was self-defence against Tutsi enemies. Alternatively, the situation confirms that the whole system was corrupt and that such defects created misunderstandings and entrenched negativity among people of the same nation.

Gerloff Roswith argues that 'If people's culture is not affirmed, they become dehumanised, as history has demonstrated. In the broadest sense culture is a 'way of life' related to people past, present and future and it is carried as baggage of a group, family or community.'[166] Archbishop Emmanuel Kolini and John Ruchahana agree with Gerloff's view that culture has a vitally important role to play in the healing of individuals and the nation, especially in unifying communities, since culture is about the values and beliefs of people translated into behaviours and patterns of living.[167] Underneath this, in essence, one's culture determines what is normal within a community and what is expected from its members, based on common sense. If so, the task for the Anglican Church is to help its members to see themselves as an integral part of one community, participating in a shared faith with a further, much broader meaning.

6.3 Deepening the Christian Faith in the Anglican Church

This thesis argues that to become fully Christian means necessarily to take on, at heart, something more than a perceived new identity. It is argued that whatever this new identity is for converts to become 'Christian', this must involve a spiritual change rather than a simple embracing of European culture, which is in some instances what it

---

[166] Gerloff, R, (1998). Truth, a new Society and Reconciliation: the Truth and Reconciliation Commission in South Africa a German Perspective, Leeds: University Press, p. 50.
[167] Interviews with the Bishops at Kigali July 1998.

appeared to suggest. Some of the new identity might mean a convert taking on the new culture, in desiring to embrace the systems of belief and norms of behaviour similar to those of the missionaries. It is further argued that Anglican missionaries shouldn't have been surprised at meeting resistance, because individuals bring with them an inherent stock of meanings with which to understand their experience and which they are likely to have treasured. These meanings were, of course, drawn from their traditional heritage, known from childhood and the culture in which they were located. This exerted pressure on them to conform to certain conventions affecting their daily living.

It is very important for the present Anglican Church to acknowledge the concepts of spiritual experience and truth that rest firmly within people's daily experience. As an earlier examination of conversion implied, this is the key to understanding how people felt and it was expressed in the many Anglican Churches visited. Thus, the main factor mentioned by Anglican Church respondents was the need for a theology related to people's situations. This is why a Christianity that takes note of culture is necessary in order to meet the need for Christians within the Anglican Church to deliver the gospel effectively to the people.[168] It is therefore essential to understand the people's faith and to locate it within the teachings of Christ. An important argument here is that to be a Christian means a personal faith, to be committed to finding Christ in the common things of life and to bring them into a working partnership with Him. Robinson developed a theme of 'pro-existence' illustrating a distinction originally drawn by Tillich between the 'manifest Church', wherein Christ is consciously recognised and worshipped and the 'latent

---

[168]Cfr. Anglican and Society, Report on World Conference, Geneva, WCC, September 1998, p.210.

Church', to which belong individuals who do not consciously acknowledge Christ and whose whole relationship with the world is implicitly if not explicitly Christ-like.[169]

As Robinson makes clear, there were good reasons for converts to resist losing their rich heritage and the cultural vitality of their tradition and there is a good Biblical warrant for this need. According to Berger and Luckmann, constructionists of reality argue that the use of familiar words and symbolic actions is important in making possible an ongoing and unfolding experience.[170] The significant thing about this observation is that, in responding to the Christian message when it is in a cultural context, individuals are not simply receiving a neutral message, but also familiar symbols assist them in interpreting meanings on the basis of their own familiar understanding of the concept of God. This is not just important for personal and idiosyncratic experience, but also where individuals are able to take in ideas, concepts, meanings, theories, attitudes and judgements that convey the message of Christian faith in ways of living and acting by its creeds.

Communication in contextual theology represents a huge repository of interpretation and knowledge, by which the ideas and the recognition of ancestors' knowledge as referenced by society is passed on to succeeding generations. In addition, for liberation and reconciliation purposes, the contextual theology of Rwanda is, to an extent, an offshoot of past neglected societal values and ideas that take a prime place in the contemporary experience of individuals. This source of religious tradition is received and examined within a critical dialogue. The point to stress here is that theological dialogue can create

---

[169] Robinson, J. A. T., (1965). The New Reformation, SCM Press, p. 48.
[170] Berger, P. L., & Luckmann, T., (1967). The Social Construction of Reality, Buckingham: Open University Press, p. 34.

coexistence within Rwandan communities without contradictions.

It is argued that the Anglican Church should analyse its theology critically, since, because there is this lack of self-criticism, the Church's theological discourse is locked into the past, constantly repeating itself, having lost touch with the reality of people's lives in various contexts. Having identified the issues surrounding the past history of the country and the Anglican mission it is argued that contextual theology is a prophetic call for the Anglican Church to assume the role of liberating its members both spiritually and materially, especially in areas of knowing what is saving life and what is not. It is a challenge to the Anglican Church to engage in the daily struggles of its members, especially where those members expect the Church leadership to help them. There is a crucial demand for a theology that can reignite a mass movement and for a social leadership to tackle the existing huge inequalities of the divisive, socio-economic situation in Rwanda.

The former is important, as the activities of people are also important in gradually developing a deeper understanding of Christianity and offering insight into how people think in local terms. God is depicted as being not far away, spending the day overseeing the entire universe, while at night He rests in Rwanda (translation of Kinyarwanda). Based on observation, there has been increasing consciousness concerning the role of culture related to everyday life, as expressed in the language of culture and distinctively associated with the world of local people. It is argued that the use of traditional mythological concepts, which can have different functions and work on an abstract level, is vitally important.

Jacob Loewen observes that the myth can give answers to fundamental questions. It has an integrating function, as, for instance, when harmony is broken it is restored by integrating ceremonies and has a sanctioning or renewal function.[171]

One of the factors that emerged clearly from the interviews was an awareness of the importance of culture in the struggle for reconciliation. How one relates to the question of Rwandan theology varies greatly according to the culture in which it arises. It is therefore designed to harmonise both Christian teaching and the Rwandan concept of God, who liberates both physically and spiritually, assisting human beings in their everyday struggles. The examples of baptism and communion are not exactly the means of a private relationship with God. They are symbolic signs of the declaration of a corporate identity with a group that follows Jesus in the fulfilment of an historical task.

Therefore, the imperative of participation is the reason why the Anglican Church was required to re-examine past failings in its mission to act as a custodian of the truth in the middle of political crisis in Rwanda, as well as the failure to protect its members. The same imperative calls for it to reflect upon the past and to make assessments for the future.

In the context of the past, I wish to argue that Rwandans cannot change history but, by challenging the past, each Rwandan can help change the future. Each should take a new look at the Christian faith in the Church and examine how that faith can be lived and practised. Before leaving this discussion, it is necessary to point out Desmond Tutu's approach was right to argue in favour of Africans finding ways to resolve their own problems in a manner appropriate to African needs.

Desmond Tutu argued that God endowed the African continent and its inhabitants with wonderful gifts.

---

[171]Loewen, Jacob, "Mythological and Mission". Practical Anthropology, Vol.16n. 4, July-August, 1969, p. 147

Likewise, Rwanda must look for Rwandan solutions to its problems.[172] Of course, Desmond Tutu's argument heightens the need for Rwandan theology to offer a meaning to complicated issues such as reconciliation and to how people can liberate themselves from the dehumanising conditions that surround them. Teresa Hinga argues that missionaries had thought to create a spiritual and cultural 'tabula rasa' upon which the new culture and spirituality could be inscribed.[173] The argument is that the content of the mind is built upon what it receives passively from the senses or through reflection. In fact, it is the evidence of irrelevance and ineffectiveness that created ambiguity in Rwandan social structures and which apparently, in local communities, still contain former elements of political propaganda and ethnic distinction. These divisive stereotypes and propaganda messages, taught by the previous Anglican Church leadership, still exist.

It is now the purpose of this study to try to find out whether the Anglican Church recognises that, in a situation of conflict, its action is essential to the creation of awareness and restoration of values that were once treasured and which 'glued' people together in the structures of society. Any collective or individual will attempt to bypass the frequently stifling rigidity of the Anglican Church authorities' discourse, which is orientated exclusively towards one perception of reality. Respondents argued that, during this period, getting involved meant following the orders of Belgian masters or missionaries;

---

[172]Cfr. Tutu, Desmond, (1996). "Troubled but not Destroyed", Unpublished Presidential Address, All African Conference of Churches, Seventh General Assembly, Addis Ababa, October, 1997; Tutu, D., Hope and Suffering. Collins, UK, Chapter one.

[173]Hinga, Teresa, (1994). "Jesus Christ and the Liberation of Women in Africa", in King (Ed.) Feminist Theology from the Third World, Maryknoll: Orbis Books, p. 263.

taking part in decision-making was important in constructing one's future and functional mechanisms.[174]

I will add that the Anglican Church and Rwandan society can no longer be separated. The Anglican Church will either allow itself to be inhibited, or it will evangelise society so that society, itself, integrates, understands and responds to the example of the Anglican Church in Rwanda.

The purpose of conversion and evangelisation is said to be the act that announces God's 'rescuing', redeeming Presence and His participation in the human struggle. Rwandans had to find God within harsh, environmental conditions and find the means to protect the moral fabric of the people. Careful treatment of the past has to be re-examined in order to discover what was lost, as well as what served as an aid to the growth of Christianity in Rwanda.

6.4 Contextual Theology

This topic is very extensive and often considered as a theoretical construction of problems inherent in the way missionaries interpreted the Bible in the context of their countries of service. The concern of central Anglican Church leadership in Rwanda is to ground Biblical interpretation in the wider context of the doctrine of reconciliation. The Revivalist mission exposed the dangerous futility of evangelism divorced from societal reality and people's history. The shallowness of Revivalism was then its lack of radical discipleship. It is argued that the model of mission and cultural encounter should have been the way Jesus commissioned his disciples with 'As the Father has sent me, so I send you' (John 20:21-23): they too are to pursue the mission which the Holy Spirit gives

---

[174]Interviews at Gahini Mission and Kigali Diocesan Office, July 1998.

them by relating to the society incarnationally.[175] It is this type of approach that takes people into a deeper level of reflection and understanding. The continuing ignorance and venality of the converts showed that weakness in the Anglican Church leadership was evident after Independence.

Thus, the mission for the present Anglican Church is to contextualise the Revivalist message and to bring it home in a fresh way. For instance, it is important for the Anglican Church in Rwanda to re-examine the meaning of ethnic diversity, to determine whether it is God's creation and to discover if He has a reason and purpose for it. It is therefore important to look for a theology that can talk to Rwandans clearly in a way that acknowledges ethnic diversity as being useful to their society. To do this, the Anglican Church will have to look back to the early days when it was laying its foundations in the country. In other words, it is a process of interpreting the gospel in today's world to meet the social situation in Rwanda, in all of its uniqueness, informing both the thought and actions taken by individuals.

Another human being might possess some part of the truth that others have not yet received. The immediate question then is self-imposed, 'How do we proceed with those who claim absolute and exclusive truth?' The phrase 'social or structural sin' is worth mentioning in the context of Rwandan theology, in order to understand what happened to that society which made people act in ways that were unexpected. Respondents at Butare National University argued that people learn their attitudes, values and views of reality from the social structures within which they are born. However, where Rwandans were bombarded daily with new ideas, the loss of society's values and moral responsibility broke down any sense of common citizenship

---

[175] Cfr. Forward, M. (ed.) (1995), Ultimate Visions, Oxford: Oneworld, p.14

and this, in its extreme form, eventually drifted into the committing of what society had forbidden as sin. Thus, arguably the Anglican Church in Rwanda must be faithful to its calling as a Godly serving Church, moving away from being a people-pleasing Church that tends to stand alongside politicians and to follow divisive policies.[176]

Like the theological notion of 'Ubuntu', Rwandan theology must focus upon 'Ubumwe' or 'oneness', combining past experience with traditional Christian doctrine to examine what went wrong in Rwandan society and to explain why people acted contrary to expectations by failing to protect each other as they would from the Ubumwe point of view. Edward Farley argues that the everyday contemporary experience of ordinary people has theological meaning and significance. It is believed that when the Anglican Church starts to consider its methods and approach, it will be the time when its theology begins to help people in their own everyday situations. It is argued that the new theology will function as a guideline to restoring the framework of society's values and expected responsibilities within communities as part of the reconciliation process.

First and foremost, according Anglican Church leadership, redefinition of a theology of national unity is needed.[177] So far the practised theology is not clear enough on the issues of uniting people. It is out of this situation that the meaning of spiritual needs is misunderstood and it becomes evident that there was even some confusion over the specific role that the Anglican Church would play in national reconciliation.

As mentioned earlier, the Revival Heritage teachings in Rwanda involve different meanings, whilst it is recognisable that each culture, in its own setting, has its

---

[176]Interviews at Gahini Mission and Kigali Diocesan Office July 1998.
[177]Mbanda, L., (1998). Committed to Conflict, The Destruction of the Anglican Church in Rwanda, London: SPCK, p.135

own moral values and special needs. Some of the views raised by members of the reconciliation seminar group at Kibungo were that, if contextual theology is developed, it might help Anglican Church members towards a better understanding of Christianity and assist reconciliation committees to choose strategies and tools best suited to the goals they hope to achieve. In this view, Christianity may show the way to how seemingly irreconcilable differences can be harmonised and caring communities encouraged and created in divided communities.[178]

The Christian mission in the world has always been to make the Word flesh (John 1:14), which is precisely the aim of inculturation theology. Schreiter, in The Faces of Jesus in Africa, quotes Pope John Paul in his encyclical 'Redemptoris Missio', where he addresses the practicalities of inculturation. Inculturation must involve the whole community, not just a few experts, since the people reflect the authentic 'sensus fidei', of which we must never lose sight.[179] The leading role of the missionary is not without its critics. Bishop Muzorewa, addressing the All African Conference of Churches in Harare, Zimbabwe in 1990, drew a link between liberation and inculturation. He criticised the negative role played by missionaries when they chose to compromise under a Belgian rule that saw oppression of converts rather than opposition to injustices.[180]

Today, as the Anglican Church in Rwanda struggles to be faithful to the culture of the people, to the human spirit and to what God says, it becomes necessary to revisit the

---

[178] A report of the three days Anglican leaders' seminar on reconciliation organised and sponsored by REACH from 25th to 28th March 1998 held at St. Joseph Centre, Kibungo Prefecture

[179] Schreiter, R. J., (1992), Reconciliation, Mission & Ministry in Changing Social Order, New York, Orbis Books, p. viii.

[180] Muzorewa, G. H., "African Liberation Theology", in Voices from the Third World, 31 January 1990, pp.190 - 97.

Bible. It can be argued that God calls us away from where we think He has been to where He wants us to be and we are called again to move on. This is why some people approach the Bible in a different way, not as having a fixed and unchanging law, but as a fallible record of where previous generations got to in their understanding of the nature of their relationship with God.

To advance this idea further, the Rwandan way of thinking and of forming religious convictions is very close to the way of thinking of Bible people, especially that of the Old Testament. The need for a theology based within a cultural context means that the Anglican Church in Rwanda can start from the ways in which people's convictions are formed and expressed. In addition, this need for the inculturation of theology is linked to the historical background of society. Dickson Kwesi asserts that a people's way of life is the means by which they comprehend reality[181] and that it is difficult to see another culture if one views it through one's own culture, especially in communication. Evans-Pritchard adds that 'cultural translation' is supremely difficult and that it is perhaps even impossible to understand another reality without becoming a part of it.[182]

The key point is that a state of inward transformation and growth is rooted in an attitude of receptivity, whereas, when people are passive in this process, they are moulded without contributing to it. This is what appears to have happened when Rwandans were treated as if they did not exist and as if nothing had happened before the missionaries and Belgian rule. In this case, the new theology in Rwanda may be described as a way of life, or a value system. The aim of this analysis, therefore, includes

---

[181] Dickson, Kwesi (1984). Theology in Africa, London: Longman and Todd, p. 3.
[182] Evans Pritchard, E. E. (1965). "Theories of Primitive Religion". Oxford: Clarendon Press, p. 7.

theological contextualisation, using familiar language and symbols in a given situation, recognised and practised in nearly every civilised and uncivilised society throughout human history, all of which is necessary in order to reach people in their own context, .

The issue of language is particularly significant. The use of the verb 'to create' shows how important this is, as language interprets the concept of the Creation and the communication within the Genesis story. The first thing that Adam did after he was created was to name all the creatures. John's gospel states: 'from the beginning was the Word and the Word was with God and the Word was God' (John 1:1–2). The uniqueness of words is summed up by Lenski and Nolan, who argue that 'without words and other symbols, human societies would differ little from the societies of other primates, for they would lack their most distinctive feature'.[183] James Woodward and Stephen Pattison reinforce this argument by stating: 'The capacity to be able to reflect upon and articulate something of the theological significance of human experience is highly valued in theology. It is implicit for this argument that it was time for the Anglican Church to respond to the voices of its members to interpret the meanings of myths and symbols that shape people's views of themselves and their world,[184] to how Christ can be found everywhere.'[185]

Another concern of younger Anglican Church respondents is the style of worship, which is still kept foreign to Church members, although a few congregations

---

[183] Lenski, G., Nolan, P. and Lenski, J., (1995). Human Societies, an Introduction to Macro Sociology, Seventh Edition, New York: McGrawHill, Inc., p. 20.
[184] Woodward, C. Vann, (1971). American Counterpoint, Slavery and Racism in the North South Dialogue, Boston: Little, Brown, p. 9.
[185] Cfc. Tutu's speech at St. Thomas's Anglican in Dublin in "Common Ground", The Journal of the Council of Christians & Jews, 13 June 1999, No.2

have made slight alterations in the liturgy. Louise Pirouet reasons that those who had found a Christian faith could have been allowed to use gestures and symbols of their old religion to express their Christianity, without implying a mixing of religions.[186]

Indeed, traditions of piety, Keswick teaching and the search for the 'higher life' all influenced Anglican Church missionaries who worked in Rwanda.[187] This hunger for a deeper experience of God in one's life was a deep undercurrent leading to the Revivalist outbreak.[188] It is also important to consider the influence of Protestant Evangelicals, who tended to identify Christian morality with a more fundamental interpretation of the Bible. This is not a feature of just one religion. In practice, regarding exclusiveness, it is 'important to keep in mind that Luther's attack on the Jews is not an isolated phenomenon, but arises out of the monotheism common to all of the religious traditions rooted in the Bible'.[189] Down the centuries, there have been groups in all the major world religions that make such claims. Islamic fundamentalists may be regarded as the most obvious today, but there are many Christians who claim a similar fundamental attitude to truth, just as missionaries in Rwanda confronted their converts with claims to absolute and exclusive truth.

Thus, what missionaries in Rwanda conceived at one level, they could not from another. The Rwandan way of making sense of the world would not be the same as that of the converts to Christianity. It was impossible for

---

[186]Pirouet, L., (1989). Christianity Worldwide, Anglican Church History 4: AD1800 Onwards, London: SPCK,
p. 105.
[187]Ibid. p. 133.
[188]Bowen, R., (1995). "Rwanda, Missionary Reflections on a Catastrophe", London: SPCK, pp. 33 – 47.
[189]Rubenstein, R. & Roth, J. K., (1987). Approaches to Auschwitz, the Legacy of the Holocaust, London: SCM Press Ltd, p. 60.

missionaries to see through traditional religious eyes without conversion to the people's ways of seeing the world around them. It is argued that this is required for integration otherwise, they would only be observing other people's reality; until it was 'internalised' it could not be real for them. The same applies to Christianity. It is not real for people as long as they lack a vital aspect of comprehension; it will always be observed from the standpoint of other people's reality. It will remain incomplete until the Anglican Church in Rwanda affirms and accepts that truths can be discovered elsewhere. If the Anglican Church does not do so, it would be as if it was turning its back upon its own greatest discoveries.

The new emphasis is upon including the positive elements of the known, but going beyond this in order to consider new, theologically related challenges, as well as offering pastoral care. The Anglican Church's burden of recovery and rehabilitation during the first phase was shared between local Anglican Churches in the communities, NGOs, local associations such as Widows Associations, Youth Associations, Co-operatives and the Government's Department of Rehabilitation. At a local level, the Department was only supposed to play a facilitative role, leaving the beneficiaries to participate fully in caring for local needs.

Unfortunately, the Government did not have the capacity to provide a link to bridge the gap between national programmes and local communities. By getting to know people in their local communities, the Anglican Church took the initiative to discover what it means to live together. The aim of the initiative is to provide a focus for the reconciliation that is currently being developed around these issues of the Rwandan people's broken relationships.

However, when I asked respondents the reasons for their overwhelming support of the palaver mode, the responses were that they believed it would help them if they met face to face with different groups affected by the conflict. The Rwandan Anglican Church termed this concept the 'palaver talks'. The talks are the prime vehicle for examining and raising major issues concerning the situations in which people find themselves. It was intended to transform people's lives through the discovery of how past communities had eradicated social problems such as poverty by acting collectively. Palaver talks are designed to provide a forum for a discussion around a number of past and present community matters. In the past, people would confront their common history and then speak about what they knew of community spirit, a source of reconciliation in itself. It is argued that part of the deficit of present-day theology in Rwanda is its inability to connect meaningfully to people's needs.[190] It was even conceded by the respondents that it was foolish to begin talking about religious commitment before addressing fundamental problems such as how to find food or employment.

This illustrates a situation of despair in a country where unemployment is chronic among villagers and health is poor in the camps. The need for pastoral support springs from a deep concern that the Anglican Church should not lose sight of its ideals. In William Temple's pastoral view, 'the only real cure for unemployment is employment. In other words, the country is challenged to find a social order that provides employment, steadily and generally and our consciences should be restive until we succeed. Christian sympathy demands this.'[191]

Today, Temple's argument is more patently relevant to the Rwandan economic situation than when it was written. Fundamentally, many people need to hear of a God who

---

[190]Maluleke, T. S., (1998). "Truth, National Unity and Reconciliation in South Africa, Aspects of the Emerging Theological Agenda", Missionalia, 25:1 April, p. 339.
[191]Temple, William, (1976). Christianity and the Social Order, (Edition), London: SPCK, p. 35.

can liberate them from the conditions in which they are trapped, allowing them to see their situation from a liberationist perspective. This is not only illustrative of the preaching of the gospel, it is a demonstration of the reality of God's love in action, a meeting of faith and works. James, in his letter says, 'Faith that doesn't show itself by good deeds is no faith at all – it is dead and useless (James 2:17b). As Ian Linden states: 'Indeed, the starting point for the thinking of the Peruvian theologian, Gustavo Gutierrez, was precisely the disjunction between the Christian message and an experienced reality, that of the Latin American poor. 'How is it possible to tell the poor, who are forced to live in conditions that embody a denial of love, that God loves them?' His implied answer was that this message would be a lie if God's love and thus the Christian Gospel, were disincarnate, not about changing the world of the poor economically, socially and politically.'[192]

With reference to Rwanda, the quest for contextual theology illustrates the significance of the need for the Anglican Church in Rwanda to share the love of God and for the Church to involve itself in evaluating the immediate issues of everyday life. Indeed, it is the task of the Anglican Church to show people the means by which to move forward and to assure every ethnic group that living in such an ethnically pluralistic culture is part of God's design to manifest the purpose of His Kingdom (John 11:52). The assumption is that a devotedly pluralistic culture will develop a theology based on normative teaching about politically sensitive issues, explaining that politics that divide cause suffering and dehumanising conditions to both the oppressor and the oppressed.

This fresh look at Rwandan theology provides the basis for a whole new sociological and multi-cultural situation. It is a spirituality that has to encompass all. It is argued that

---

[192]http://www.sedos.org/english/liden2.htm/12/8/07

Rwandan theology has to be slightly different from that of South Africa or Latin America due to the fact that people in Rwanda have their own unique experiences and cultural needs. The first thing for Rwandan theology to address is the effect of the period of Belgian dominance, wherein people were taught to undervalue their own culture, customs, values and beliefs, beliefs that were deemed unacceptable. The main task for Rwandan theology is therefore to analyse the theology under which the Anglican Church operates, whereas in the case of South Africa's 'Ubuntu' notion, with its links to theological thinking, its main objective was to deal with apartheid or racial segregation. Self-segregation, driven by fear of others, is a belief that this is the only way to promote, retain and protect self-interest, power and identity.

As mentioned earlier, the use of religion for political purposes is not unusual. In the segregation policy of apartheid it was classified as a theology that advocated the relationship of oppressor and oppressed, while, at the same time, being classified as an ideology of social and economic oppression that one Rwandan described as 'a form of blindness'.[193] The purpose of Ubuntu theology was to offer an alternative way of living in a hostile world. Further analysis of the theological meanings of Ubuntu and 'Ubumwe' stresses the importance of unity in a shared image of God between people of all races or ethnicity in society. Similarly according to Canon Andrew Kaizari the Rwandan initiative known as 'Ingando' promoted unity. Today it is especially linked with the image of God as Advocate for any person rejected and discriminated against.[194] The only difference between these theologies is that each has developed under different social, political and theological circumstances.

---

[193]Interviewing Provincial Secretary: Canon Andrew Kaizari at the provincial headquarters in Kigali, July 1994, who sadly later died.
[194]Ibid.

Rwandan theology recognises that people live in a world that houses a mixture of good and evil, right and wrong. Holding this view, it argues that the Christian Anglican Church in Rwanda has the power to tilt the balance, encouraging good and discouraging evil. Part of the Anglican Church's role is to be custodian of the gospel, to teach it clearly to all, putting the word of God into practice within society in order to equip its members with teaching that illuminates. Rwandan 'Ubumwe theology' explains and challenges ethnicity in the same way as Ubuntu exposed the injustices of apartheid, creating a voice for the voiceless millions whose political leadership was forced into exile.[195]

Ubuntu (humanity) theology is viewed in the context of apartheid and is concerned with Afrikaner and African cultures. Desmond Tutu argued that 'a person is a person through other persons. I am a person because you are a person. If I undermine you, I undermine myself.'[196] In other words, forgiveness is the highest form of self-interest and therefore of interest in others. The main objective for Ubuntu is to restore the integrative side of humanity that seeks to promote the dignity of all–'the bundle of life'.[197] He states that 'we are bound up together and it is in our own interests that harmony is restored'.[198]

Ubuntu is a word from the Xhosa language, in which the expression 'Ubuntu Ungumuntu' translates as 'a person depends on other people to be a person'. Ubuntu theology proclaims that people rejoice in the way that God created

---

[195]Battle, M. J., (1977). Reconciliation: The Ubuntu Theology of Desmond Tutu, Cleveland: The Pilgrim Press, pp. 8–17; compare Tutu, D., (1993). "African Theology and black Theology: The Quest for Authenticity and the Struggle for Liberation", in African Challenge, edited by Kenneth Best, Nairobi: Trans Africa Publishers, pp. 3-8.
[196]Battle, M. (1977), Reconciliation: The Ubuntu Theology of Desmond Tutu, Cleveland: The Pilgrim Press, pp. 8–17.
[197]Ibid.
[198]Ibid. pp. 8–14.

them differently. As Adam and Eve discovered, new meanings and identities are always possible.[199] The important elements of Desmond Tutu's Ubuntu theology can be applied as a guide: firstly, to build up interdependent communities, secondly, to recognise people as entities and individuals, thirdly, to combine the best of Christian teaching and African cultures to produce a new and distinctive theology and fourthly, if it is strong enough, to address and even overthrow the social evils in society.[200]

Desmond Tutu states that God does not love us because we are loveable, but that we are loveable precisely because God loves us. God's love is what gives us our worth. So, we are liberated by the price paid by His beloved Son. Ubuntu theology states that race is an irrelevance, apart from an understanding of Ubuntu. He concludes by saying 'we hope that in a very short time, people will ask: 'Why were we so stupid for so long?'[201] Rwandan theology encompasses Ubuntu in its approach. Its theological base is to reflect back upon old ways of living in a community with its values, which in the past had united groups of people together, to examine what had gone wrong with the diversity that had always existed.

The process of analysing diversity influences people to put aside political differences and to look at the similarities that hold communities together. A Bible college tutor commented that going 'back to roots' meant examining the foundational parts of Anglican Church theology.[202] Rwandans have a very different reaction to their past. As

---

[199] Battle, M., (1977). Reconciliation: The Ubuntu Theology of Desmond Tutu, Cleveland: The Pilgrim Press, p.40.
[200] Ibid.
[201] Egan, Meg, a member of the Corrymeela community in Northern Ireland, reports on Tutu's speech at Thomas's Anglican in Dublin, Common Ground, The journal of the Council of Christian s and Jews, June 1999, No.2, p.7
[202] Interviewing tutor at Butare training College for ordinates, May 2004.

the Old Testament puts it, 'we sinned against you, only against you – and [have] done what you consider evil' (Psalm 51:4). Together, Rwandans might learn more about how differences were formed and by whom they were encouraged.

The task is to move from aversion to embrace, within an unfolding vision of what is good for all. Examining the changes in society requires going back to the roots to look at the Anglican Church ministry to see if it meets God's standards, then, when the Church finds where people have gone wrong, to seek God's forgiveness and to return to His ways.[203] The intention behind all this is a reconstruction of the Christian way whereby once again people 'stick together', in Ubumwe, to restore those values that had united Rwandans, to share the memory of their traditions and to examine what went wrong in the past. This may mean going to local communities and to rural Anglican churches where the remains of the community concepts of living together are buried. To restore past community values may mean listening to the composition of people's prayers, songs and stories. This is one way the Bible can be re-introduced to its readers, in a cultural context and where emphasis is laid upon the community.[204]

Conclusion

This chapter has attempted to explain the need for an expanded and more meaningful theology and faith response. It has explained that during the missionary days, a social process was needed through which to comprehend and articulate the features and dimensions of the Christian faith. The Anglican Church's urgent mission is to promote those social values that had, in the past, united Rwandans in

---

[203]Interview at Butare, July 1998.
[204]Mbiti, J. S. (1991). Concepts of God in Africa. London: S.P.C.K, p. 90.

the service of God towards their neighbours. In response to the current situation in Rwanda, the restoration of community social values is urgently needed as part of the reconciliation process in this new theology.

In order to be effective, this sort of contextual theology has to be committed to and founded on a study of the Scriptures. This requires the Anglican Church in Rwanda to examine the Scriptures systematically, while those who teach must commit themselves to an analytical and expository teaching of the whole Bible, relating Biblical messages to society's needs. Louise Pirouet argues that dependence on overseas development aid also creates a kind of bondage.[205] He argues that Rwandan contextual theology must involve Rwandans in their communities in the process of mutual support. It is 'above all, a new way of doing theology rather than being itself a new theology'.[206] Its social theological theory arises from the use of 'action-reflection', a model that sees the Rwandan Anglican Church's current theology as divorced from its obligation to fulfil the Christian mission in the world.[207]

This emphasis is most important if the Rwandan Anglican Church is to develop a theology capable of delivering a meaningful gospel based on people's needs. While encouraging theological debate, the Anglican Church can help to build a civil society within the cultural framework of the traditional social set-up. Utmost importance is placed on respondents' views and their realisation of how important it is to restore and to cultivate traditional and community values. These values should be seen as building blocks in the process of resolving,

---

[205]Pirouet, L., (1989). Christianity Worldwide, Anglican Church History 4: AD1800 Onwards, London: SPCK, p.174.
[206]Cfr. Kirk, J. A., (1979). Liberation Theology, An Evangelical View from the Third World, England: Marshalls Theological Library, p. 23
[207]Biggar, N., (1988). Theological Politics, Oxford: Latimer House, pp. 29–30.

managing and fostering reconciliation in the country. The approach of the Anglican Church should be to understand people and to bring a message of the reconciling Saviour in the gospel message that will transform the Rwandan people's outlook on the world and offer them hope and confidence for the future.

The next chapter examines various methods that the Anglican Church in Rwanda can employ in the process of reconciliation after the genocide. In this exceptional situation, the purpose is to illustrate some of the ways in which reconciliation theology might infiltrate everyday life. It is argued that the Anglican Church's use of 'palaver' talk as an approach to reconciliation may assist people in discovering where the current Rwandan political problems lie. This may then help them to find a way forward to resolve their differences.

Chapter Seven

The Anglican Church and Reconciliation

7.0 Introduction

The purpose of this chapter is to explore the theology and practice of (Ubwiyunge) reconciliation in Anglican Churches in Rwanda. It has already been mentioned that the situation in the early days after the genocide was very volatile; groups still blamed each other, though reconciliation was still essential. That chapter was mainly based upon a combination of observation and interviews with diocesan reconciliation group workers and painted a graphic picture of the extent of the reconciliation progress in parts of the Anglican Church in Rwanda.

During my last visit in May 2004, to my surprise the situation had changed and there was a need for the Anglican Church to provide for people to be able to be in control of their own political destiny for the country's future. I was put in touch with Anglican Church leaders, through the recommendation of individuals and learnt, thereby, about other places to visit (snowball format). I soon discovered that there was a network of people who were concerned with the role of reconciliation, some of whom knew each other and kept in touch.

I was welcomed into this network and the most impressive thing was the willing help given by everyone approached and the interest they showed in the task of reconciliation. During this time, the first task was to assess the people's feelings about the possibility of reconciliation. The second task was to analyse the arguments from both sides: those who argued in support of reconciliation instead of vengeance and those who objected to the idea. The third task was to examine what the Anglican Church was doing about reconciliation, both theoretically and practically. The aim throughout the interviews was to assess the Anglican Church's approach to see if they had considered reconciliation theology as a strategic mission, in order to understand how the Anglican Church was preparing to handle the challenges ahead. For instance, one of the other roles of the Anglican Church is to hold trauma recovery classes for the counselling of both Hutu and Tutsi survivors of the genocide, the training of counsellors, providing psychological support to genocide victims, providing survival kits to those who need them, resettling the displaced and providing free discussion, which is an essential element in a reconciliation process.

The Anglican Church, at the heart of the community, is called to bring people together as part of reconciliation within the community. Therefore, the issue of how to welcome and reintegrate those who participated in the genocide is important. It is possible for the Anglican Church to assist in the reconciliatory process in order to stimulate public debate about the roots of the problem and possible courses of action.

From a theological point of view, these arrangements are a call to the 'integrative' side of the political process. If there are difficulties with the integrative arrangements, divisions will persist and the legacy of ethnic distinction will continue for as long as people live this way. It is a call for action on a broad front; this study argues that the Anglican Church and other Churches in the country must make a joint effort in the reconciliation process. This is the only way forward, so that the traumatised population can be reconciled. So far, evidence shows that although the Anglican Church was in favour of reconciliation, it still fell far short of the task.

7.1 The Anglican Church's Commitment to Reconciliation

At this point, it is necessary to return to the public acceptance of reconciliation in Rwanda. One positive thing was that as time passed, survivors gradually began to realise the consequences of what had happened and to see the necessity of moving on with life. This contrasts markedly with the situation immediately after the genocide, when there was a general aversion to this idea. First, at this early stage, people were still suffering, to the extent that even thinking about the possibility of reconciliation seemed impossible. Second, the blanket amnesty proposed by the government was unpopular and in the view of many survivors was a physical impossibility.

On a return visit to Rwanda ten years later, the situation had changed. At this time there were organised offices dealing with reconciliation programmes that provided guidance on the formulation and implementation of policies for good practice. In March 1999, a Unity and Reconciliation Commission (NURC) was created by Parliamentary law. On 4th June 2003 Article 178 was enacted in the National Constitution.

This department of reconciliation is situated in the Presidential Office and is responsible for national reconciliation. Another reconciliation department operates under the Ministry of Justice and is mainly responsible for the Gacaca court trial programme. These two departments were umbrellas of the national network, represented at the local level. I mostly used the Église Épiscopale au Rwanda and Butare University Reconciliation Centre as my sources, which have a collection of literature on the Gacaca trials. In addition, academic staff at Butare University provided me with up-to-date information about reconciliation programmes.

There were four dioceses that had clear objectives. These are Byumba diocese, Gahini diocese, Kigali diocese and Shyira diocese. Somehow, they lacked a clear strategy to engage local communities in a constructive programme for reconciliation. It is argued that a genuine reconciliation is when those involved are encouraged to understand what is involved in the convergence phase of the task.[208] At this period, the Anglican Church was in an early stage, still organising the process that allows participants to understand and to receive instruction in what is involved in the search for peace; that is, to engage people in an exercise where survivors and victims of genocide are willing freely to share their pain with others and to search for a way forward through joint effort, breaking the chains of the past to build new roads to reconciliation.

What is important is that the Anglican Church in Rwanda was beginning to realise that reconciliation is a precondition for the reconstruction of the country.[209] Anglican Church leaders argued that, in order to develop people's capacity to ask questions about what happened and to search for alternative ways forward, it helps to create the right combination of involvement and detachment that is required for the reconciliation process. It is argued that the psychological theory used to describe this kind of involvement in the other person's state of mind is the quality of 'empathy'. This implies the ability to put oneself in the other person's position, an 'emotional involvement...which acknowledges neighbours as living human beings with equal rights'.[210] One of the aims

---

[208] A report of the three days Anglican leaders' seminar on reconciliation organised and sponsored by REACH from 25th to 28th March 1998 held at St. Joseph Centre, Kibungo Prefecture
[209] Interviewing Bishops at the Provincial Assembly of Église Épiscopale au Rwanda, August 1998.
[210] Gerloff, R., (1998). Truth a New Society and Reconciliation, London: SPCK, p. 23.

claimed as fundamental in the process of reconciliation in Rwanda is that assumption that reconciliation theology is able to empower both individuals and communities with certain transforming capabilities. These are expected to bring about positive quantitative and qualitative change that would not occur if there were no reconciliation.

Every community, therefore, will have to identify its needs and to clarify them as aims and objectives for reconciliation. However, the Anglican Church cannot pretend to provide a solution to all problems. The pattern and the varied options open for bringing people together and related directly as it is to the survivor's own perception of the seriousness of the conflict will determine the emphasis placed by the Anglican Church in its approach to reconciliation.

This approach must be based on two points. First, one assumes that the principal task of reconciliation is to ensure that all citizens participate as fully as possible in making concessions. Second, through knowing the causes of conflict, individuals are allowed to re-examine what went wrong for people and, in a full sense, to discover this for themselves. It was mainly the Anglican Churches that set the process in motion, offering support for comprehensive debate. In particular, the Anglican Church in Rwanda recognised that the strife that afflicted the country derived from divided communities. Therefore, the way to redeem the situation and for people to live together peacefully again would be through an extended process of reconciliation.

During the Anglican Church seminar's talks, most participants stressed that it was necessary for the Anglican Church to take an active role in assisting the process of reconciliation and unity in the country.[211] Pastor Antoine

---

[211] A report of the three days Anglican leaders' seminar on reconciliation organised and sponsored by REACH from 25th to 28th March 1998 held at St. Joseph Centre, Kibungo Prefecture.

Rutayisire of the National Unity and Reconciliation Commission (NURC) argued that it was extremely important for the Anglican Church to play a leading role so that people could unite again, rather than living in pretence as if there were no bad feelings. One of the early resolutions passed by participants was the decision to have more seminars on reconciliation. It was argued that seminars should not only involve Anglican Church leaders, but also those in government and other non-governmental organisations, because the idea of reconciliation must spread beyond Anglican Church members themselves.

The seminar elected new committee members to co-ordinate similar seminars in other parts of the country. In less than a month, there was another reconciliation conference that attracted thousands of people from all over Rwanda and, this time, Protestant Church pastors from different denominations attended as well. It was organised by the Anglican Archbishop's Office of Kigali Diocese and held at the National Stadium. The speakers included cabinet ministers from the Rwandan government, Anglican Church and other Protestant Church leaders and the African Evangelist Enterprise. On this occasion, the Catholic Church leaders and the Seventh-day Adventists turned down the Archbishop's invitation.[212]

The participants were urged to carry out their discussions openly, without bias or fear or avoiding suspicion. There were seven discussion groups and eleven questions used in all groups. Each group discussed strategies and methods that should be used in local and national reconciliation programmes. Église Épiscopale au Rwanda stressed the need for promoting reconciliatory values designed to articulate the following:

---

[212] A report for Protestant Anglicans on the Reconciliation Seminar, July 1998.

- Palaver talks in local communities;
- Anglican Churches to encourage the spirit of forgiveness;
- Anglican Church support for a pluralistic society;
- Protection of the people's rights;
- Reconciliation and social integration.[213]

The conference enabled people from different dioceses and ethnic backgrounds to meet with others who shared similar views about reconciliation and for Hutu and Tutsi Anglican Church leaders to come closer and discuss vital strategies for how to begin the process of reconciliation. There were countless testimonies from respondents, women and men of all ages, who had survived the genocide. During the interviews, I discovered that the idea of reconciliation was still received with mixed feelings in the country. In fact, I noted that after the genocide, any proposal for reconciliation was unconceivable. It was explained to me by some respondents that it was unrealistic to think about reconciliation and that it was too early to restore relationships, bearing in mind that immediately after the genocide there were several attempts; for example, the REACH group had initiated reconciliation programmes in Kenya, Tanzania and Rwanda for reconciling Rwandans in exile and in Rwanda itself. At this early period, survivors shrugged off the idea, because the general public was still angry even just to hear the word 'reconcile'.[214]

At this period in Rwanda there were various reactions to reconciliation, some survivors questioned even the reason for it.[215] During the early attempts for reconciliation after the genocide there were still fleshy scars and visible

---

[213]Interviewing staff members of 'Seeds of Peace Centre – Anglican Church', Gahini Diocese, July 1998.
[214]A report for Protestant Anglicans on the Reconciliation Seminar, July 1998
[215]Ibid.

memories of damage that made it quite hard for many victims and survivors to trust anyone. The general feeling was still one of tension and distrust between groups that made it harder even to wonder what a reconciliatory process could do to help.[216] For others, the immediate response was to 'reconcile with whom'? Augustin Nzamwita's response, 'I see no point in me being reconciled with anyone because I am no longer a person. The only thing that I have chosen to do, is to pray until the end of my life'.[217]

Given that people, in the aftermath of the genocide in Rwanda, were still very traumatised by what they had endured, it was even difficult and perhaps inappropriate to keep moral indignation out of the question of why the genocide had begun and the pain of those who were wronged. The choice for reconciliation over vengeance was even harder to justify, as is evidenced by the 42% of respondents who disagreed with the idea that people had free will to kill during the genocide. The genocide was beyond imagination, where neighbour had killed neighbour, teachers had killed their pupils and doctors had left their patients to die. No-one who saw the corpses of men, women and children, twisted in pain and lying in their hundreds beside the altar and all over the grounds of the parishes of Rwanda will ever be able to forget the sight.[218]

In order to assess the situation, I paid another visit to Rwanda in July 2004 to try to see if there was any progress towards reconciliation in the preceding ten years, specifically observing which methods had been used by

---

[216]Mbanda, L., (1998). Committed to Conflict, The Destruction of the Anglican Church in Rwanda, London: SPCK, p. 123.
[217]African Rights, Resisting Genocide at Bisesero, April-June 1994, p.80
[218]Cf. African Rights, The Protestant Churches and the Genocide, Appeal to the World Council of Churches, Meeting in Harare contains a copy of the Bishop's Report 1999, p.1

both the Anglican Church and the government. The descriptions and observations made in this chapter are based on the reconciliation approach used during this time by the Anglican Church.

In my first visits in the aftermath of the genocide, I saw bodies lying in churches and classrooms and it was extremely hard for me to accept how a human being could do to another human being. What I saw - it was too cruel to describe in words. Certainly it was a very difficult situation, especially for survivors who were still recovering from the loss of their loved ones. It was, indeed, obvious that people needed time for grieving. Objecting to the idea of reconciliation was quite natural in the circumstances.

On the other hand, we need to bear in mind that in such complicated situations there is no one clear, effective and set way of finding the answer. The critical point to raise here is that forgiveness can be problematic when survivors are still demanding that the perpetrator suffer too, or perhaps that the victim forfeits the right to revenge, risking future suffering. Timothy Longman's conclusion in his findings in Rwanda noted: 'His study demonstrates that traumatic exposure, PTSD symptoms and other factors are associated with attitudes toward justice and reconciliation. Societal interventions following mass violence should consider the effects of trauma if reconciliation is to be realised'.[219]

It is argued that if people don't trust each other, they cannot listen to each other. At a conceptual level, an alternative approach was to prepare the good soil in every person's heart before engaging in reconciliation. At the same time, the Rwandan government came up with the

---

[219]http://search.live.com/results.aspx?srch=104&FORM=AS4&q=Timothy+Longman+Rwanda+genocide/5/08

misguided and ill-advised idea of a blanket amnesty, which, naturally, received an angry reaction from the survivors.[220]

Virtually every interviewee complained about the blanket amnesty proposal. It became clear that this policy was not popular, especially for survivors who lived in camps with those who had been involved in the genocide. The large number of those who opposed the blanket amnesty argued in favour of the government developing tougher procedures to allow genocide victims to seek redress and for perpetrators to be brought to justice and punished. In the view of the respondents, reconciliation and blanket amnesty did not offer a lasting solution to the conflict. It was seen as a 'sell out' and it was argued that you cannot grant amnesty for an unacknowledged crime. In a sense this contradicts the expectations of those who felt that the perpetrators of crimes must be brought to justice and punished in order to deter others from becoming perpetrators.

The main shifts in opinions shown by the survivors saw reconciliation as bringing perpetrators to justice, offering a degree of reparation for victims or relatives in cases where loss of life had occurred. Whereas, in table 6, 48% agreed that it was important to bring the perpetrators to justice in order to properly address issues of ethnic conflict and in view of the damage it had caused to victims. This suggests that some Anglicans, while they held to faith in reconciliation they were unwilling to let killers go free. On the other hand, the positive thing that came out of the Anglican Church leaders' seminar, as the testimonies of participants revealed, was that it then helped them to alleviate the suspicion that had previously existed among Church leaders themselves and this, in turn, helped to demolish the wall of mistrust. To those who supported the

---

[220] A report for Protestant Anglicans on the Reconciliation Seminar, July 1998

idea of reconciliation, it was their dream of a new society in which people would be reconciled.

The Anglican Church leaders' call for a resolution was seen by many to be a wise move, in that, taking the lead in calling for support for peace and reconciliation, would provide avenues of communication so that matters concerning different groups could be talked about.[221] Respondents stressed that the burden should not be upon the victims, asking them to forgive people who have not asked for forgiveness. In my view, forgiveness cannot be demanded or coerced. When it is granted it is a gift.

Another group of women from Ibuka, a group of genocide survivors, stressed the importance of teaching and rehabilitating ex-prisoners to acknowledge that they have done wrong and to approach the victims for forgiveness. There was no dispute that the basic idea behind reconciliation is a noble one.[222]

During the conference, Anglican Church leaders agreed that Christian unity is not identical with uniformity. It does not allow division, but it does not exclude variety. In the body of Christ, there are many members. This unity grounded in Christ leaves scope for diversity of action and function; the only conformity is to the mind of Christ and the direction of the Holy Spirit. And collectively all members agreed that ethnic distinction should be condemned and ethnicity should be treated as an extended family system, acting as a moral force offering security to its members. Pierre Grimes succinctly explains this when he asserts that human existence is normally a dialogue

---

[221] A report from Anglican Church leadership's seminar at Kibungo on the Reconciliation, July 1998.
[222] Interviewing Anglican Ibuka members at Anglican leaders' seminar on reconciliation organised and sponsored by REACH at Kigali in.May 2004.

(Imibonano) that prepares human beings for a more profound existence.[223]

Furthermore, Anglican Church leaders asserted that people have the power to transform their thoughts into physical reality and that Rwandans were capable of dreaming and making their dreams come true. One view that was supported by most Anglican Church leaders was that the best way of opposing such a conflict, which generated hatred and ended in genocide, is spiritual renewal. One evangelical clergyman's central argument was that to miss this message of spiritual renewal was to miss the whole point of Christ's teaching.

During the reconciliation seminar at Kibungo, respondents argued that making positive steps along the long road to reconciliation is good for communities and support for this process is believed to be the most effective way of opposing any future repetition of atrocities.[224] The Anglican Church had taken this task on board and fully committed itself to the ministry of reconciliation. At this point it is right to say that the Anglican Church was using any means available in local communities to search for a way forward.

However, an immediate obstacle slowing down the pace of reconciliation was a lack of financial resources. The main challenge was that of a lack of easy access to and for people in rural areas. There is no easy road access and most rural communities are scattered, distant villages, on steep hills and in valleys. This meant that the early stages of disseminating vital information about future reconciliation meetings proved difficult. Coming up against the inadequate road network and frustrated participants meant that the process had a long way to go. The Anglican Church and its members in rural areas and the rural interior of the

---

[223]Cf. Grimes, Pierre, "Dreams and the Philosophers" in http://www.philosphicalmidwifery.com/dandphilo.htm26/0/00
[224]Interviewing seminar participants at Kibungo Diocese, July 1998.

region is still almost entirely Hutu. The latter were extremely poor and lacked quick means of communication.[225] The only means of being informed about future meetings for reconciliation was through word of mouth from the local leadership. The problem with word of mouth is that it may be distorted and seem negative in some instances, while in other places it may be positive – it all depends upon the 'messenger'.

7.2 Methods and Initiatives of Reconciliation

Any exploration into the process of reconciliation discovers whether respondents have confidence in its possibilities. Are the people concerned sceptical about the whole process and do they think that it is not possible? In order to answer such questions we explored matters of concern helped by Anglican Church members and its leadership. The Anglican Church's restoration of the structure of leadership began to respond to community-related crises. They worked in partnership with relief organisations already engaged in restoring peace and rehabilitation.

To date, there are working committees responsible for reconciliation programmes in nine dioceses. These programmes varied from fully constituted committees with an officer, to lead committees or ad hoc groups with a part-time officer or with none at all. In four dioceses they had set up a committee responsible for a reconciliation

---

[225] According to local respondents at Gisenyi, the reason for Ruhengeri being entirely occupied by Hutus was that it was done deliberately by Habyarimana's regime between 1959 and 1961 and Tutsis from northern areas of Ruhengeri and Gisenyi were forcibly relocated to Bugesera in order to make the north an exclusive area of Habyarimana's supporters. Tutsi refugee returnees were either resettled in refugee camps or in urban areas, which is the reason why there were less Tutsis in the rural areas.

programme, where each diocese had a fully paid co-ordinator at the Anglican Church headquarters of the Archbishop's Office. In five other dioceses, issues of reconciliation were the responsibility of the Diocesan Board for Social Responsibility and Rehabilitation, though these included individuals who did not seem to have much interest in the process.

The reason for this lack of commitment to the process of reconciliation was that there were some clergy who had served in the previous Anglican Church leadership who still kept allegiance to their previous bishops in exile and others were bishops who had served as well under a previous leadership. The latter were still suspects for having participated in genocide. All these allegations raised feelings that made it very difficult for the clergy and bishops to work as they would have liked to do. On the other hand, the Rwandan government and the Anglican Church decided to restore positive aspects of traditional institutions such as Gacaca and the Palaver talks.

68% of respondents agreed that Rwandan community life had been eroded and that the role of elders in community governance had diminished. They felt that there should be a more substantial restoration of traditional structures that were clearer and more community oriented. So far, the Anglican Church in Rwanda seems to have opted out of the palaver mode of reconciliation.

The two approaches of palaver and Gacaca are both traditional methods that had been used in Rwanda to resolve local disputes. The differences between the two are minimal and both put emphasis upon community participation. The only difference is that Gacaca uses judicial methods to achieve reconciliation, while the Anglican Church palaver talks are centred on analysis of the background of the conflict. The palaver is a method of dispute resolution that does not depend in any sense on a 'duel' between the parties. Rather, the aim of palaver is a reconciliation of views to provide, or attain, a uniform perception of a dispute, perceptions shared both by the participants and even the parties to the dispute. According to tradition, a successful palaver is one in which a perception is reoriented so that it is shared by all. The Rwanda Anglican palaver theological approach is a means for the Anglican Church to apply a tool to help reconciliation groups to be in control of future progress. This is because, as reconciliation of the parties is an important goal for the Anglican community, the disputes approach can prove to be is a healing balm for Rwanda's wounds.

Throughout the country today there are visible Gacaca and Palaver groups, some of which I was able to attend specifically for ethnographic observations in seminars and to listen to the discussions of Anglican clergy. Following these, I contended that there was a clear theological approach to the reconciliation process likely to operate in the Anglican Church in Rwanda. The question of palaver talks especially is discussed in more detail later in line with the findings in the table below.

From the Anglican clergy's point of view reconciliation was associated with two ideas: a greater sense of concern on wide ranges of issues such as reconciliation theology and a greater sense of being able to make a positive contribution to human relations.

Let us now look in more detail at what the respondents' figures reveal.

Table 6: The Question of Reconciliation and Forgiveness

	Agree %	Disagree %	Uncertain %
Is it wise to propose reconciliation in the present situation?	68	29	03
Do you agree with those who say that revenge is justice?	15	78	07
Do you see any sign of hope for reconciliation between Hutu and Tutsi?	55	29	04
Does your Church address the issue of reconciliation?	48	47	05
Is it possible to forgive perpetrators of genocide?	45	48	07
Do you agree with returnees reclaiming their properties?	47	48	05

The table shows that with regard to reconciliation, 68% preferred reconciliation (Palaver talks) but not the path of revenge as justice: 55% saw signs of hope for inter-tribal reconciliation and that it could happen. The warm and friendly atmosphere of this form of fellowship is one that many will find attractive once contact has been made. The friendly perspective was stressed in a reconciliation seminar at Kibungo, as important hopes need to be captured by Church leaders and members alike, so that they can begin to gain confidence and trust of each other in small winnable steps. This would encourage the Anglican Church in setting goals together and working towards them. Also the table shows that there is a significant minority of 15% representing the group that supports seeking revenge as a form of justice.

However, this group was not a national sample; they only represent the few Interahamwe in the prison whom I was able to interview. This 15% of responses was mainly from prisoners who included Hutu 'hardcore' extremist politicians who opted for revenge. I was interested in the views of this group of imprisoned genocide suspects and, at the same time, wanted to compare how large and enthusiastic the group was for taking revenge, I listened to one suspected perpetrator of genocide who remarked, 'If I survive, I can do anything.'[226]

In looking at the perceptions that each of the respondents had in interpreting events, the Anglican Church throughout is trying to prevent conflict and sees reconciliation and forgiveness as a viable and necessary alternative to revenge. Given the above survey results, it might seem that this 15% of responses suggest that Belgian ideological theories of divide and rule in Rwanda can still give rise to the possibility of long-term conflict in the future. For instance, interviews of suspects uncovered a sizeable number of hardcore prisoners who maintained that whatever time it took they would have to start from where they stopped in the conflict. This group of prisoners suspected of involvement in genocide was sizeable and represented those political activists who were seen as the greatest challenge facing reconciliation groups and prison staff, people who were trying to get them to re-examine their convictions. Although they denied being involved in genocide, it is reasonable to propose that their reactions to questions revealed this to be far from the truth.

Looking in detail at the choice of reconciliation and whether they thought it was achievable, overall 68% were confident in the wisdom of proposing reconciliation and another group of 55% were hopeful that Hutu and Tutsi would participate in the process. 29% of respondents were somewhat doubtful about them doing so. 3% were either

---

[226]Interviews at Byumba, August 1998.

uncertain or were disillusioned and unenthusiastic about being involved in the reconciliation process. Unsurprisingly, the analysis shows that the Anglican Church members were distinctly positive towards it. Nevertheless, when asked whether survivors would forgive the perpetrators, there were different responses. 15% agreed that they should be prosecuted. The majority (78%) disagreed and argued that they should be forgiven and clergy should leave the population to decide whether they should be granted amnesty. However, findings vary between congregations; where there were more Hutus, they disagreed with punishment and argue that the Church's role is to forgive and where there were more Tutsi survivors, they argued that responsibility for reconciliation and tackling political extremism in all its forms lies within the rule of law and justice. I looked in detail at a group of 1959 returnees interviewed at Mutara camps and at Gahini Mission to assess the differences of opinions from returnees to see how they differed on issues of reconciliation. The first group argued that no one should force the pace, because reconciliation cannot be realised overnight. Instead, the Anglican Church should concentrate on creating conditions that give people the confidence to come together and take the necessary steps towards reconciliation.[227]

While the second group within an internally displaced refugee settlement in Nyamatimba, made up of young men and women respondents, totally rejected the idea of forgiving and argued that simply forgiving without solving the question of justice was not enough.[228] Considering all the various groups examined in this analysis, seminar participants regarded as irrelevant the fact that the 78% majority came from the Anglican Church, in comparison

---

[227] Interviews at Mutara and Gahini, July 1998.
[228] Interviews at Nyamatimba, July 1989

with a similar majority drawn from other denominations in the country. They argued that reconciliation was the only way for people to live together and must be an inevitable way forward towards a peaceful solution. [229]

This clearly demonstrated that people were still in a state of shock, wondering why the wider Church had not prevented its Church leaders in Rwanda from getting involved in the genocide. Intuitive experiences were involved in the process of reconciliation, which meant that recovery might continue to be a challenge. Nonetheless, the challenge had to be faced and this process was an opportunity to respond in a way that was constructive, inclusive, positive and forward-looking. There were other voices in the Anglican Church wondering whether achieving genuine reconciliation in a theological context does not first require reconciliation with God. It is argued that these are the challenges that reconciliation will have to encounter.

In this case, the process of reconciliation may be slow or quick, but conflict batters and bruises and frequently gives people, whether Christian or not, countless memories, whether in Croatia, Iraq, South Africa, Sudan, Sierra Leone, or many other parts of the world where atrocities are still experienced. All of these examples offer a challenge to those who are involved in achieving reconciliation. This requires the realisation that when conflict arises, different people react in different ways. Some fiercely confront each other, some recoil from each other and others may seek a compromise. This is why it is important that those engaged in reconciliation have to recognise and evaluate the reactions to forgiveness.

Harriet Lerner Goldhor argued that our responsibility lies in our ability to observe ourselves and others in interaction and to respond to a familiar situation in a new

---

[229]Interviewing seminar participants at Kibungo Diocese, July 1998.

and different way. She added that we cannot make another person change his/her steps to an old dance, but if we change our own step, the dance can no longer continue in the same predictable pattern.[230] This thesis flows directly from the views expressed by those in favour of reconciliation, not only in seeking to understand how people react as they do, but to go one step further – to determine the natural and wise response. In this case, reconciliation it is seen as a building block in the process of resolving, managing and preventing further conflict and in fostering good human relations.

For example, there was hope in some small groups that they 'had defied the logic of their past and broken all the rules of ethnic theory'.[231] And respondents at Kibungo Diocese argued that 'to forgive is a powerful spirit of unity from a shattered nation'.[232] It was once said by the former Secretary of State for Northern Ireland that 'we can dwell on the past, we learn from the past but we can't live in the past'.[233] In contrast to her speech, the Anglican leadership in Rwanda is poised to confront the ethnic animosity directly through reconciliation workshops and community healing initiatives and, indirectly, within the context of their other programmes.[234] It is argued that reconciliation is a confrontation with evil. It is therefore imperative for the Anglican Church not to expect secular leaders to 'cross Jordan to the Promised Land' of political solution unless the religious cross it first.[235]

---

[230]Goldhor, L. H. (1990). The Dance of Anger, (Wellingborough, Grapevine), p. 14.
[231]Waldmeir & Holmam, *Financial Times* (London), 18 July (1994), p. 1.
[232]Interviewing seminar participants at Kibungo Diocese, July 1998.
[233]The Church Times, Church of England News paper, July 2001.
[234]http://jha.ac/greatlakes/b001.htm/11/9/04
[235]Interviews, Byumba, Kigali and Cyangugu, July 1998.

It is argued that if the Anglican Church in Rwanda takes its mission seriously, then it must play a role in working towards the goal of encouraging survivors in forbearance. This process includes a refusal to repeat the enemy's crimes and anticipates a new outlook on the situation. Furthermore, refusal to take revenge must be coupled with an accurate remembrance of the past. This is partly because the decision for reconciliation was made through considering an end to warfare and the realisation that vengeance could not resolve the conflict. The experience may lead to the conclusion that avoidance of war may serve the best interests of humanity at all levels, from individual interests to national unity. On the other hand, considering the political bankruptcy in ethnic politics, one of the elements of reconciliation is empathy for the enemy, even though society at large may still be hopelessly corrupt.

African Rights provided an independent, unbiased report representing the general feelings of wider groups of respondents in Kinigi, who stressed the importance of teaching the awareness groups to acknowledge that they had done wrong and to approach the victims for pardon.[236] This group stressed the importance of teaching infiltrators and insurgents to recognise the pain and grief they had inflicted upon others and to seek forgiveness from the individuals they had inflicted suffering upon. They argued that this applied as much to the RPF who had wronged the Hutus.[237] However, refugees who left the country more recently (such as those who fled in 1994) do have the right to their properties. If they return and find their house occupied by an illegal occupant, that occupant has two months to leave. When occupying an empty property, the

---

[236] African Rights, Rwanda – Killing the Evidence: Murder, Attacks, Arrests and Intimidation of Survivors and Witnesses, April 1996, p. 10.
[237] International Alert Index: AFR 02/01/1996, p 25; compare with African Rights, April 1996.

occupant signs an undertaking to give up the house at the end of the two-month period if the legal owner returns.[238]

Another important issue is how old conflict persists between moderate Hutus and extremist Hutus. The first conflicts were provoked in the context of property disputes between extremists who looked at moderate Hutu as traitors who betrayed their fellow Hutus to support RPF in its return to Rwanda. The second new conflict arose intermittently between the 1959 'old refugees' (Tutsi returnees to Rwanda from exile in 1994) and 'new refugees' (Hutu returnees from camps in Tanzania and Zaire in 1996–97). Some had been threatened and they were also under threat with increasing fears for their safety.

According to respondents in Kigali, this conflict is likely to continue between the two 'sets' of refugees who hold jealous and contradictory opinions on which set is receiving preferential treatment. For instance Tutsi returnees believed that Hutu returnees received preferential treatment. Some Tutsi returnees believed that Hutu returnees were privileged in that they could return to their home area and reclaim their property and land whereas the Tutsi themselves were resettled by the government in areas where they did not want to live.[239] However, the Anglican Church in most areas visited appeared to have a real concern for fellow human beings in that the humanity of Christians in the Church was coupled with forgiveness.

Some churches went further, displaying posters that read, 'Forgive and you will have peace.' Also in table 6, 47% of elderly Tutsi agreed that Hutu returnees should reclaim their properties, whereas 48% in table 6 disagreed. This refusal to acknowledge Hutu returnees' rights of property served to delay the process of reconciliation. Almost equal percentages of agreement and disagreement

---

[238] Ibid.
[239] Amnesty International Index:AFR01/02/96, p.25

over property rights illustrates the deep-seated nature of the problems to be faced. This has a delaying effect on the progress of the reconciliation process for the Anglican Church as well as the communities outside. On the other hand, George Trevelyan in the Woodstock report put it realistically, when he observed that history is made in the first instance by those who see one side of a question, but it requires those who see both sides to effect a settlement.[240]

The point I am trying to highlight here is how tensions rose between the RPF government and genocide survivors in that the latter felt as if they were being asked to forget and forgive too quickly. The RPF government was seen as having overlooked the demands for serious retribution from the culprits. The argument for retribution was a reminder that the punishing of the deviant person bolsters people's moral consciousness. On the matter of punishment respondents in table 6, an overwhelming 78% disagreed with punishment as a solution. It is argued that it strengthens social solidarity through a reaffirmation of moral commitment among victims who witness the suffering of an offender.[241]

I will be quick to add that the punishment of offenders does not necessarily offer a solution to the problem, however much it may satisfy the victims. In a real sense, it may either help the perpetrators to realise their faults, or push them into becoming hardcore criminals. The evidence for this came from those interviewed in the prison. Those with an alternative outlook see forgiveness as associated with the teachings of Christ, central to the sacrament of penance that helps to define forgiveness as a personal, individual, secret and anything but political transaction.[242]

Rwanda has recently channelled its efforts into palaver talks' about reconciliation, adopting a whole new approach

---

[240]Shriver, D. W., Woodstock Report, March 1996, No. 45, p.2
[241]Interviews at Kigali August 1998.
[242]Shriver's, D. W., Woodstock Report, March 1996, No. 45, p.2

by restoring perpetrators to the community. This has led to the development of community networks, where perpetrators are rehabilitated through discussions and through examining what went wrong in society. Doing this accomplishes two objectives: first, community service is in harmony with the concept of rehabilitation or restoration and second, it enables the perpetrators to integrate back into communities. Volf interpreted the motif in a Christian context by looking at the story of the prodigal son in the Bible story. Central to the story are the themes of repentance, forgiveness and grace.

In Volf's interpretation of reconciliation and its relevancy to Rwanda, rehabilitation is a process of assisting perpetrators to move away from the path of self-destruction and towards a realisation that it is through forgiveness that the relationship with the enemy can be healed. In short, to be at peace with your enemy is a process of turning enmity into friendship. This proposal of forgiveness provoked several reactions during the Anglican Church seminars. For some perpetrators it implied 'to forgive and forget'.[243] But the word 'forget' is used unrealistically; because it is doubtful whether the Hutu and Tutsi differences can be squarely phased out. It is one thing to say, let us forget the differences in the interests of Christian unity. In that case, the differences are likely to come to the fore again. It is something entirely different to accept the differences and attempt, as Christians on both sides of the political argument, to find a permanent solution. Volf argued that, in the case of unjust suffering, to be forgotten is the final indignity that a person can experience.[244] This, according to Miroslav Volf, is what he terms 'the fundamental injustice of grace'.[245] At this time, the appropriateness of the idea of forgetting differences was still debatable.

---

[243]Ibid.
[244]Ibid.
[245]Ibid. p. 147.

Indeed, Volf's argument made sense to some of participants in the reconciliation seminar during the early period of debates in that doubts were expressed about the wisdom of such a strategy of forgiving and forgetting. In this research, I was able to attend diocesan meetings in the areas where the Anglican Church was planning for reconciliation, in order to get first hand information on how the reconciliation process was carried out and what was being done.[246] The feeling among minority respondents during the first reconciliation seminar debates seemed one of disillusionment that argued that enthusiasm for reconciliation was naive idealism. This consequently led to doubts about forgiveness and raised questions during the initial stages for Anglican Church leaders about where to start.

This caused division among respondents. The minority (15%) of respondents were in favour of forgiveness and argued that the signs suggested that the Anglican Church leaders could facilitate meetings in order to bring together groups of people who still had problems with their neighbours, to encourage and support community leaders who had been reconciled with their victims and others who had not done so.[247]

During my visit to Rwanda in May 2004, I was able to listen to some of the hopes for the future and also the problems related to the activities embarked upon by the Rwandan Anglican Church. The Église Épiscopale au Rwanda was thought to be evangelical, because of its foundation by the Anglican Church Missionary Society, an evangelical wing of the Anglican Church of England. The clergy who returned from exile to Rwanda thus held many

---

[246] A report of the three days Anglican leaders' seminar on reconciliation organised and sponsored by REACH from 25th to 28th March 1998 held at St. Joseph Centre, Kibungo Prefecture

[247] Analysing questionnaires and responses from interviews in Kigali Diocese, December, 2001.

divergent theological views. There is not only a duty to forgive, but also a challenge to the Anglican Church to understand salvation theology in context and to explore, from people's experience, how they are able to forgive each other's mistakes for the sake of the future.[248]

My argument is that the Anglican minority gave a sense of purpose for Rwandan people in fostering a process whereby they might come to terms with the questions facing a post-genocide Rwanda and, in a wider context, the experiences of individuals feeling remorse. Furthermore, Bayingana argued, 'When people reconcile with God, they will also reconcile with one another. Please forgive us.'[249]

In the early debates in 1997, the Anglican Churches were still bogged down in the role that the relevant theology has to play in reconciliation and in building a peaceful future in which coexistence might be possible. The Anglican Church created reconciliation groups that were set up to examine the scope of multi-agency approaches towards reconciliation. A series of recommendations from different diocesan committees were beginning to follow their own style of Anglican theological reflection and deepening their Christian understanding naturally from their own beliefs. At this point, they were developing a theological way of understanding the daily concerns of people that sprung from their personal experiences. These differed from the usual Anglican teaching.

The findings suggest that, despite the desire for reconciliation, a realistic expectation is that people must be prepared to take the process of reconciliation slowly, to ask gentle questions rather than make antagonistic remarks. In this local community approach, learning by example rather than precept is emphasised. What may not be achieved by

---

[248]Cfr. Kalilombe, P. A., (1979). "The Salvific Value of African Religions", Afer, 21, pp.143 – 157.
[249]Bayingana, Ng. E., Art., (1994). 'Reconciliation: Foundation for Reconstructing a New Rwanda', Nairobi: Evangel Press, p. 23.

theorising or moralising may be achieved through the examples of community leaders. The findings revealed that the theology of reconciliation was still in the process of forming strategies of what could be done. During this period, there remained varied arguments. Some suggested that any action taken required a great deal of preparation, involving the examination of the reconciliation strategies that could be created and maintained.

During the last 14 years, the Anglican Church's goals for reconciliation have been defined, methods determined and responsibilities allocated. During the initial stages of forming reconciliation committees, there was an issue that called into question how forgiveness could be attained. 78% of respondents agreed that there could be no reconciliation without forgiveness, even if there still remained some individuals obsessed with revenge and justice.

At this point, the Anglican Church was particularly anxious to avoid the existence of 'no go areas' in rural districts, where an atmosphere of fear and insurgency rendered it impossible for people to reconcile. Through seminars, the Anglican Church realised that there was more than one theological point of view about reconciliation.

As a matter of concern, the Anglican Church had to access these views before anything else could be done, because they seemed to agree on the use of traditional methods for resolving disputes. They argued that the starting point for any approach towards reconciliation, in response to the threat of revenge being taken, should be for each local Anglican Church parish to offer full commitment to the process of reconciliation in the form of a comprehensive, national mode of approach. They insisted that this mode should be accompanied by a process of continuous consultation with community groups at every level.[250]

The Anglican Church's function and relevance in society was a serious concern for many. Members also agreed on such issues as social, economic and political policies in the process of reconciliation. Nevertheless, through listening, theological views only differed in the emphasis attached to the Anglican Church backgrounds of the clergy, rather than in the Biblical implementation of reconciliation.[251]

As previously mentioned, there were significant differences between two viewpoints: that of the clergy who described themselves as traditionalists and that of evangelicals known as the 'Seeds of Peace'.[252] These talks stimulated lively debate with participants, with the intention of providing strategies for approaching the reconciliation process. The traditionalists' emphasis was on the relationships between faith and theological themes in society, which required consideration of the theological context involved.

From these discussions, traditional Anglican Church leaders argued that common experience has a legitimate place in the contextual theological scene and that there were signs of such an approach being taken seriously in the contemporary wider Anglican Church. Traditional clergy, whose theology stems from contextual theology, argued for a theological approach to reconciliation in the general context of reconciliation, particularly related to people's culture. Meinrad Hebga's argument is for the use of one of

---

[250] A report of the three days Anglican leaders' seminar on reconciliation organised and sponsored by REACH from 25th to 28th March 1998 held at St. Joseph Centre, Kibungo Prefecture
[251] Ibid.
[252] The Seeds of Peace Centre at Gahini Diocese, June 1998.

the critical and creative tools articulating the Rwandan people's own questions and pursuing their own answers.[253]

In this respect, a paradigm for 'contextual theology' is required, a theology that demands the Christian to reflect upon the Anglican Church's tradition and mission and to explore contextual dialogue and Scripture. On the other hand, in the light of the extreme poverty existing, the greatest challenge of all is now adapting a combination of methods for reconciliation and for the Anglican Church to consider the theological dimensions of its mission. It is important to realise that poverty affects everything people do and think and it is argued that the Anglican Church is required to try different approaches in the process of reconciliation, because people must be reached in their actual living situations if faith is to be a live option.[254]

However, the Église Épiscopale au Rwanda's reconciliation theology seems to have its present focus upon the belief, emphasised in Paul's letters in the Bible, that all people are sinners. Nearly all evangelical clergy in this seminar contended that Paul's interpretation was needed for two reasons. First, they argued that if the Anglican Church failed to take Biblical pronouncements seriously, the Anglican Church would have failed in its mission.[255] Second, they argued further that the Bible story of the Good Samaritan was not told primarily to show the importance of helping others, but to expose the evil of discrimination against others. Their Biblical interpretation focuses on Satan's past career as Lucifer and therefore it is

---

[253]Hebga, M., 'Penance and Reconciliation in African Culture', African Ecclesiastical Review 25, 1983, pp. 347-355.
[254]http://www.amazon.co.uk/gp/product/0860121569/2002-52011-26-8050237?v=glance&n=266239
[255]Interviews, Gahini and Kigeme, at the time of these interviews there were debates in Anglicans about reconciling people in Rwanda and in their view, genocide was an influence of Satan, July 1998.

in him that the source of conflict rested, misleading people.[256]

In an objective sense, it is argued that evangelicals had reasons founded on more than the facts that the Bible teaches. Jesus is the example and His teaching condemns discrimination in all its forms. However, Cormack put it realistically: 'From the tranquillity of Eden's tree to the eternal peace of God's new City in Revelation lies a path of everlasting unresolved conflict'.[257] Satan caused the fall of the human race as the serpent (Gen. 3). His judgement was predicted in Eden (verse 15) and was accomplished at the cross (John 12:31–33).

The evangelical explanation is that the conflict is rooted in satanic influence. They argue that when people forgot God and became entangled in perverted and horrible acts of ethnic division, they lost the power to fight secularism. Furthermore, they stressed that during genocide, no one could know who were Christians and who were not. They also added that Satan was hiding throughout in the form of ethnic politics in Rwanda.

There is the temptation in the work of reconciliation to condemn and judge others, based on what was heard and seen in some places during my visits to Rwanda. The visit covered the communes of Rwerere, Kanama and Mutura in Gisenyi and the communes of Nkuli, Kinigi, Cyabingo and Nyamutera in Ruhengeri. A considerable part of the working group's discussion focused upon interpretation of the Bible concerning forgiveness. 78% of respondents showed concern that revenge might be seen by some as justice and were against this view. This was shared by reconciliation groups who, during the reconciliation debates, were of the opinion that reconciliation might be seen by some as built on a premise of forgiveness, without

---

[256]Ibid.
[257]Cormack, D. (1989). Peacing Together, London: MARC Europe, p. 9.

having to admit the crime committed. This, they felt, would mean to 'fix' but not to truly reconcile.

At the early stages of convergence, it was argued by participants in Anglican Church reconciliation seminars that to be reconciled was to practise acceptance of one's own 'mess' and that of others. In other words, reconciliation is a process of accepting each other, not fixing each other. Moreover, reconciliation is central to the teachings of unconditional love that lie at the core of the gospel message. Thus, ethnic divisions in Rwanda got so deep that the community values of love and caring for one another were lost. Returning to the ideology of the old conflict (Chapter Two), divisions still existed not only between Hutu and Tutsi, but also in one refugee group of returnees after another in different parts of the country.

After the genocide, there were many questions surrounding the conflict that subsequently led many Anglican Church members to distrust the Anglican Church's leadership. It was understandable that some people who endured the trauma of the loss of loved ones during the genocide lost their faith in the work of the Anglican Church. The prospect for goodness existing and being fostered was destroyed. It therefore became a necessity for the Anglican Church to heal such memories. At Mutara and Gahini, respondents stated that they found themselves in a moral wilderness, especially when Anglican Church leaders defended secularism. They described this, at best, as nothing other than confusing.[258]

Accordingly, nearly all the Anglican Church respondents interviewed (96%) were of the view that the kind of reconciliation approach required for active and responsible participation should involve all people in the community, both young and old. The Anglican Church was viewed as an important tool for instigating change in

---

[258]Interviews at Mutara and Gahini, July 1998.

society. Respondents argued that for this to happen there must be a continuing dialogue between reconciliation groups, who identified the Anglican Church as the vehicle that should play the greatest role, ranging from personal encounters to national reconciliation. There was a feeling that if reconciliation was to be taken seriously, the process required humility. It was therefore argued that a constant emphasis upon reconciliation and compromise should be encouraged in the communities.

Similarly, R. Banks observed that the Anglican Church's role must be of a therapeutic nature, 'gently' persuading the parties to merge their perception of what had occurred.[259] Banks' argument offers hope in the form of the Christian concept of the seed of love providing the means of reconciliation. It must be made clear that this reconciliation reorientation is then sealed by a delicate exchange of gifts of love and forgiveness. The situation is delicate in that the level of gift giving is intended not to embarrass the giver, who then becomes the recipient of a gift of love from the other party.

According to O'Connell and McCullum, 'reconciliation grows stronger where forgiveness is not only given but made known'.[260] Once love is shared as a gift, then one has reconciled with God and fellow human beings. Here love becomes a sign of the Kingdom's advent. The Kingdom that Christ introduced, one that He continues to build today, brings 'good news to the poor and sets at liberty those who are oppressed' (Luke 4:18ff).

It is further argued by O'Connell, in agreement with supporters for reconciliation that it is through reconciliation that a new community is born with a fresh perception of what he terms the 'New World'. Its foundation is the

---

[259]Banks, R., (1994). Reconciliation and Hope, London: Paternoster Press, p. 116.
[260]O'Connell, J., (1995).The Essence of the Forgiveness, Month CCLV (September/October), pp. 354–358.

communication of shared values, which may be found through mutual understanding and recognising the image of Christ in each other's eyes.[261] For instance, taking South African apartheid as an example; it was not just a challenge to the country, but also to the wider Anglican Church and the entire human race.

In the theological context, the Anglican Church has to treat ethnicity and race as a challenge to Christian teaching. In theory and in practice, to discriminate against another person on the grounds of ethnicity is another form of apartheid and the Anglican Church in Rwanda must continue to challenge ethnicity so that it is not acceptable in society and so that its practise is seen as evil.

Therefore, the Anglican Church in Rwanda will need to act not only by paying attention to past political influences in Rwandan society, but also to the theological differences that treated the same people unequally. It is therefore imperative for the Anglican Church to respond to such situations that impose unlawful conditions and demands.

In her teaching, the Anglican Church in Rwanda must reflect and develop a deeper, new theology that can create understanding. Functional imperatives for this are found in Rwanda at present. The reconciliation process demands that the population be self-examining, since memories may be very long, incorporating old resentments and involving entrenched attitudes and unresolved feelings.[262] This means that the task of reconciliation is, intrinsically, more difficult and will need to take place over a longer period.

---

[261]Ibid.
[262]Interviews at Mutara refugee camps, August 1998.

7.3 The Anglican Church Palaver Mode of Reconciliation

I was drawn to the 'palaver' approach precisely because its assumptions and ideas offered a role for the Anglican Church (Église Épiscopale au Rwanda) in the reconciliation process. In this case, the palaver was described as existing before Belgian rule in Rwanda. The palaver was a cultural, social-political institution that was mostly practised in pre-colonial Rwanda. It is an assembly where a variety of issues are debated and important decisions concerning community matters are taken.[263] The major purpose of palaver talks is to resolve latent and overt conflicts in specific situations. The resolution of problems occurs by using reasoning in an atmosphere of respect and mutuality between participants. The facilitator sets a pace for dialogue about a particular problem. It is a critical and dialogue means towards affirmation and is stressed responsibly through a joint, holistic approach, shared by all in what may be called a 'philosophical circle of minds'.

If theology is always a matter of deduction, drawing upon specific principles in order to respond to certain questions, then it might be reasonable to argue that the palaver model of reconciliation talks must be applied by the Anglican Church in Rwanda. In view of the great need for reconciliation, each of the approaches is used and their value varies according to the situation. It requires no theological argument to assert that the misery, suffering and despair that Rwandans experienced demanded a practical response to current situations in Rwanda. Therefore, this section argues for a practical theological approach to ensure that Rwandan people can engage freely and safely in

---

[263] Sapova, Jasmina, "in the shade of the palaver tree" UNESCO, Courier Jouranalist.http://www.unesco.org/courier/1999/05ur/singnes/txt2.htm. 11/7/06.

reconciliation talks. It is clearly important for the people reconciling to understand the history of the conflict and the cultural relevance of traditional resolution dispute mechanisms. It is therefore argued that the Anglican Church must organise and encourage alternative methods, such as palaver theory.

I will start, perhaps, with asking what is palaver and how does it work? Etymologically, the word 'palaver' comes from the Spanish 'palabra' and means speech, discussion or endless, idle conversation. It is a structure for the organisation of open forums, for expressing different views, offering advice, using different dissuasion in the form of an arbitration mechanism. In Rwanda this form of the 'palabre' had been used over the centuries as a suitable framework for conflict settlement. The same conception of the "Gacaca" was used before to deal with the odd differences, in which its sacred character, authority and knowledge were interlinked, the latter being personified by the elders who accumulated wisdom and experience over the years.[264]

A genuine institution, the 'palabre' is governed by established norms and the main actors have to be highly competent. The key role played by mediation is seen in abundance in the oral tradition, where 'sages' incarnated as old men intervened. The function of a mediator in traditional society called for notable qualities of wisdom, neutrality and level-headedness, a profound knowledge of customs and traditions and, above all, a great talent for oration and communication. The mediator has to be a master of dialectics and clever at 'palaver' dialogue.[265]

Therefore, palaver is not a new practice in Rwanda, but rather a traditional cultural and social institution, mostly practised in pre-Belgian Rwanda. In the historical

---

[264]http://www.oecd.org/dataoecd/47/36/3851593.pdf/06/07
[265]Cfr. http://www. Caas.concordia.ca/htm/caasasapng.doc/06/07

mythology of Rwanda, the palaver tree was a symbolic gathering place for elderly people of wisdom who sat to debate a variety of issues and important decisions concerning the community. The theological palaver mode of reconciliation is another way to acknowledge the divinity of Christ incarnate through reconciliation and for people to recognise each other and discourage any form of ethnic superiority. It is a formal approach where participants gather under 'a palaver tree'.[266] The palaver tree is a therapeutic model for the formal settlement of disputes.

The relevance of the palaver approach to resolving conflict is based on a common sense understood by all Rwandans. Its importance lies in the way the gathering provides everyone with the right to speak and to be given an audience. It emphasises and promotes dignity of the individual, because dignity is a matter of equality, with consideration of each other during the process of (Imishikirano) negotiation. The equality of treatment for all citizens is part of the ingredient in palaver and should therefore be seen as an ideal goal rather than an absolute. It was further argued that equal treatment might help to separate out all those differences and inequalities that originated from Belgian differentiation policies.

The palaver theological argument is a process whereby many new ideas evolve from traditional mythology, which is central to the past cultural values of communities. Palaver involves participation in understanding one's life and taking the courage to change the ethnic propaganda that fuelled the conflict. Indeed, Socrates argued that an unexamined life is not worthy of living.[267] Rwandan

---

[266]Sopova, Jasamina, "In the shade of the palaver tree", UNESCO Courier Journalist.http://www.unesco.Org/courier/1999/05/ur/singness/tx12.htm . 11/7/06.
[267]http://www.wsu.edu/~dee/GREECE/SOCRATES.HTM/07

palaver theology becomes an important tool in answering fundamental questions about the Rwandan people's past and future.

In sharp contrast with the Rwandan situation, theological palaver is based on the argument that a person who does not take part in his or her own community life decisions is a prisoner to circumstance. The prisoner hears echoes and sees shadows and the prisoner interprets these shadows and echoes as the whole reality. This is in comparison with the situation where people have a voice, but have no choice. The implication of this is that people need to be in charge of their own destiny and develop an understanding of ideological politics and the reasons why ethnic propaganda was promoted in politics. Therefore, analysis of the Belgian economic structure is seen as a major hindrance in the process of reconciliation and a prerequisite for addressing the irrelevant, false structures in Rwanda. Generally, respondents saw an immediate need to analyse the past, in order to devise a reconciliation process to deal with the crisis and for there to be an awareness of the problems that need to be faced.

The purpose of this section is to explore and, hopefully, illuminate a debate between the ideas of theological palaver that have arisen out of the argument that people need help to critically and rationally explore their past experiences and that they need to pause for thought when making assumptions about the decisions they make. Palaver theology argues for the Rwandan people to learn more about their history, a history that prepared them for genocide. It is important for people to share memories and to morally judge the past. The line of reasoning here is that Rwandan history can highlight ethnic distinction ideology and help us to recognise how, under the Belgian period of rule, it was fixed deeply in the minds of the people. We need to cultivate the idea that diversity consciousness can be a beneficial resource, specifically, if it leads to learning from each other and getting to know each other better. It was further argued that an understanding of Rwandan history is required in order to better get to grips with Rwandan problems. It is important to see clearly how differences emerged and how political ideology, policies and practice contributed to this deviance in people's behaviour. The decline in tolerance was caused by the pressure upon people to turn to the use of violence. In the view, of how ethnic conflict developed in Rwanda, the findings of this study provide strong support for the view that, for example, people such as (Interahamwe) who, when caught up in certain situations they did not understand, acted purely according to their own motives and concerns and were the subject of familial, cultural, social and political influences of the day.

Palaver analysis, as opposed to causal analysis, focuses on a very different perspective. It asks not only what the cause of a problem is, but also what is the condition one wants to bring into being? Therefore, the aim of palaver is not just to talk about the experience of survivors or about the torture of the militia, but also to talk about the issues of those who were indirectly involved, especially the younger generation. This will help to build a dynamic and, most importantly, sustainable reconciliation process. The process allows people to embrace those with opposite views who find themselves unable to accept the path and commitment to reconciliation. Participants in the palaver talks can share a uniform perception of what happened in the past. Reconciling people, too, involves constructive communication that builds on the important teachings of the Rwandan Anglican Church.

A successful palaver is one in which the talks are people-oriented and involve all participants. The purpose of the dialogue is to build and foster Christ's love and to deepen both understanding of the problem and each other's position. The debate will be an 'avenue' to discover common experiences, mysteries and meanings that are fundamental to reconciliation. A reconciliation palaver is a straight talk that recognises the need for honest debate about differences and that in God's eyes all Rwandans are unique individuals with special gifts and abilities. This atmosphere of mutual understanding is very important, in that a palaver tree may promote the well-being of individuals, but also encourages people in taking personal responsibility into consideration. Furthermore, its aim is not to decide who the guilty party is, but to offer a process that seeks to interpret history and visualises the future they want, in order to sustain lasting reconciliation.

In seeking to resolve existing differences through the 'home-grown' palaver approach to disputes, local problems can be understood and people can know themselves in the full sense. It is argued that to be in charge of one's destiny requires the capacity to rationally think about one's existing relational circumstances. It is a belief that through reason, people can work together to resolve their differences and any manifestations of discrimination. The palaver theological idea is based on the principle that all participants have experiences that form a body of knowledge. This body of knowledge helps, in turn, to demystify the causes of their differences. It argues for a mode of practice or process that the Anglican Church can use in debate, in order to work for the common interest that particularly arises when people bring their own special experiences, actively cooperate and communicate in response to the common problems of living together. Thus, it is vitally important to know that there was an indigenous and traditional way of reconciliation.

It is often too easy to blame someone else or to leave the problem to others. However, what happened in Rwanda in 1994 cannot be ignored. This idea to develop the palaver theological mechanism suggested that the Anglican Church should look to traditional modes of practice as a starting point, to then examine the mechanisms that had been part and parcel of Rwandan society for generations in order to resolve and manage conflict through reconciliation.. The Anglican Church's choice of palaver talks is based on the view that people are expected to engage in dialogue with each other. People are encouraged to reach areas of compromise and. understanding, see things from a different perspective, realise that they are all a product of the same society and that they need to accommodate their differences.

Theological palaver does not pretend to have all the answers to the conflict. Rather, its aim is to create an understanding in order for the Anglican Church to debate the challenges for how live together. In the Rwandan sense, palaver is a process of co-operative effort in the critical interpretation of assumptions held; a rediscovery of the past allowing participants to focus upon the present and the future. The importance of theological palaver is manifested in the people's search to discover how to re-imagine perplexing human relations and social-political implications with others over time. It thus has relevancy to the mysterious complexity of human relations.

Clergy in seminars had argued earlier that ironing out contradictions contributed to the fruitfulness of the palaver theological debate. Palaver theory suggests that the participants' history and cultural valuation are fundamental things to recognise in the process of reconciliation. In order to explore the cultural richness of the past in the search for conflict resolution, it is important that the Anglican helps communities to focus on the fundamental principles and aims of palaver. They had also argued that participants in palaver talks must not dwell on past politics, nor regard the process as something peculiar, but rather to accept the method as a traditional tool that Rwandans used in the past to resolve disputes. The talks thrived as a result of the open atmosphere and the potential for fruitful relationships between people who have to live together, where they all have an equal opportunity and all ethnic groups have a role and purpose.[268] Indeed, Robert Nisbet argued that people do not live together merely to be together, but in order to do something together.[269]

It is this idea of living together and doing things together that must be the Anglican Church's approach to educating communities, in order to promote co-operation through participation and to learn the values of respect for others and living together. It is argued that in the past this practice had always been used at village level, based on an understanding of community life. In the past, Rwandans believed that human life was full of mysteries that aroused their curiosity to find meaning in life and to interpret reality.

As argued elsewhere in the thesis, it is important that people who are afraid of each other must find out what created the fear and why and to challenge the causes. The whole internal psychological mechanism needs to be tackled in order to know the source of the problem. If people fear the search for the meaning of these differences, how is it possible to refer to the actions of those who are not understood as 'abnormal'? In fact, it is argued that without faith in people, without the belief that they can settle their affairs through positive, bold and democratic action, people always move from one timid mistake to the next and into ultimate failure.[270]

---

[268] Interviews at Mutara refugee camps, August 1998.
[269] Nisbet, Robert, (1962). Community & Power, New York: Oxford University Press, p. 61.
[270] Cfr. Shriver, W. D., Woodstock Report, March 1996, No. 45.

Figure 7.3 Youth in attendance at a unity and reconciliation seminar where they are taught how to live in harmony.

Source:[271]

In practice, the palaver approach is an assembly where a variety of issues are debated and important decisions concerning communities are resolved. Its purpose is to find a resolution to latent and overt conflicts in specific situations. In this sense, many respondents saw the palaver tree as one of the Anglican Church's innovations for locating the reconciliation process through community discussion, as in the past. This method is best developed since all ethnic groups have something to contribute, but, obviously, there needs to be some discussion and compromise. To discuss differences and not avoid them and thereby arrive at a workable agreement to a way forward serves the mission not only of the Anglican Church, but for

---

[271]

http://www.enteruganda.com/brochures/kagameaniversarypage8.htm/2 3/8/07 all people, not just one group. This focuses upon the present as the best way for people to work out their future. The community was concerned that the Anglican Church was now promoting community ideals aimed at the development of a national philosophy for (Ubumwe) unity.

7.4 Lessons from Other Reconciliation Groups

The Unity and Reconciliation Commission of the Republic of Rwanda (URC) joined with groups from South Africa to learn from the reconciliation experience there.[272] During the initial stages of the search for ways in which the Anglican Church could engage in the process of reconciliation, participants recommended that, for the Anglican Church to attain genuine reconciliation, it would have to learn from other countries' experiences, such as South Africa, Argentina and Chile. For example, the challenge of the Commission of Truth and Reconciliation was how it handled its process of reconciliation. In response to the question of reconciliation, these are essential procedures that need careful consideration.

Maluleke pointed out that South Africa compared other models to find out what might work for Argentina and Chile. Whereas Catholics were well acquainted with penance, confession and absolution, these approaches would not work in South Africa.[273] On the other hand, it seems to me that Rwanda does not have to regard these models of reconciliation as empirically existing realities, but rather as ideal types in the reconciliation process.

Testimonies gathered at the first seminar held at St. Joseph's Anglican Church Centre, Kibungo Prefecture

---

[272] http:www.rwandanews.com/gov/08-24-00news-Learn;from-SA.htm/16/01/01

[273] Maluleke, T. S., (1998). 'Truth, National Unity and Reconciliation in South Africa, Aspects of the Emerging Theological Agenda', Missionalia, 25:1 April, p. 76.

clearly showed how both Tutsi and Hutu Anglican Church leaders were particularly willing, open and frank about discussing the question of reconciliation. All seminar presentations, group discussions and plenary seminar sessions focused on the need for reconciliation, arguing that without a genuine realisation that there was something wrong, there would be an impression formed that there was no need for reconciliation.

For Rwanda to be successful in achieving reconciliation, it was important to consider the history of different places and how they shaped their political experiences, experiences such as the Holocaust and massacres in Latin America and South Africa.[274] These countries have something to teach Rwanda in terms of the reconciliation process. For example, the Chilean government and the Anglican Church decided that everything must be known, but not everyone must be prosecuted. This was one of the facts that helped strengthen the requirement for people to learn to live with each other in spite of past failures.

It is argued that South Africa preferred to set up the Truth and Reconciliation Commission in order to uncover the worst of the human rights violations under apartheid: the killings, abductions and torture. Likewise, Rwanda needs to uncover all the hidden atrocities by using the same methods that have been successful in Latin America and South Africa. Frost argued that 'South Africa's search for reconciliation has a global resonance, for healing, restitution and repairing, as well as for love, remembrance, reconciliation and repentance.'[275]

---

[274]Cfr. Rubenstein, R. & Roth, J. K., (1987). Approaches to Auschwitz, the Legacy of the Holocaust, London: SCM Press Ltd, pp. 59 – 63; Cfr. Tutu, D., (1999). No Future Without Forgiveness, London: Rider, pp. 2-11

[275]Frost, B., (1991). The Politics of Peace, London: Longman and Todd Ltd, p. 15.

In Rwanda, there were initially many voices that suggested the replication of South Africa's Truth and Reconciliation Commission, but little had been acknowledged about the great hindrance of literacy needs in educating the public about sowing the seeds of sustainable peace and reconciliation. Due to these hindrances, Rwanda had to use traditional Gacaca methods that the population were more familiar with, in order to promote forgiveness as an important precondition for peace. It was hoped that reconciliation could be approached first via a gradual process of education and training.

The participants' emphasis was on the fact that reconciliation should begin with the Anglican Church leaders and then move to other members in order to clear away any fears and hidden feelings at the start. During the process of finding appropriate methods, the Anglican Church highlighted wider issues that needed attention and one of these was the influence of mediation (Uguhuza) through loyal attachment to the family. Families not only mediate in disputes, but also perform most of the social, economic and political functions of communities in the absence of centralised state government. The system was gradually pushed out of operation until Belgian administrators abolished it. The 'kin-based' family system was quite effective in conflict mediation. For example, it was the custodian that was responsible for allocating the roles of individuals in community and determined attitudes towards conflict, the style of (Ugutumanaho) communication, expectations in communities, victimisation and forgiveness.

7.5 Theological Bases for Reconciliation

Overall, the purpose here is to examine the Anglican Church's theological interpretation of the process of reconciliation in a broader context, from both Biblical and Rwandan contextual theological searches for peace. As part of my study of reconciliation theology, I have considered a number of theological arguments such as H.G.Lerner, W.D. Shriver and Hort's social theological approach that will contribute to this discussion. It is argued that from St Paul's teaching down to that of contemporary theologians, the term 'forgiveness' has found a home in theological and secular treaties on political ethics. Even theologians have treated 'forgiveness' as an orphan in the realm of reconciliation.[276]

There are numerous passages in St Paul's epistles to the Corinthians where words of reconciliation are used with primary reference to God acting through Christ. Paul's doctrine serves as the foundation of the Anglican Church and in particular his use of the metaphors of the body and the building to explain his beliefs, in which it suggests the interdependence of Christians to one another with Christ as the head (1 Corinthians 12:12–27). The relevance here is that no one may read about the Church divisions at Corinth (1 Corinthians 1:10) without realising how vital to his thinking was the unity of Christians in the early Church as within the Anglican Church fellowship today. In Paul's mind, the good life was the reconciled life. The uniqueness of Christ, therefore, depends upon whom He claimed to be and what He achieved rather than what He taught. Or perhaps, more accurately, His teaching was the expression that He had come to reconcile people and God in the Kingdom of God.

Donald Shriver argued that Arendt, a secular Jewish modern political philosopher, once a refugee from the Nazis, was one of those who disregarded forgiveness as an effective way of a achieving a long-term settlement and

---

[276]Shriver, W. D., Woodstock Report, March 1996, No. 45.

reconciliation.[277] However, Arendt acknowledged the religious contribution of forgiveness when she advanced her theory that in order to effect change in social relationships, humans can firstly make new agreements or covenants and secondly, reckon with the evils of the past through the releasing power of forgiveness.[278] Arendt's argument emphasises the importance of forgiveness and the Christian effect of discovering the healing power of forgiveness on the cross. Arendt gave clear confirmation when she said, 'the fact that Christ made this discovery in a religious context and articulated it in religious language is no reason to take it any less seriously in a strict secular sense'.[279]

It was further stressed by seminar participants at Kibungo that the Anglican Church in Rwanda must develop theological theories that are more helpful in order for Church members to understand the effectiveness of Christ's mission in reconciliation and human redemption. However, this is not suggesting going back to Rwandan ritualistic worship and ancient sacrificial days, but the approach similar to Israel's theory, whereby both salvation and life were redeemable by making the appropriate payment. In contrast to the knowledge for God in Rwanda, it was therefore argued that the traditional categories of the theology of salvation are much more amenable to a fully interpersonal interpretation of the way of salvation.

It is this need for people's salvation that begs for Rwandan Anglican Church theology to demonstrate the characteristics that reveal Christ's mission. More precious than revenge, this reminds people that salvation was purchased at a great personal cost, for Christ gave up His own life for our sins in order to save others. This is relative to what Reformers taught of effectual calling, justification,

---

[277]Shriver, W. D., Woodstock Report, March 1996, No. 45.
[278]Ibid.
[279]Ibid.

adoption and sanctification, all descriptive of the activities of God in the redemption of humanity, while repentance and faith define a response that is truly his own.[280]

I argued in the previous chapter that if the Anglican Church doesn't act, it is a serious mistake for Anglican Church leaders to expect politicians to reconcile the people ahead of the Church's response. It is precisely liberationists like Shriver who argue that there can be little hope for communities and national reconciliation without the Body of Christ showing the way and 'paying the price'.[281] This redemption idea of purchasing certainly emphasises the cost of reconciliation, but includes the hope of forces opposing reconciliation being overcome by a faith in Christ. In the context of this faith in Christ, life here and after is a life in God; it is for everyone already participating in this life. There is also, therefore, a personal response to God, with a personal responsibility in life, in human relations, in labour and in politics. This is important in the sense that 87% of Rwandans are Christians, but for almost 100 years they have failed to put Christian teachings into practice; to show love, forgiveness and to act as peacemakers in Rwanda.

It is notable that the New Testament exalts peacemakers (Matthews 5:9; 5:20). Theologically, it is argued that the sinner is constitutionally ignorant, having lost the pristine knowledge of God in the Fall and without a knowledge of how to effect peace (Romans 3:23). It therefore becomes important for the Anglican Church to act as mediators between competing groups and to assist them to overcome their state of confusion and animosity. It is also argued that in a dual society, with 87% of the population in Rwanda professing Christianity, there is the

---

[280]Shriver, W. D., Woodstock Report, March 1996, No.
[281]Ibid.

hope that the Anglican Church can help these competing groups to develop an attitude towards a common purpose.

According to Romans 8:29, God's plan for the redemption and renewal of the whole of creation starts with the building of a people in which men and women of all nations, classes and types will be united in Christ (Galatians 3:28). The doctrine of human redemption involves taking both the divinity and the humanity of Jesus Christ very seriously. Due to its concealing as well as revealing nature, Christ used the title 'Son of Man' (Dan. 7:13; Mark 8:38; Matt. 10:23). It thus was a title that stressed Christ's humility. The title also reveals the divine authority that Christ possessed as the Son of Man, who came to judge the world, having come from the Father (Mark 2:17; Matt. 5:17). Moreover, Christ *is* God. In Christ, God, the God of all nations, came near to us, 'Emmanuel', 'God with us' and chose to be involved in human salvation (Philippians 2:7), revealing that Christ wants to be known, loved and honoured by all. All humankind has a right to get to know this.

To be more specific, considering the big difference between the faith of the people and the faith represented in the Anglican Church, it is argued that it is not merely a matter of retracing Christ's path. Trying to adhere to His ethical behaviour challenges our behaviour. The Anglican Church has always had to rediscover that path, i.e. that it is in Christ that the fullness of human divinity can be restored.

To believe in God incarnate is to believe that God has chosen this way of making Himself known and drawing people to Himself. Hort, as a historian and theologian, expressed the concern that the Christian faith must be related to the whole of life in numerous practical ways. In the demand for social change Hort is more appropriate than any other modern theologian to challenge the Anglican Church today in Rwanda. The Christian's regard for his fellows must cross all barriers. This means that the social behaviour of every Anglican Church member is significant, especially if it lays the groundwork for how people should respond to each other. In this respect it is the Rwandan Anglican Church's responsibility to assist every member to establish patterns of behaviour that can modify the generation's social conduct and relationships.[282]

As mentioned earlier, respondents at Butare, in discussing reconciliation, partly look for how they can change the way that people see things, especially when those people have been brought up to believe that the accumulation of wealth and success is satisfying in itself.[283] In fact, Hort's interests were based very firmly on the theological convictions of how to live a Christian life in a practical way. Hort and Westcott believed that the doctrines of Incarnation and Redemption had practical implications. It is argued that the theological concept of God's incarnation includes the sociological implications of the 'The Lord's Supper', which is seen by them as the sharing of the material resources of this world (Matt. 26:26-30; Mark 14:22-26). The whole essence of incarnation theology is a self-sacrificing love laid down to achieve a right relationship. Thus, entering into such a relationship with those who wronged you, or those you wronged in the past, involves giving support to those who seek to change and repair the past. This implies a very positive attitude to the world.

In other words, God's way of expressing this concern is in His claim that the Incarnation brings heaven and earth together. This is very important and as such it is the Incarnation or 'embodied' character of Christ that must be understood as relating to human concerns, not thought by some to leave out consideration of the physical and social

---

[282]Cfr. Hort, A. F., (1896). Life and Letters of Fenton Anthony Hort, 1 & 2, London: Macmillan, p. 390.
[283]Interviewing tutor at Butare training College for ordinates, May 2004.

conditions under which people actually live. St Paul represents the work of Christ as the creation of a new humanity, one that Christians 'put on' like a robe in baptism, when the old nature – fallen, corrupt human nature – is put away. This is Paul's conception of the Church as a newly created humanity in Christ, both eschatological and incarnate (Romans 8:29; Galatians. 3:28).

This emphasis derives from the doctrine of Christ entering human life and thus giving worth to all that is human. Christ's incarnate life made clear God's sovereignty over the earth and implies our positive attitude towards it.[284] In the middle of conflict, it would appear to suggest that an understanding of the love of God, events around us and individual cognition might help to control and improve our sense of responsibility to each other. Lerner defined responsibility in this way: 'The ability to observe ourselves and others in interaction and to respond to a familiar situation in a new and different way'.[285] In addition, this makes it possible for those involved to design messages that are context specific. This eventually helps them to modify behaviour and encourage the development of desirable community habits.

In theory, it is a profound mission of the Anglican Church's commitment to Christ to contribute to social development and play a positive role in spiritual renewal. The fact that weak theology leads to weak involvement, on the other hand, encourages people to seek a truly incarnation-authentic understanding and practise for the task of reconciliation. Related to this, the Anglican Church is constantly called upon to take an active part in caring for both the bodies and minds of people.

Again, in Hort's analysis, he is a great advocate of social reconciliation, asserting firmly that redemption is

---

[284]Cfr. Hort, A. F., (1977). Just Men, London: Epworth Press, p. 400.
[285]Lerner, H. G., (1990). The Dance of Anger, Wellingborough: Grapevine, p. 17.

related to the whole of life and not only to be understood as a purely spiritual matter. Christ has redeemed men and women's bodies as well as their spirits. Hort stressed that 'to deny the redemption of the body is to deny Christ and relapse into heathen despair; and the redemption of the body carries with it the redemption of the world to which it belongs'.[286] It was argued by Evangelical clergy that, when the stress is on the rule of God, the incarnation aspect of relationships with the world comes to the fore, since God is the omnipotent Lord of all. This is where Christ's mission is also to be seen as a concern for social issues and where the Church must learn to minister to community needs. As this view suggests, there are a number of different ways in which the Anglican Church can theologise relationships within its environment. It is a ministry rooted in where people live and how they live out their faith in any given historical and social context.

There is, therefore, a need to marshal all our tools in order to help people understand others, as well as helping them to understand themselves. This ministry reflects an intrinsic tension in the Christian gospel, summed up by Paul as the need to be 'in the world but not of it' (Romans 12:2-8). Similarly, incarnation's emphasis derives from the doctrine of Christ entering human life and thus giving worth to all that is human. It is in this concept of the incarnation and reconciliation that Christians are fully expected to be involved in the life of the world. Hort, significantly, is very important today in his role as a theologian, as in the past, because his interest was based firmly on theological conviction. While he could not accept the Christian Socialist position, he remained convinced that there was a social dimension to the Anglican Church playing her role in society. The other argument, actually articulated in the Rwandan context, is that the Anglican

---

[286]Cfr. Hort, A. F., (1977). *Just Men*, London: Epworth Press, p. 74

Church has to validate acceptable attitudes and received conceptions and to be careful to resist wrong innovations.

This understanding comes from a careful analysis of the past and such analysis is an important task of the Anglican Church. This is based on the fact that past innovations reconstructed a new order in Rwanda, controlled it and set up functional structures; all these changes became law, based on approval by Belgian administrators. Belgian innovations ignored, marginalised or destroyed societal structures and ways of living and in the process created contradictions and led to conflict in Rwanda – this is the concern for contextual theology today. This contextual theology stresses that there is no basis in Christian teaching for the belief that one ethnic group is, in any way, intrinsically superior to another. This challenges the concept of entitlement to wealth and to own a power that treats others as sub-human and nothing more than a higher class of animal.

What is crucial is that, in the definition of the form of reconciliation needed to sustain stability, it should be based on the principle of the constant exchange of ideas between the rulers and the ruled. Being open to criticism means that a system provides the opportunity for each individual to contribute to the best of their ability and knowledge. Linden was right to argue that the Anglican Church must have courage in situations like that of Rwanda, to challenge ethnic boundaries and to imagine new identities with new content and so redefine development in terms of social reconciliation.[287]

This suggests that the Anglican Church's teaching must be based on the doctrine of Incarnation, which expresses the conviction of Christians that God has made Himself known fully and personally to humanity. God

---

[287]Linden, Ian, (1978). Church and Revolution in Rwanda, Manchester: Manchester University Press, pp. 41- 43.

incarnate lived among us, because Christ took our human nature on Him and came among us as a particular person, without in any away ceasing to be the eternal and infinite God. In both the Old Testament and the New Testament, to be a community within which our common humanity is recognised, all human-made barriers are broken down and sinners are saved only by God's grace. In the new humanity of Christ, the deepest, divisive, political ideologies and social divisions are done away with.

In the New Testament, the early Church is a community marked by love and reconciliation within itself, demonstrating and proclaiming love and reconciliation to the world. Therefore, the work of atonement, or reconciliation, is not only the satisfaction of what has been done, but includes the entire work of God incarnate. This is how the Anglican Church must take on 'the mind of Christ'. In the New Testament, the cross plainly occupies the central place and it is insisted upon that this is God's way of bridging the gap through reconciliation and salvation. In addition, out of the two He has created 'one new person' and has reconciled them both in one body. It can also be argued that, in the Biblical perspective, sin is not an act of wrongdoing, but a state of alienation from one another and God.

The sinful state of our being builds a barrier separating people from each other and God, a barrier that humankind was able to erect, but is unable to demolish. In the Old Testament, sacrifice has a large place. It is valid, not because of any merit it has of itself, but because it is given in the New Testament that insists that God has dealt with sacrifice through Christ. If it fell upon Christ to spare us from the punishment from all the evil committed in the world, reconciliation demands that the cross has an absolute moral claim over humankind.

The cross is presented to humanity as something infinite, something eternal. Atonement for sin is mediated through Christ's sinless life, whereby death is a triumphant resurrection. From the outset the Bible associates obedience with safeguarding life and denotes the means by which reconciliation restores everlasting life. The reconciliation theology that comes out of a study of Genesis, Chapter Two, does not obscure the fact that Adam and Eve's fall created a struggle for survival. The process of reconciliation began in the Garden of Eden and reconciliation theology is a continuation of this process of salvation.

Of course, by comparing the fall of Eden with the Rwandan situation, there is no doubt that Rwanda's hopes for the future as a nation and its ability to rise from the ashes of genocide lie in its response to the reconciliation message of the Cross and the subsequent resurrection. The Rwandan struggle for reconciliation can achieve little, unless Rwandans' reconciliation becomes a struggle at the foot of the Cross.

It is further argued that before the Fall, humankind occupied a different level of existence in its relationship with God, but after the resurrection, took on the fallen nature or death-prone body-soul of Adam. Through Christ's obedience, humankind was able to receive and live out the imperishable body-spirit of life in Christ (1 Corinthians 15:35–50).

It is therefore argued that it is in Christ where there is the perfect realisation of the ideal of a new life of spiritual communion with God. This is also a possibility for all those who are drawn into fellowship with Christ in the Anglican Church in Rwanda. Through reconciliation, the believer can obtain the realisation of a commitment to another, in the service of Christ in the new fellowship (Rwanda). The resurrection of the crucified Christ highlights love as the key to redemption and proposes a synthesis of the divine presence through Christ. The idea of ransom is commonly given as a metaphor, pointing to a price paid by Christ, a transaction made to obtain the freedom of others.

This metaphor of money payment is used several times in the New Testament. Twice St Paul tells the Corinthian Christians, 'You are bought with a price' (1 Cor. 6:20; 7:23). The paradox that St Paul is proclaiming is that, although God looks upon sinful human beings as enemies, He reconciles them to Himself and has done this by the one decisive act of the crucifixion of Christ on the cross. All that Christ has done and all that He is doing now, is a part of His work for reconciliation. Another key virtue explains that the meaning of the cost of reconciliation is love, used to denote the self-giving of God, for the salvation of the human race, of which Christ's earthly mission was held to be the embodiment.[288]

To reconcile is to unite, to bring back that which pertains to relationships in social reality or the political sphere; to change from anger, hostility or alienation to love, friendship or intimacy. In other words, the Anglican Church's effort is to make the Word of life present in a world of oppression, in reconciliation and death.[289] God's concern for reconciliation is shown right at the beginning of the Biblical story, when God begins to reveal His will. The central doctrine is that God had revealed himself in all of creation and supremely in Christ so that humankind may conform to His image.[290]

In addition, His will is reconciliation rooted in the nature of God and an attribute of His manifest holiness. For the Hebrews, righteousness did not consist of living in accordance with our higher nature, but in doing the will of

---

[288]Cfr. Linden, Ian, (1978). Church and Revolution in Rwanda, Manchester: Manchester University Press, pp. 23 – 29.
[289]Gutierrez, G., (1988). A Theology of Liberation, 2nd (Edn), Maryknoll, New York: Orbis, p. 57.
[290]Cfr. Farmer, H. H. (1935). The World and God, London: Nisbet, p.139.

God, made known to Israelites in the Torah Law. In the Old Testament, the Scriptures' righteousness is, in origin, an ethical and political term and is better translated as reconciliation.

7.6 Incarnation Theology for Reconciliation

I intend under this subheading to explain the purpose of the theology of incarnation in such a way that it can help people in Rwanda to engage in the process of healing the wounds of their differences. It is a Biblical argument that, since we are all sinners, we need to accept each other without confrontation, praying for people until they change their minds or waiting for them to repent. It is an argument that St Paul anticipates when he responds in his classic explanation of grace. It expects involvement with Christ where people are suffering and inevitably leads to reconciliation between people. As far as we can fix people at all or get them to sin less, we do it by being vehicles of grace and leading them to the loving grace of God.

The meaning of Christ's incarnation is found in His total immersion in a historical situation of conflict or human oppression. It is within incarnation acts that Christ's life makes absolute the values of the Kingdom with His unconditional love, universal forgiveness and continual reference to the mystery of God. Therefore, the definition of incarnation significantly draws our attention to the accounts of God's involvement in human affairs to reconcile the world to Himself. The doctrine of incarnation affirms this.[291] It has been advanced, therefore, that the incarnation of God in the Christian life and the Christian message becomes a principle that animates, directs and unifies the people. Theologically, in this view God's

---

[291] Rubenstein, R. & Roth, J. K., (1987). Approaches to Auschwitz, the Legacy of the Holocaust, London: SCM Press Ltd, p. 63.

experience transforms and remakes people's views to bring about a new creation.[292]

It is argued that St John gives a captivating picture of the order of God's reign (Revelation 21:22–26). The vision speaks of God's purpose for the whole of creation, of people of diverse ethnicity and nations dwelling together in the unity of God's design with God as their light. In the new community there is unity with God and each other, without the indifference that tears apart humanity or the global drive that destroys identities. The story of Pentecost constantly reminds the Anglican Church to take part in promoting the common good through a public commitment to the salvation of the world. When Rwandans say that God is love, they mean His nature is to act in the way Christ acted in His mission of reconciliation for humankind. It is evident that the political and social context in towns and villages in Rwanda was becoming influenced, if not wholly determined, by contextual theology and practice and these issues are on many Rwandans' minds today.

In the first place, God in Christ took upon himself responsibility for the entire world's ill. Christ on the cross gives a clue as to God's purpose in enduring suffering and subjecting Himself to human cruelty and horror in order to be reconciled with humankind. Christ's suffering on the cross is in contrast with the Anglican Church in Rwanda. The mission of the 'suffering servant', wrought through the Christian experience of salvation, reveals that reconciliation theology's mission is rooted in the very nature of struggle and confrontation with sin. Therefore, the Anglican Church in Rwanda is called to this mission of a 'suffering servant', to display the characteristics revealed in Christ as the ultimate ground for saving Rwandans.

---

[292]Cfr. Gutierrez, G., (1974). "Praxis of Liberation and Christian Faith", San Antonio, p. 49.

It is on the cross that He revealed, as He could in no other way, the reality and depth and costly nature of God's forgiving love. By God's identification of Himself with the human predicament, He draws people to Himself in an utterly moral and personal way. The task of reconciliation illustrates that this process is costly and this is nowhere truer than in the matter of the teaching on atonement. The Scriptures clearly teach, through Christ's death, that atonement for sin will result in the salvation of the world. It is important that the Anglican Church's commitment in Rwanda is for the people to know that reconciliation is essential, costly and not an easy path to follow.

7.7 The Difficulties with Reconciliation

During his interview, Bishop Alexis Birindabagabo asserted that peace and reconciliation are much harder than making war. It takes time and requires endurance. The RPF government, Non-Government Organisations and the Anglican Church have all placed emphasis upon reconciliation. To meet this challenge several suggestions were made. Under this subheading, the overall assessment of the reconciliation process shows how the Anglican Church's role in reconciliation was to be a long painful task.

In my view, there are two compelling reasons for this. First, most people liked the idea of reconciliation and the sound of the word, but not the hard work of putting its abstract meaning into actual practice. Like sunshine and fresh air, reconciliation does not demand more than the fact that it is supposed to be good for many and perhaps it could be for all. The second reason is that reconciliation is a very messy business and anathema to those who seek revenge as their form of justice.

There are two main tasks for reconciliation groups. Firstly, a constant and total commitment to the challenge, until there is acceptance of people's behaviour and its consequences and direct responsibility for both. However, Gerloff sounds a warning always to be aware of some people who might act not consciously out of a realisation of what went wrong, but as an act of imitating attitudes.[293] It also means that groups involved in the task have to make contingent plans to include educating everyone as to the value of the process of reconciliation. Secondly, it is argued that education is one of the dependable tools for the construction and restoration of peace in the minds of people. Peace is a deep-seated value, attributed to an orderly process that can be entrenched in families and communities. The search for total peace therefore has its foundation in communities.

It was also reasoned that the process of reconciliation must aim to educate the population about the root causes of violence, poverty, powerlessness and exclusion, which are all characteristic of the Rwandan conflict, symptoms of underdevelopment and the consequent rivalries between different ethnic groups over meagre resources in the poorest areas. Having seen the state of exclusion, the government and the Anglican Church decided to make it a priority to invest in conferences for schools. Commenting on the relevance of the seminar to Rwanda, the Minister of Education, Gahakwa, recently said that the Ministry would ensure that national programmes of unity and reconciliation are disseminated early enough in primary schools, in order to prepare young people for an active and responsible citizenship that promotes tolerance and unity. It is a process of making all the allowances for a solid path to reconciliation under identifiable conditions and includes patience and pressure, as well as the common sense realisation of 'being in the same boat'.[294]

---

[293] Gerloff, R., (1998). *Truth a New Society and Reconciliation*, London: SPCK, p. 21.
[294] New Times, Monday 3rd November 2008

Conclusion

This chapter has found abundant theological precedents that have stressed the need for people's repentance and renewal in the light of gospel teaching and for the Anglican Church to engage actively in the promotion of social conditions under which that renewal may lead to reconciliation in Rwanda. This chapter has attempted to examine the ways the Anglican Church in Rwanda can engage in the process of reconciliation from the Rwandan point of view, rather than using imported modes of reconciliation that may very be difficult for people to use or irrelevant to Rwandan needs. As for the answer to the question of forgiveness, there were several arguments from those opposed to the idea of reconciliation, mainly those from surviving groups of genocide who saw reconciliation as a 'sell out' and an injustice.

On the other hand, the analysis of these developments has suggested that the task of the Anglican Church in the reconciliation process is to unite all forces to challenge all forms of destruction, isolationism, withdrawal, distrust, animosity, sectarian psychology, the intent of the division and confessional tension, all of which were and are extremely dangerous for Christianity and society at large. So far, what has been promising is how it has established bridges among Anglican Church leaders, bridges that could become strong grounds for reconciliation in the future. I believe the concept of a bridge between the different communities and ethnic divisions in the Anglican Church is one that has been reflected on by different congregations. It is a concept that responds to the Anglican Church's reconciliation mission. The future make-up of the congregations will provide strength and direction for the Anglican Church's reconciliation process in Rwanda.

It has been argued that the task for palaver groups is to decipher the social implications of the past, engaging communities to discover the causes of their differences through reconciliation talks. In the actual process, the reconciliation palaver talks centre upon the origin of the deviance of people's behaviour, linked to Belgian policies of divide and rule, in which people were entangled and fundamentally bound up within ethnic ideological propaganda.

During all the visits made to Rwanda, through observations, there was a clear indication that the Anglican Church and the government were both committed to the policy of reconciliation, making the public recognise the reality of the problems and taking measures to work towards freeing them from lives lived in fear. The Executive Secretary of the National Unity and Reconciliation Commission (NURC), Fatuma Ndanginza, recently commended Oxfam for its contribution to the unity and reconciliation program since 2001, especially in the Western province where it has registered many achievements ranging from the eradication of poverty to conflict resolution.[295]

However, for reconciliation to be successful it needs continuous and consistent effort. As a matter of urgency, in my view, consideration needs to be given by all the Anglican Churches to assist the rehabilitation of those considered to be politically opposed to reconciliation, such as militia groups. As part of the reconciliation process the Anglican Church will also have to be an advocate for the rights and protection of disadvantaged groups. The history and theory of conflict suggests that when people are deprived of hope or social assistance from society, people are more likely to resort to violence.

---

[295] New Times, Monday, 3rd November 2008

The overall findings indicate that despite all the failures of the Anglican Church in the past, people still look to the Anglican Church for guidance. People still have faith in the Anglican Church to play a role in the process of reconciliation. Respondents argued that if the Anglican Church is not living up to its duty towards a people in serious danger, then the 'wider Anglican Communion' should fraternally call that Anglican Church in Rwanda to order, to stick to Anglican moral teaching.[296] Secondly, the Anglican Church should engage with agencies such as the Mothers' Union, Youth Clubs, the Church Army and Missionary Societies in order to develop close collaboration with Anglican Churches operating in the area and negotiate carefully with dioceses to promote reconciliation. Thirdly, exchanges of visiting speakers between Anglican Churches should be promoted as channels of change. Finally, I have described the ways in which reconciliation theology should be treated as both genuinely contextual and authentically B23iblical theology.

The task of the last chapter is to explain why local voices have offered different interpretations of the 1994 genocide in Rwanda, explaining that they believe poverty should be seen as contributing to the political crisis in the country. It analyses the possibility for a specifically Rwandan approach to resolving the conflict. The idea is for the Anglican Church to offer a contextual theological approach to the reconciliation and liberation process, whereby the Church can assist in restoring a caring mechanism within the social setting of individual communities.

---

[296]Interviews at Kigali and Butare Diocese, July 1998.

Chapter Eight

Conclusion

8.0 A Review of the Study

This study has examined the nature of the ethnic conflict to establish the Rwandan point of view concerning the cause of the genocide in Rwanda. This thesis has served its purpose in bringing forward the comments of eyewitnesses to show the relentless suffering experienced by people during and after Belgian rule in Rwanda. It includes stories narrated by local eyewitnesses who trace the source of the conflict and its causes in order to explain why people become killers. Particular attention has also been paid to the political nature of conflict propaganda, so as to highlight the danger of propaganda impacting upon people's attitude towards relationships. It outlines how the conflict created fear and hatred between Hutus and Tutsis. This fear generated an explosive mix between growing rural poverty and urban resentment at the lack of political freedom.[626] It is argued that under existing social, economic and political situations, the reliability of behaviour varies over time, based on particular situations.

The various reactions and theological types of reconciliation and approaches are discussed and the effects of social change. The implications of social change in relation to the process of developmental change and the social nature of the disintegration of community have also been closely examined. The role of the Anglican Church in the process of reconciliation has been discussed and various theological and sociological interpretations, along with the theological imperatives of the Anglican Church involvement, were examined. The ways in which the Église

---

[626]http://ww7.news.bbc.co.1/hi/world/africa/7/4/2004

Épiscopale au Rwanda restored its credibility in society and the problems that faced the Church in the aftermath of the genocide were described. The theological and contextual perspectives of reconciliation regarding the role of the Anglican Church in the process and in society in general have been explored.

However, the process of behavioural change in Rwanda is still being debated, bearing in mind that not all this may be due to variations in the level of transgression, but to variations in the likelihood of resources being spent on community improvements and essential services. Thus, to the extent that such factors can determine and influence changes in human behaviour, when adversely affected, the pace of such changes can be similarly impaired. The fear is that economic factors may continually push the country deeper into poverty and lopsided development.

8.1 The Poverty Trap

This study has discovered that a growing number of people feel excluded by a lack of support, or feel powerless to participate in the national recovery. Past social-economic policies related to Belgian administration have kept poor people in a state of poverty. Latent poverty has also been on the rise due to political breakdown and a decline in the possibility for employment, especially for those in rural areas. Therefore, these findings cast serious doubts upon the wisdom of the country's strategies and whether reconciliation is likely to be jeopardised.

What is important to realise is that if poverty continues to loom large, national reconciliation will need to be accompanied by economic investment in the poor and other forms of reconciliation.[627] If the RPF government

---

[627] Cfr. Maluleke, T. S., (1998). "Truth, Natio.al Unity and Reconciliation in South Africa, Aspects of the Emerging Theological Agenda", Missionalia, 25:1 April, pp. 322–243.

implements good policies, making more resources available, this may address some of the existing social problems and improve human behaviour. The significant and worrying situation in rural areas is that the majority feels left out of development and is subjected to forms of social control. This is accepted as part of the means to control insurgency in insecure times, but the question is for how long this will be tolerated?

As mentioned above, the research findings documented in the nine dioceses were quite disturbing. These findings covered poverty and the lack of necessities such as education and health and the fact that the level of inequality had worsened, mostly in rural areas. These findings revealed the collective failure of Rwanda's economic structures to provide appropriate development. This was in part because of past policies. Even before the political crisis, the situation had worsened after the genocide in such way that even the government could not contain the violence, let alone reverse it. It is impossible to imagine how they could do so without a net increase in expenditure. The state of the economy hit the poor the hardest, as they depended upon national healthcare, itself gravely impaired and they struggled with poverty, psychological injury and stress, which often resulted in death. The failure was overwhelmingly attributed to economic shortcomings that amounted to discrimination. Evidence presents the possibility of undue prejudice in an extreme form of Belgian rule and ethnic stereotyping.

Referring to the question posed at the beginning of this thesis that asked why people in Rwanda acted the way they did, there are three main factors. Firstly, through analysis of past Belgian ideological indoctrination, violence became an integral part of political practice. An institutionalised culture of impunity facilitated this violence as a legitimate means of resolving disputes. Secondly, it has been exceedingly burdensome for Rwanda to compete in the economic game with the West. Thirdly, monetary policy has been a significant constraint, because it deals in perception, not fact; and is linked to the economic problems of the country. Political propaganda was engineered based on ethnicity and the Belgian legacy left a political climate that proved difficult to reverse after independence. This legacy created permanent divisions, where the minority Tutsis lived under discrimination and persecution. Therefore, considering the above factors – conditions of poverty, accumulated propaganda of political regimes and ethnic categorisation – a social reality developed where everyone knew whom to kill.[628]

The study also described the size of the problem and emphasised the importance of the Anglican Church in Rwanda accepting and meeting these challenges. Addressing ethnic ideology and the dangers involved in the process of reconciliation is fundamental, in order to assist the search for peace and to resolve the causes of the Rwandan conflict. Local responses offered valuable explanations about the Belgian legacy, debt, capitalism and globalisation, all of which were argued to have contributed to the weaker state of the economy, corruption and the moral vacuum that led to the ethnic crisis and genocide.

The role of ethnicity as a politically relevant element has been extensively argued as the main contributor to the political crisis through a broad analysis of ideological policies. It is argued in Chapters Two, Five, Six and Seven that recovery from ethnic conflict is a long and complex programme that embraces questions of political democracy, economy, leadership accountability, Anglican Church theology, rule of law and how to deal with social deviance. In fact, any analysis would be incomplete without a

---

[628] Cfr. Brandstetter, Anna-Maria, (1998). "Ethnic or Socioeconomic Conflict? Political
Interpretations of the Rwandan Crisis", Institute for Ethnology and Africa Studies, Germany: Mainz University, p. 432.

consideration of Mamdani's observations. Mamdani observed that the crucial challenge for Rwanda was to find a way to break out of the notion of the state of representation of the permanently defined majority and how to move from an order based on conquest to one based on consent.[629]

The reconciliation process must therefore proceed in two ways. Firstly, the people must transcend the micro-level approach toward offenders or community victims. This means that family neighbourhoods and communities may continue to be organised along ethnic lines, but are increasingly devoid of distinctive ethnic content. The most crucial demand upon the leadership is to settle ethnic differences and allow all Rwandans to participate in the process of liberating themselves from a lack of education, professional skills, poverty and from all sorts of issues currently under intense sociological interrogation, such as how to deal with the AIDS' epidemic and provide for the large number of young widows and orphans.

Secondly, the starting point for reconciliation must recognise ethnic identities without reproducing dualities. It is seen as essential to find ways to engender a sense of 'togetherness'. On the other hand, evidence of the ethnic conflict was not associated with a culture rooted in ethnicity as such, but was a result of ideological policies. It is argued that unless people learn to recognise each other as Rwandans with each group able to empathise with the other, they will never be able to be reconciled.

The challenge is to develop an imagination that also involves recognition of the absences and distortions within the public debate and for those missing voices to be heard. It is important that reconciliation is based upon reforming and eradicating any ideological policies, divisive structures

---

[629]Mamdani, Mahmood, (2001). When Victims Become Killers. Colonialism, Nativism and the Genocide in Rwanda, Oxford: Currey, p. 17.

and economic differences. It was even doubted whether reconciliation was achievable while these factors were still begging for an answer, despite the hold on the present political situation. It is essential that reconciliation must address issues with a much wider historical lens, whilst recognising each ethnic group's existence.

Another worrying problem expressed by respondents, but not directly related to the current ethnic problem, was that of overpopulation and the constant threat of destabilisation from across its borders.[630] International efforts to control overpopulation have only proved successful when governments have focused upon improving the population's welfare at a micro-level, rather than through grand announcements from the centre. According to the 2000 UN's human poverty indicator, 67.5 percent of the 8 million people in Rwanda live below the poverty line, compared to 20.2 percent in South Africa.[631] Another indicator of development is that of per capita income, which was $230 in Rwanda, contrasting with $630 in Zimbabwe and $3310 in Botswana.[632]

With the 2020 objective of combating poverty, the government is embarking upon a comprehensive programme of privatisation and liberalisation, with the goal of attaining rapid and sustainable economic growth. In this regard, the RPF government is both morally and legally obliged to defend the human rights of its own citizens and protect their lives. It was argued that respect for human rights was the key to any successful resolution and the only way to break the cycle of violence that has occurred over the last four decades. This must be addressed in an equitable manner. Any limited or partial approach to addressing the abuse of power in the past has simply

---

[630]Hastings, A., "The Tribal Contest behind Africa's Bloodbath" The Tablet, 5 September 1998, p. 1152.
[631]UN Global Agenda human poverty indicator, 2000.
[632]Ibid.

deferred the problem to a later date in many post-conflict settings. If leaders attempt to ignore these problems, nothing will have been learnt from the past.

The challenge before the Anglican Church now is the search for reconciliation and to develop the liberation theological debate to show how the reconciliation agenda can provide an opportunity for the Anglican Church in Rwanda to unravel the complex patterns emerging from ethnic conflict issues. The Anglican Church's goal is to assist the people to transform the country's social-economic conditions from its 90 percent dependence upon subsistence agriculture into a modern, broadly based economic engine, welcoming investors and creating employment.[633]

According to the Rwanda Development Plan 2001, 75.2 percent of the rural population are farmers, but the country's annual use of fertiliser was only 100 grams per hectare.[634] This compares with 6100 grams per hectare in Burundi and 27,800 grams per hectare in Kenya. This is added to the fact that 65% of the Rwandan population live on less than a dollar per day, but this percentage is expected to fall to 32.5% by 2015. If Rwanda can combine developmental programmes directed towards the real needs of the poor, especially in rural areas, with adequate financing from international donors, it will then see rapid achievement, helping the 89%without any legal income in rural areas.[635]

Clearly, there is a need for an outline programme dealing with national recovery. The level of poverty faced by many Rwandans is worrying, especially for those in rural areas, which explains why the economy forms such an important part of the agenda for post-conflict governance and reconciliation.

---

[633]http://www.rwandatourism.com/economy.htm/2007
[634]http://www.jhuccp.org.puhs/sp/19/English/19.pdf/2007
[635]Ibid.

8.2 A Lesson for the Anglican Church in Rwanda

This thesis analysis offers an alternative point of view, closer to the local interpretations of the Rwandan conflict that have been argued as often absent or distorted within journalists' reports. History highlights that Belgian ideology underlay the crisis of ethnic conflict. The study has argued that the virtual monopoly over education offered by the missionary Anglican Church created a nominal Christian society, with considerable influence. As a result, the Anglican Church allowed itself to be led down the wrong path in support of ethnic politics. Subsequently, this wrong path led some Anglican Church leaders to create a political alliance with politicians, whose influence dominated the country up to the last days of the genocide.

The Anglican Church in Rwanda has been described in Chapters Three, Five and Seven to be already engaged in the process of reconciliation. This thesis has argued in various ways how the Anglican Church can create awareness of how Rwandans can move towards a solution, eradicating the political differences in order to promote reconciliation. The challenge for the Anglican Church is not only to read the signs, but to develop a theological imagination that will involve interpreting the signs and distortions within the public debate. The Anglican Church can play a salient role by working towards the goal of liberating people from a poverty that hinders both spiritual and human progress. It is argued that in the period from 1962 to 1994 the Rwandan Anglican Church's prophetic voice in society was largely lost at a time when the Anglican Church was predominantly Hutu in leadership.

The findings show that the Anglican Church, instead of sticking to Revival Heritage Christian love drifted into party politics. It aimed at approving everything suggested by the national political leaders in order to lend divine blessings to their actions. It supported the principles of the revolution and enjoyed much greater favour from the Kayibanda and Habyarimana regimes than had been the case during Belgian rule in Rwanda. The wider view expressed by respondents was that this time the Anglican Church should stay free of politics and allegiances, in order to preach fearlessly against the evil of corruption and other crippling practices revealed in past developments in Rwanda. In the light of this exploitation and economic and political (as well as cultural) dependence the Rwandan Anglican Church effort must be dedicated to a proclamation of God's truth, a challenge to injustice and especially to inclusive theology.[636]

Apparently, politicians still use the argument that Church leaders should not interfere in politics and, if they do, politicians further suggest they should leave the Anglican Church and become politicians. Such dangerous, subversive arguments provide little in return and are used with the intention of drawing Anglican Church leaders' attention away from the real problems facing people. Politicians hope that these leaders may have no time to attack and criticise their policies. If the Anglican Church is swayed from its purpose, it is as capable of becoming as corrupt as any other part of society. On the other hand, Anglican Church leaders stressed that they consider their focus on unity as essential and that ethnic diversity is a very strong foundation upon which equally strong bonds can be rebuilt.

Leaders argued that to do this effectively it was necessary for Anglican Church teaching to emphasise applying Christian values in daily living, in order for people to be reconciled. It is argued that in this process of reconciling people, the Anglican Church in Rwanda would have to be aware of its boundaries and act effectively in an

---

[636]Kirk, J. A., (1979). Liberation Theology, An Evangelical View from the Third World, England: Marshalls Theological Library Kirk, p.26

advisory capacity so as not to repeat past mistakes in being too close to the government. Instead, Anglican Church leaders found themselves largely joining the cause and accepting opinions mooted by politicians.[637] In fact, this was the juxtaposition of people and relationships that reached its head in the crisis. In the view of those interviewed, there was a feeling that a section of refugees should be denied the opportunity to return and settle.[638]

This means that both the government and the Anglican Church still have the enormous task of addressing all sorts of social problems, related to corruption, arms and power. Chapter Eight further described the essential characteristics of a social infrastructure that shows an increasing need for the Anglican Church's advocacy and its experience with contextual reconciliation theology. The question is, how relevant is this Anglican Church theology in engaging members in the reconciliation process? In this respect, an estimated 50,000 Rwandan refugees, still living in neighbouring countries, still hesitate in choosing in repatriation due to the lack of public services such as education and health, or due to fear of litigation upon their return.[639] The conclusion, however, is that some of these concerns could be alleviated. What is apparent is that those most critical of the RPF, especially those in villages and elderly people, are growing weary of deep-seated divisions based on misinformation and a lack of clarity surrounding historical facts.

So far, the Anglican Church in Rwanda has been busy recently encouraging all ethnic groups and the government to co-operate in the process of change, in order to reconcile and engage in national rebuilding. At present, the Rwandan Anglican Church is making great efforts to pursue

---

[637]Interviewing Rwandan Anglican bishops and community leaders, July 1998.
[638]Ibid.
[639]http://wwwjubileecampaign.co.uk/world/rwanda.pdf/20/9/07

reconciliation, assisting in interpreting the issues for communities, conveying the necessity of reconciliation and deploying strategies with insights allied with approaches suggested by local communities. The major problem at the time of this research was the lack of skilled people to be involved in this.

Given the characteristics of the ethnic conflict, there are still fears and suspicions, but the implication is that the Anglican Church has initiated strategies that consider all the constraints, but not in such a way that they hover around the issues out of hyper-sensitivity, for fear of reaction. The Anglican Church leadership takes seriously issues of sensitivity and honesty and positive ideas represent a change for all. It is even argued that within the interplay and creative action of the Christian spirit, the leadership is discovering each time God's guidance, which stimulates the imagination and makes suggestions for genuine reconciliation.

Furthermore, it is argued that to effectively enhance the process of reconciliation is to use available resources, including training local Anglican Church members to engage in programmes of reconciliation, administration, liaison with communities and voluntary groups. Communication should account for the common interest, but with outward-looking concern and continued foreign support, not to recreate dependency, but so that local resources can be tapped more fully. This study began with questioning what happened in Rwanda for people to have acted the way they did. I wish to end by arguing that just as physicians recognise the importance of good health and promoting a healthy way of living rather than waiting to treat illness, the Anglican Church in Rwanda ought to recognise the importance of creating confidence among Hutus and Tutsis, to trust each other and return to their long abandoned community values. In the past, these community values had united them and prevented them from resorting to conflict. However, this first requires the poverty crisis to be addressed in rural areas and for equal opportunities to be promoted. This is all in response to those in rural areas and refugee camps who expressed that help was urgently needed for people to be able to sustain themselves.

It is argued that the desire to tackle the ethnic divide and conflict must wait until there is an improvement in the poverty situation. The ethnic problem comes down to one thing: a lack of support for communities struggling in with need. The Anglican Church plays a vital role in national consciousness and in influencing the way that the government and the international community should invest in communities in order to helps people. In this respect, the Anglican Church's role is to encourage people to understand their need for togetherness in order to develop the country and improve their own lives.

8.3 The Crucial Challenge for the Anglican Church in Rwanda

I will now turn the focus on the same conditions within which the conflict arose and still exists. For example, people in rural areas are not yet fully participating in the economic development of the country and it is not surprising that a desire for help is on many people's minds, especially those still trapped in refugee camps or in a hopeless state of unemployment. A persistent energy crisis continues, with increases in global fuel prices pushing inflation in Rwanda up to 13.6 percent in 2004/05. The 2005/06 budget indicated that the country's total expenditure was much higher than internal revenue. In post-conflict analysis it is argued that unless economic reform and the poverty crisis are dealt with, they will still pose a very serious threat to the country's stability. Social-economic recovery is still the greatest challenge to maintaining macroeconomic stability without incurring more debts, following $1.4 billion of debt relief from international financial lenders.[640]

It is argued that this type of economic situation demands that the leadership listen to voices of dissent that are legitimately expressed, as the tendency to resort to violence will increase if no one pays attention.[641] Alison Des Forges argued that, 'It could be violence within the elite, itself in the form of a coup, or it could be violence in terms of a rural uprising, or an uprising in the city streets'.[642] Although life is a gift from God, the Scriptures suggest that we have an essential role to play in affecting the present and even the country's future for its good in the service we give it. Anglican Church leaders like Anglican Archbishop Emmanuel Kolini see signs of hope. Koloni's words provide some comfort to practitioners and theorists alike. Kolini spoke from the Christian point of view that signs of hope are everywhere, whether strong, hidden, or little known. It is true and convincing to see people's resilience being increased in communities. This slight improvement is attributed to improved coffee prices, security and aid.

Overall, the study observed improvements in the suburbs of the Kigali area. It is now 13 years after the genocide and the country has indeed undergone tremendous change. If there is no great disturbance within it, this may lead to economic and social development and sustainable democracy. It may be argued that if people do not consider the issue of moral values seriously, similar problems will continue to arise in Rwanda. Therefore, looking to the future, although some gains have been made in meeting the

---

[640]Cfr. Lemarchand, Rene, (1994). Managing Transition Anarchies: Rwanda, Burundi and South Africa in Comparative Perspective, The Journal of Modern African Studies, 32, 4, Cambridge: University Press, p. 587.
[641]http://www.news.bbc.co.1/hi/world/africa/7/4/2004
[642]Ibíd.

objectives of the political agenda, the implementation of equal opportunity policies is still uneven across sectors. Institution building, too, continues to be a challenge. This failure is interpreted as a threat to the country's future.

Human rights organisations have increasingly criticised the RPF government for its brutal leadership style. However, RPF's public speeches have constantly argued that the future of the country lies in all Rwandans regarding themselves as Rwandans first and Hutu and Tutsi second. This theory, if put into practice, can form the basis for a fair and sustainable settlement for reconciliation that would enhance the stability of the country as a whole and lead to a better future for all communities. However, it appears that there were issues of concern that have not been adhered to by RPF, such as the persecution of the press, the imprisonment of political dissidents and the failure of the trials of their assassins.[643]

The Jubilee Campaign argued that just wishing away ethnic awareness is futile and counterproductive and that you can remove ethnic identification from identity cards, but not from memory. The crucial problems to address are coexistence, mutual respect and power sharing.[644] For this to happen there is a need for leaders to recognise that human rights are not a personal moral choice for some countries, but a universal obligation for individuals and states.

What are people really worried about? Are they simply worried about how they get on with others? At present the major concern is for RPF to address worries created by its policies. There has been little room for positive criticism of RPF's performance and there are restrictions upon journalists. Journalists say that prominent critics of the government have been imprisoned or forced into exile and

---

[643] http://www.jubilleecampaign.co.uk/world/rwanda.pdf
[644] Ibid.

human rights groups have added that many Rwandans are afraid to speak out against their government.[645] Further evidence has been uncovered that both Hutus and Tutsis who speak out against the RPF system are either forced into exile or imprisoned. This suggests that many Rwandans are still denied freedom of expression, afraid, for example, to speak out against the RPF government.[646]

Evidence from the questionnaires and interviews shows that the RPF government's 'tinted glasses' need to be removed in order to review the way forward for long-term political strategies. Many respondents still felt that they had a say, but that the RPF government had its way. Widespread responses from both Tutsis and Hutus argued that, with the RPF government, they have a voice in a vote, but not a choice. It is argued that the electoral system can be deceitful when it is used more or less to confirm those in power. This is another form of political exploitation.

For many, getting involved has come to mean filling out voting forms and yet at all levels of society, people still lacked participation, which is still an issue of concern for many. Respondents interviewed argued that there was nothing like an opposition possible and there was no one that could criticise the government. Insofar as the question of the media was brought up, opinions from the Anglican leadership reflected that they must be allowed to act as agents to build bridges and trust during all the phases of reconciliation. The government, in turn, must allow the media to play a proper role in drawing attention to areas of mutual trust, respect and the promotion of group aspirations.

Another issue of greater concern is one raised by Alison Des Forges, that the Tutsis have so far been the greatest beneficiaries, holding important posts in the

---

[645]Cfr. http:// news. bbc.co.uk/1/hi/world/africa/7/4/2004.
[646]Ibid.

economy.[647] Forges added that Tutsis, especially English speakers, occupy the most important positions in the army and the civil administration.[648]

If the RPF is committed to its course of liberating Rwanda, economic power cannot be concentrated in the hands of a few people who freely use it for their own benefit. Therefore, based on this evidence, the economy cannot yet be working effectively while it is connected to a system that still retains past structural mechanisms and policies. These are apparent obstacles to future stability and a hindrance to reconciliation, but are not the source of tribal hatred. Others argued against this, claiming that most issues will get a hearing in a pluralist system. Judging from these arguments, there is still a long way to go towards any full commitment to the political project of promoting democracy by strengthening national institutions for democratic leadership.

In fact, the crisis is still there even if the media have stopped talking about it. The political situation can still be manipulated by extremists in the former army or by Interahamwe and events and views can change things with passion put behind them. For this very reason, expressed by the leadership, it still 'tries to keep the media out of these views as much as possible'[649]. Finally, this study draws the conclusion that whatever impact missionaries or Belgian rule may have had on the country, the political situation, being propagated and grown in the fertile soil of certain political and ideological principles, has left the greatest mark on Rwanda and best explains what became the root of the genocide.

---

[647]Cfr. Http://www. News. bbc.co.uk/1/hi/world/africa/7/4/2004.
[648]Ibid.
[649]Ibid.

Bibliography

Affidavit of Nicholas Martin Cavender, (1994). 9, The Precincts, Canterbury, Kent England.

African Rights, (1994). 'Rwanda, Who is killing; Who is dying; What is to be done'? May.

African Rights, (1994). 'Rwanda Death, Despair and Defiance'. London: September.

African Rights, (1995). Issue1: 'Backwards and Forwards: The Struggle for Justice, Father Wenceslas Munyeshaaka is arrested and released in France', October.

African Rights, (1996). 'Rwanda –Killing the Evidence: Murder Attacks, Arrests and Intimidation of Survivors and Witnesses', London: April.

African Rights, Issue 3: (1996). 'Presumption of Innocence: The Case against Innocent Mazimpaka', May.

African Rights, (1996). Issue 4: 'Jean Paul Akayesu: First Prosecution by the International Tribunal at Arusha', Tanzania, September.

African Rights, (1997). Issue 7: 'Antoine Sebomana and His Supporters: Burying the Truth in the name of Human Rights', September.

African Rights, (1999). 'An Appeal to the World Council of Churches', Harare: December.

Aguilar, M. I., (1996). The Rwanda Genocide and the Call to Deepen Christianity in Africa, Uganda: AMECEA GABA Publications Spearhead Nos. 148 – 150.

Allen, R. and Borror, G., (1982). Worship: Rediscovering the Missing Jewel. Pórtland: Multnomah Press.

Amelia, French,(1997). 'Militias Raid Camps as New Offensive starts in the Killing Fields,' The Independent, 16 December.

Amnesty International Rwanda, (1995). 'Arming the Perpetrators of the Genocide', London: Amnesty International Report, Index: AFR47/17/94, June.

Anglican and Society, (1997). Report on World Conference of Churches, Geneva, WCC, September.
Anglican Communion, (1997). News Service, 21 March.
Atta-Bafoe, Victor, R. and Tovey Philip, (1990). 'What does inculturation mean', in Liturgical Inculturation in the Anglican Communion, ed. David R. Holeton, Grove Books, Nottingham.
Banks, R., (1994). Reconciliation and Hope, London: Paternoster Press.
Barham, E. L., (1961). Ruanda, a Bird's Eye View, London: Ruanda Mission CMS.
Barnett, Michael N., (2002). Eyewitness to Genocide: The United Nations and Developing society. Ithaca, N.Y. Cornell University Press.
Barrett, D. B., (1968). Schism and Renewal in Africa, Oxford: University Press.
Barrette, M. & McIntosh, M., (1980). 'The Family Wage: Some Problems for Socialists and Feminists', 11 Capital and Class 51.
Battle, M., (1977). Reconciliation: The Ubuntu Theology of Desmond Tutu, Cleveland: The Pilgrim Press.
Baum, G. and Wells, H., (Ed.). (1997). The Reconciliation of Peoples, Challenge to the Churches, Geneva: WCC.
Bauman, Z., (1992). Intimation of Post Modernity, London: (Routledge & Kegan Paul).
Bayingana, Ng. E., (1994). 'Reconciliation: Foundation for Reconstructing a New Rwanda', Nairobi: Evangel Press.
Beattie, J.O.C., (1968). Other Cultures, London: Hodder.
Bennett, J., (1994). Zur Geschichte und Politik der Rwandischen Patriotischen Front, in: Schurings, H., (Ed). Ein Volk VerlaBt sein Land: Krieg und Volkermonrd in Ruanda, Koln: Neuer ISP Verl.
Berger Peter, (1966). Invitation to Sociology: London: Penguin.

Berger, P. L., & Luckmann, T., (1967). The Social Construction of Reality, Buckingham: Open University Press.
Berger, R., (1969): 'Is Traditional Religion Still Relevant?' Orita, 3, 15-26.
Biggar, N., (1988). Theological Politics, Oxford: Latimer House.
Birinda, L., (1996). The Colour of Darkness: a Personal Story of Tragedy and Hope in Rwanda, London: Hodder and Stoughton Ltd.
Bournique, J., (1967). 'Good Tidings', July – Oct., East Asia Institute Manila.
Bowen, R., (1995). Rwanda, Missionary Reflections on a Catastrophe, London: SPCK.
Bowen, R., (1996). Revivalism and Ethnic Conflict Questions from Rwanda, Transformation, Vol. 12, No. 2.
Bowie, F. (2000). 'Ritual Theory, rites of passage and ritual violence', The Anthropology of Religion, Oxford: Basil Blackwell, 151-85. ISBN 0631 20848
Braeckmann, Collète and A. Guillaume, (1994). La Poudrière Rwandaise, in Le Soir (Brussels), 1 J'une.
Brandstetter, Anna-Maria, (1997). 'Ethnic or Socio-economic Conflict? Political Interpretations of the Rwandan Crisis', International Journal on Minority and Group Rights 4: 427 - 449, Institute for Ethnology and Africa Studies, Germany: Mainz University.
Branford, S. and Kucinski, B., (1989). The Debt Squads, London: Zed
Branson, Roy, 'Never Again', (1996). Spectrum, Vol. 25, No. 4, June
Briggs, S. M. & Chen, L.C., (Eds.), (1999). Humanitarian Crises, The Medical and Public Health Response, London: Harvard University Press.
Brixton, (1986). Anglicans and Racism, British Council of Churches Report.

Brown, I. C., (1963). Understanding Other Cultures, Prentice Hall, Inc., Englewood Cliffs, New Jersey.
Burdon, C.R., (1964). 'Theological Expository Times', February Issue
Byrd, Anita, (1996). 'Sabbath Slaughter: SDA's and Rwanda', Spectrum, Vol. 25, No. 4, June.
Cassidy, M., (ed.), (1997).A Witness Forever, The Dawning of Democracy in South Africa, Stories Behind The Story, notes.
Chopp, R., (1997). 'Latin American Liberation Theology', in D. Ford (Ed.). The Modern Theologians, Oxford: Blackwell.
Chrétien, J. P., (1991). Presse libre' et Propagande Raciste au Rwanda: Kangura et 'Les 10 Commandements du Hutu, Politique Africaine 42
Chrétien, J. P. (1993). ''Tournant Historique au Burundi et au Rwanda'', in Marches tropicaux et méditerranées, Paris, Octobre.
Chrétien, J.P., (1995). Appela'laconscience des Bantu, Paris.
Classe, L. P., (1935). ''Ils Trébuchaient dans les Ténèbres'', Grands Lacs, no. Spécial, 1 March.
Coleman, Alice, (1988). Design Désavantage and Design Improvement; The Criminologist, vol. 12
Conn, H. M., (1984). Eternal Word and Changing Words, London: ECUM.
Cormack, D., (1989). Peacing Together, London: MARC Europe.
Cumberland Lodge, (2004). A Residential Conference Essay, 'Minority Rights and Reconciliation in the Commonwealth', 11th – 13th February.
Dallaire, Roméo, A., (2004). Shake Hands with the Devil: The Failure of Humanity in Developing society. Toronto: Vintage Canada.

Dalton, G., (Ed.), (1967). Tribal & Peasant Economics, Readings in Economic Anthropology, Texas: Press Sourcebooks in Anthropology.
Danzig, R. and Lowry, M., (1975). 'Everyday Disputes and Mediation, Law and Society Review', Volume 9 Number 4, pages 675-694

David, S. and Anders, N., (Eds),(1999). 'Development as Theory and Practice', Harlow. Longmann.
Denzin, N. K., (1970). The Research Act in Sociology, Chicago: Aldine
Des Forges, Alison, (1999). 'Leave None to Tell the Story', Genocide in Developing society. New York: Human Rights Watch.

Desouter, Serge A. (1995). Tyangombe-rituelen als buffer tussen de machtigen en horigen in het oude Rwanda. Wereld en Zending 24(2):58- 64

Destexhe, Alain; Showcross, William,(1996).Translated by Marschner, Rwanda and Genocide in the Twentieth Century, New York: New York
de Waal, Alex, (1994).'The Genocidal State', in the Times Literary Supplement, London, 1 July. University Press.
Diamond, S., (1971). 'The Rule of Law versus the Order of Custom' 38 Social Research 42
Dickson, K. A., (1984). Theology in Africa, London: Lutterworth
Diener, E. and Crandall, R., (1978), Ethics in Social and Behavioural Research, Chicago: University of Chicago Press.
Djereke, Jean Claude, (1995), 'Peace and Reconciliation in Rwanda, What can the Church do'? Vidyajyoti Journal of Theological Reflection, Vol. 59, No 4, April.

Donoghune, Joan, (1994). 'Freedom of Information Act release' by the Department of State, 16th May

Dorsey, L., (1994). Historical Dictionary of Rwanda, London: The Scarecrow Press.

Doyle, Mark, (2004). 'Ex-Rwandan P.M. Reveals Genocide Planning', BBC News. 26 March

Duignan, P., (Ed.), (1971). Belgianism in Africa 1870-1960, Vol. 1: The History and Politics of Belgianism 1870-1914, London: SCM.

Duly, G., '(2000). Creating Violence – Free Society', The Case of Rwanda', Journal of Humanitarian Assistance, July 20.

Dussel, E., (1976). History and Theology of Liberation, New York: Orbis Books.

Erickson, J., (1996). The International Response to Conflict and Genocide: Lessons from Rwanda Experience, Odense: SCLEAR.

Evans-Pritchard, E. E., (1937). Witchcraft, Oracles and Magic Among the Azande, Oxford: Clarendon Press.

Evans-Pritchard, E. E., (1965).Theories of Primitive Religion. Oxford: Clarendon Press.

Farley, E., (1996). Deep Symbols: Their Post-modern Effacement, Minneapolis: Fortress Press.

Farmer, H. H., (1935). The World and God, London: Nisbet

Fieldhouse, D. K., (1961). 'Imperialism; an Historiographical Revision'; Revision; Economic History Review, X1V, 2

Forde, D., (1954). 'African Worlds', Oxford: Oxford University Press.

Forward, M., (ed.) (1995), Ultimate Visions, Oxford: Oneworld,

Franche, D., (1995). Généalogie du Génocide Rwandais: Hutu et Tutsi; Gaulois et Francs? Les Temps Modernes 582(50ᵉ année).
Frank, A. G., (1981). CRISIS: In the Third World, London: Heinemann.
Frankel, S. H., (1955). The Economic Impact on Underdeveloped Societies, Cambridge: Harvard University Press.
Frisby, D., (1984). George Simmel, Chichester: Ellis Harwood.
Frost, B., (1991). The Politics of Peace, London: Longman and Todd Ltd.
Gana, A. T., (1994). The African Political Crisis and the Church in Africa, London: SPCK
Gatwa, Tharcisse, (1995). 'Revivalism and Ethnicity', The Church in Rwanda, Transformation, Vol. 12, No.2, April/June.
George, S., (1988). A Fate Worse than Debt, London: Penguin
George, S., (1992). Debt Boomerang: How Third World Debt Harms Us All, London: Pluto
Gerloff, R., (1998). Truth, a new Society and Reconciliation: the Truth and Reconciliation Commission in South Africa a German Perspective, Leeds: University Press.
Gill, Robin, (1985). A Textbook of Christian Ethics, Edinburgh: T & T Clark.
Gillingham, Richard, (2005). 'Quodlibet' Journal: Vol. 7, Number 2, April June.
Gitari, D., (1994). 'The Kanamai Statement', in Anglican Liturgical Inculturation in African, ed. David Gitari, Grove Books Limited, Bramcote, Nottingham, pp.37-48
Gluckman, Max, (1945). 'Seven Year Research Plan of the Rhodes – Livingstone Institute: Human Problems in British Central Africa': The Rhodes – Livingstone Journal, No. 4, December.

Gluckman, Max, (1965). Politics Law and Ritual in Tribal Societies. Oxford: Blackwell.
Goldhor, L. H., (1990). The Dance of Anger. Wellingborough, Grapevine.
Goodhand, J. and D. Hulme, (1999). 'From Wars to Complex Political Emergencies: Understanding Conflict and Peace Building in the New World Disorder', Third World Quarterly 20 (1).
Goose, S. and Smyth, D., (1994). 'Arming Genocide in Rwanda' Foreign Affairs 73 (5)
Goulet, Denis, (1971). 'International Journal of Social Economics', 2411 Development Ethics, a new discipline, University of Notre Dome, Indiana, USA.
Goulet, Denis, (1971). The Cruel Choice: A New Concept in the Theory of Development, Centre for the study of development and social change, New York: Atheneum.
Gourevitch, Philip, (1998). We Wish to Inform You That Tomorrow We Will Be Killed With Our Families: Stories from Rwanda, New York: Farrar Straus and Giroux.
Government of Rwanda, (2000). 'Capacity Needs Assessment and Capacity Building for Rwanda's Economic Management Institutions', Kigali June.
Government of Rwanda, (2002). 'Poverty Reduction Paper, Ministry of Finance and Planning Kigali', June.
Gray, R., (1997). This is a paper originally submitted to the conference 'on Changing Society', held in August to mark the quincentenary of Uppsala University.
Green, J. B, Mark, D., Baker, (2000). Recovering the Scandal of the Cross: Atonement in New Testament and Contemporary Contexts, London: Intervarsity Press.
Green, R., (1990). A Step Too Far, Exploration into Reconciliation, London: Longman and Todd.
Greene, L., (1988). The Power to the Powerless, Basingstoke: Marshall, Morgan and Scott.
Graham, S. J., (1965). Theology of St. John. London: Hodder

Guichaova, A., (1997). ''Les Antécédents Politiques de la Crise Rwandaise de 1994'', Arusha.
Gutierrez, G., (1974).'Praxis of Liberation and Christian Faith', (San Antonio.
Gutierrez G., (1988). A Theology of Liberation History Politics and Salvation, London: SCM Press Ltd.
Harris, D., (2001). 'The world's nations knowingly did nothing about the slaughter of one million Tutsi and moderate Hutu' in Church Times, Newspaper, 31st August.
Harris, E. H., (1968), A Ministry Renewed. London: SCM Press Ltd
Harris, Richard, (Ed.), (1975). The Political Economy of Africa, Cambridge, Mass: Schenkman.
Harvey, Cox, (1965). The Secular City, London: SCM Press.
Hastings, A., (1998). 'The Tribal Contest behind Africa's Bloodbath' The Tablet, 5 September.
Hebga, M., '(1983). 'Penance and Reconciliation in African Culture'', African Ecclesial Review 25, pp. 347-355.
Hegba, M., (1962). Article, ''un Concile a I' Heure de I' Afrique'' in 'Personnalité Africaine et Catholicisme', Paris.
Hillman, E., (1975). Polygamy Reconsidered, African Plural Marriage and the Christian Churches, New York: Orbis Books.
Hinga, Teresa, (1994). 'Jesus Christ and the Liberation of Women in Africa', in King (Ed.) Feminist Theology from the Third World, Maryknoll: Orbis Books.
Hirst, R. J., (1959). The Problems of Perception, London: Allen & Unwin.
Hodgson, **P. C. and H. King,** (Ed), (1988). Readings in Christian Theology, Fortress Press Philadelphia.
Hort, A. F., (1896). Life and Letters of Fenton Anthony Hort, 1 & 2, London: Macmillan.
Hort, A. F., (1977). Just Men, London: Epworth Press.

Huband, Mark, (1994). 'Church of the Holy Slaughter', the Observer, 5 June
Hughes, A. J., (1963). East Africa: The Search for Unity, New York: Penguin Books.
Human Rights Watch, (1994).Report, UN Human Rights Commission of 11th November
Hurley, M., (1974). 'Reconciliation, in Religion and Society', Belfast: Institute of Irish Studies.
Ilongu, E., (1973). 'Indigenization of Imported Religious', Journal of Asian and African Studies, XIV, 1-2, 121-128.
Kaldor, Mary, (2003). Global Civil Society, An Answer to War, Oxford: Blackwell Publishers Ltd.
Kalilombe, P., (1991). Black Catholics Speak, Reflection on Experience, Black Catholics Speak, Reflection on Experience, Faith Theology, London: Catholic Association for Racial Justice.
Kalilombe, P. A., (1979). 'The Salvific Value of African Religions'. Afer, 21, pp.143–157.
Kamukama, D., (1993). 'Pride and Prejudice in ethnic relations, Rwanda', p.133-160, in: **P. Anyango** (Ed.) Arms and Daggers in the Heart of Africa: Studies on internal conflicts. Nairobi: Academy Science Publication.
Kant, E., (1934). The Critique of Pure Reason, trans. Meiklejohn, J. M. D. London: Dent.
Kimenyi, A., (1989). Kinyarwanda and Kirundi Names, The Edwin Millen Press.
Kirk, J. A., (1979). Liberation Theology, An Evangelical View from the Third World, England: Marshalls Theological Library
Kirk, J. A., (1980). Theology Encounters Revolution: Leicester
Knight, Frank, H. and Merriam, Thorton, (1947). The Economic Order and Religion, Kegan Paul Tench Trubner Co. Ltd.
Kofi, Annan, (2001). Fellowship, April, Vol. 6, No.2.

Kolini, Emmanuel, (1995). 'Towards Reconciliation in Rwanda', Transformation, Vol. 12, No2, April/June.
Kritzinger, J. J., (1996). The Rwandese Tragedy as Public Indictment of Christian Mission, London, SPCK.
Lakeland, P., (1997), Post Modernity: Christian Identity in a Fragmented Age, Minneapolis, Minn.: Fortress.
Lemarchad, Rene, (1970). Managing Transition Anarchies: Rwanda, Burundi and South Africa in Comparative Perspective, London: Marshall Morgan & Scott.
Lemarchand, Rene, (1994). 'Managing Transition Anarchies: Rwanda, Burundi and South Africa in Comparative Perspective', the Journal of Modern African Studies, 32, 4, Cambridge: University Press.
Lenski, G., Nolan, P. and Lenski, J., (1995). Human Societies, an Introduction to Macro Sociology, Seventh Edition, New York: McGrawHill, Inc.,
Lerner, H. G., (1990). The Dance of Anger, Wellingborough: Grapevine.
Lewin, Hugh, Compiled, (1987). A Community of Clowns, Testimonies of People in Urban Rural Mission, WCC Publications: Geneva
Linden, Ian, (1977). Church and Revolution in Rwanda, Manchester: Manchester University Press.
Linden, Ian, (1997). 'The Church and Genocide, Lessons from Rwandese Tragedy', in Baum, Gregory & Wells, Harold (Des). The Reconciliation of peoples, Challenges to the Churches, Maryknoll, NY: Obis Books; Geneva: WCC Publications, pp.41-43.
Loewen, Jacob, (1969). 'Mythological and Mission'. Practical Anthropology, Vol.16n. 4, July-August.
Longman, Timothy, (2006). Justice at the Grassroots? *Gacaca Trials in Rwanda* in Naomi Roht-Arriaza and Javier Mariezcurrena, (Ed). Transitional Justice in the Twenty-First Century, Beyond Truth versus Justice. New York: Cambridge University Press.

Luzbetak, L. J., (1963). The Church and Culture, an applied anthropology for the religious worker. Divine Word Publication Techny. Illinois USA
Maluleke, T. S., (1997). 'Truth, National Unity and Reconciliation in South Africa, Aspects of the Emerging Theological Agenda', Missionalia, 25:1 April, pp.59-86.
Mamdani, Mahmood, (2001). When Victims Become Killers. Belgianism, Nativism and the Genocide in Rwanda, Oxford: Currey.
Maquet, J.-J., (1954). Le Système des Relations Sociales dans le Rwanda Ancien. Tervuren: Musée, (Annales du Musée royale du Congo belge, Sciences de l'homme, ethnocide, 1).
Markowitz, M. D., (1973). Cross and Sword: the Political Role of Christianity Mission in the Belgian Congo, 1908-1960. Stanford.
Martey, E., (1993). African Theology, Inculturation and Liberation, New York: Orbis Books.
Maxwell, G. and Morris, A., (2001), 'Putting Restorative Justice into Practice for Adult Offenders', Howard Journal of Criminal Justice, Vol. 40
Mbanda, L., (1997). Committed to Conflict, The Destruction of the Church in Rwanda, London: SPCK.
Mbiti, J. S., (1991). Concepts of God in Africa. London: S.P.C.K.
Mbonigaba, Elisha, (1988). 'Indigenization of the Liturgy' in A Kingdom of Priests: Liturgical Formation of the People of God, ed. Thomas J. Talley, Grove Books, Bramcote, Nottingham, p.41

McCullum, Hugh, (1995). The Angels Have Left Us. The Rwanda Tragedy and the Churches, with a foreword by Desmond Tutu, Geneva: World Council of Churches.
McKinnley Jr., (1997). 'International Herald Tribune', 16 December.

Melvern, L., (2006). Conspiracy to Murder: The Rwandan Genocide, London: Verso Books.

Minasse, H., (1961). United Nations Consideration of domestic questions and of their International Effects, Columbia University.
Molt, P., (1994a). Der Pyrrhussieg der 'Patritischen Front' in Ruanda, Konrad-Adenauer-Stiftung Auslandsinformationen/KAS-AI 5:3-38
Mudimbe, V.Y., (1994). The Idea of Africa, Bloomington and Indianapolis: Indiana University Press, London: James Curey.
Muzorewa, G. H., (1990). 'African Liberation Theology', in Voices from the Third World, 31 January, pp.190-97
Nash, M., (1967). In Tribal & Peasant Economies, Readings in Economic Anthropology Texas, Press Sourcebooks in Anthropology, London: University of Texas Press.
Neckbrouck, V. (1971). Afrique Noire et la Crise Religieuse de I' Occident'. T.M.P. Tabora, Tanzania: Book Département.
Newbigin, L., (1989). The Gospel in a Pluralistic Society, London: SPCK.
Newbury, Catherine, (2002). Genocide, Collective Violence and Popular Memory, the Politics of Remembrance in the Twentieth Century, Ethnicity and the Politics of History in Rwanda, New York: Schoerly Resources Inc.
Newbury, Catherine and D. Newbury, (2000). 'Bringing the Peasants Back, in Agrarian Themes in the Construction and Corrosion of Statistic Historiography in Rwanda', AHR105, 3.

Newbury, D., (1998). 'Understanding Genocide', ASR 41

Newbury, M., C., (1988). The Cohesion of Oppression: Clientship and Ethnicity in Rwanda 1860 -1960. New York: Columbia University Press.
New Times, (2008). the Rwandan English daily newspaper 15 September
Nguema, I., (1994). ''the Challenges for Peace Making in Africa, Conflict Resolution, Addis–Ababa, Ethiopia'', London: International Alert Report, September
Nisbet, Robert, (1962). Community & Power, New York: Oxford University Press.
Nkundabagenzi, (1956). Article, ''Les chefs du Rwanda expriment leur loyalisme envers le Mwami''', Le Courrier d'Afrique (1 Octobre 1956), Rwanda Politique
Nothomb, D., (1965). Un Humanism Africain, Editions Lumen Vitae, Bruxelles.
O'Connell, J., (1995). 'The Essence of the Forgiveness', Month CCLV (September/October).
Okoth, P. G., (Ed.). (2000). Africa at the Beginning of 21st Century, Nairobi: University Press.
Oliver, R., & Fage, J. B., (1962). A Short History of Africa, London: Penguin African Library.
Onimode, B., (1987). The Political Economy of African Crisis. London: ZED.
Ordway, T., (1945). Democratic Administration, New York: Association Press.
Osborn, H. H., (1965). Revival – A Precious Heritage, Winchester: Apologia Publications.
Pabanel, J.P., (1995). Bilan de la deuxième République Rwandaise: du Modèle de développemental a la violence générale, Politique Africaine 57:112-123.
Parsons, T., (1951). The Social System, New York: Free Press.
Parsons, T., (1969). Politics and Social Structures, New York: The Free Press.
Perry, B., (2002). Hate Crime and Identity Politics, London: Thousand Oaks.

Pirouet, L., (1989). Christianity Worldwide, Church History 4: AD1800 Onwards, London: SPCK
Pocock, J.G.A., (1969). Burke and the Ancient Constitution: 'A Problem in the History of Ideas', Vol. 3, No. 2, in The Historical Journal, xiiv, 2, pp. 285–301.
Popper, K., (1945:1). The Open Society and its Enemies, London: Routledge and Keegan Paul.
Présence Africaine, (1957). Rencontres: Des Prêtres noirs s'interrogent, Paris: 3me éd. Paris.
Prunier, G., (1995). The Rwanda Crisis: History of a genocide, New York: Columbia University Press.
Randall, J., (1994). 'News Post on Rwanda', Washington Post, 29 June.
Rawson, David, (1995). 'Rwanda: analysis by the US ambassador'. *Evangelical Missions Quarterly* 31(3): 320-323
Reith, C., (1956). The Blind Eye of History, London: Oliver & Boyd.
Resistance, (1986). 'As a Form of Christian Witness', Geneva, WCC/CWME-URM.
Reyntjens, Filipe, (1985), Pouvoir et doit an Rwanda, Tervuren, Musée Royal de l'Afrique Centrale, Paris.
Reyntjens, Filipe, (1993). 'The Proof of the Pudding is in the Eating': in the Journal of Modern Africa Studies, Cambridge, 31, 4, December, pp. 563-83
Reyntjens, Filipe, (1994a). L'Afrique des Grands lacs en Crise: Rwanda, Burundi, 1988–1994, Paris: Karthala.
Reyntjens, Filipe, (1995). Rwanda: Trois Jours Qui ont Fait Basculer L'histoire. Bruxelles, Paris: Institut africain - CEDAF/Afrika institut-ASDOC; L'Harmattan.
Robinson, A. R. and Borror, G., (1982). Worship: Rediscovering the Missing Jewel, Portland: Mutnomah Press.
Robinson, J. A. T., (1965). The New Reformation, SCM Press.

Roosens, E., (1989). Creating Ethnicity: The process of Ethnogenesis, Newbury Park: Sage Publications.
Rosenthal, James, M. and Currie, Nicola, (1997) 'Being Anglican', compiled by James M. Rosenthal and Nicola Currie, Anglican Consultative Council X, Panama City.
Rubenstein, R. & Roth, J. K., (1987). Approaches to Auschwitz, the Legacy of the Holocaust, London: SCM Press Ltd.
Russell, B., (1968). The Autobiography of Bertrand Russell, 3 Voles, London: George
Russell, B., (2002). Research Methods in Anthropology: Qualitative and Quantitative Methods. Walmit Greek: Altamira Press.
Sanders, E. R., (1969). 'The Hamitic Hypothesis: its Origin and functions in time Perspective', Journal of African History 10, 4: 521 – 532.
Sapir, Edward, (1949). Selected Writings of Edward Sapir in Language, Culture and Personality, David G. Mandelbaum, Ed. Berkeley, USA: University of California Press.
Scheer, Gray, (1995). 'Rwanda, Where was the Church?' Evangelical Missions Quarterly, Vol. 31, No.3, July
Schreiter, R. J., (1992), Reconciliation, Mission & Ministry in Changing Social Order, New York: Orbis Books.
Sheppard, D., (1983). Bias to the Poor, London: Hodder and Stoughton.
Shorter, A., (1973). African Culture and the Christian Church, London: G., Chapman.
Shorter, A., (1975). Prayers in the Religious Traditions of Africa, Oxford University Press.
Shriver, D. W., (1996). 'An Ethnic for Enemies: Forgiveness in Politics', Woodstock Report, Oxford: Oxford University Press, March, No. 45

Smith, A. C. Stanley, (1946). Road to Revival. The Story of Ruanda Mission Forwarded by Canon M.A.C. Warren, London: CMS.
Smith, J. C. and Hogan Brian, (1992). Criminal Law, Seventh Edition, London: Butterworths.
Southall. A., (1961). Social Change in Modern Africa, London: Oxford University Press.
Taylor, J. V., (1963). The Primal Vision, London: S.C.M
Tedaro, M. P., (1977). Economics for a Developing World, an Introduction to Principles, Problems and Policies for Development, London & New York: Longman.
Temple, William, (1934). Nature, Man and God, London: Macmillan.
Temple, William, (1976). Christianity and the Social Order, (Edition), London: SPCK.
The Church Times News, (1997). London: Church House, 5 September, p.2
The Church Times News, (2001). London: Church House, 31 August, p.4
The New Yorker, (1998). Magazine, New York: 26 May, p.4
Tillich, P., (1954). The Interpretation of History, New York: Scribner.
Tillich, P., (1959). Theology of Culture, New York, OUP
Tonkin, E., (1992). Narrating Our Pasts: The Social Construction of Oral History, Cambridge: University Press.
Trainer, T., (1989). Developed to Death, London: Green Print.
Tschury, T., (1997). Ethnic Conflict and Religion Challenge to the Churches, Geneva: WCC Publications.
Turner, Harold, W., (1969). 'The Place of Independence Religious Movements in the Modernisation of Africa': Journal of Religion in Africa, 2, p.43-63.
Tutu, D., (1993). 'African Theology and black Theology: The Quest for Authenticity and the Struggle for Liberation',

in African Challenge, edited by Kenneth Best, Nairobi: Trans Africa Publishers.
Tutu, Desmond, (1997). 'Troubled but not Destroyed', Unpublished Presidential Address, All African Conference of Churches, Seventh General Assembly, Addis Ababa, October, 1997
UN Global Agenda, the human poverty indicator 2000.
United Nations consolidated Inter-Agency Appeal for persons Affected by the crisis in Rwanda January – December 1995 Vol. 1.
UNHCR (1984).Representative Report, Kampala, Uganda, June.
Uvin, P. and Warren, M. A. C., (1994). Aiding Violence: The Development Enterprise in Rwanda, London: Church Missionary Society.
Vold, G., Bernard, T. and Snipes, J., (2002). Theoretical Criminology, Oxford: Oxford University Press.
Volf, M., (1996). Exclusion and Embrace: A Theological Exploration of Identity, Otherness and Reconciliation, Nashville: Abingdon Press.
Vygotsky, L. S., (1978). Mind in Society: the Development of Higher Psychological Process, in M. Cole, V. John Steiner, S. Scribner, E. Souberman (Eds.). Cambridge, MA: Harvard University Press.
Waldmeir & Holmam, (1994). Financial Times, (London), 18 July, p.1
Walsh, M. and Davies, B., (Ed.). (1984). Proclaiming Justice and Peace, Document from John xxiii to John Paul ii, London: Collins Liturgical Publications.
Watson, C., Issued paper, (1991). 'Exile from Rwanda: Background to an Invasion'. Washington: The U.S. committee for refugees, February.
Welbourn, F. B., (1965). East African Christian, London: Oxford University Press.

Wiesel, Elie, (1986). Speech while receiving, Nobel Peace Prize, Evangelical Missions Quarterly, Vol. 33, No. 4, October.
Woodward and Pattison, (2000). The Blackwell Reader in Pastoral and Practical Theology, Oxford: Blackwell Publishers Ltd.
Woodward, C. Vann, (1971). American Counterpoint, Slavery and Racism in the North South Dialogue, Boston: Little, Brown.
World Bank, (1989). 'World Bank Debt Tables 1989/90 First Supplement', Washington DC: World Bank.
Yoder, J. H., (1974). 'Exodus and exile: the two faces of liberation', Missionalia, Pretoria: 2, 1.

Unpublished dissertation

Beattie, Tina, (1994). Dominant Discourse and Silence Rebellions: Christianity, Culture and Liberation in the lives of African Women, Dissertation Presented to the University of Bristol towards a BA Degree.

Consulted Electronic Sources between July 1997 and July 2009.

http://www.Ambarwanda.org.uk/genocide/arusha/htm/07

http://www.ambarwanda.org.uk/genocide/index.htm//07

http://www.answers.com/xenophanes&r=67/01

http://www.BBC/NEWSWORLD/Africa/UN/chiefs Rwanda genocide regret/01

http://www.BBC/NEWS/World/Africa/Rwandastilldivided 10yearson/04

http://www.bcedu/Schools/law/law/07

http://www.bcedu/Schools/law/law/07

http://www.beyondtv.org/nato/crap/craps.htm/8/00

Cfr. http://www.
Caas.concordia.ca/htm/caasasa.png.doc04/11/08

http:www.catholicculture.org/news/features/indexcfm?recr um=47719/01http:www.bmj.com/cgi/content/324/342?look upType=volpagefp=3".v"B4#4/08

http://www.cwi.org.uk/Jewishpeople/Atonement.htm./7/00

http://www.cypnet.co.uk/ncyprus/history/republic/makarios speech.html/06

http://www.developments.org.uk/data/issue 24/localjustice.htm/04

http://www.econ.econ.worldbank.org/external/defult/main? Page=64165298pipk/02

http://www.enteruganda.com/brochures/kagameaniversary page 8.htm/07

http://www.en.wikipedia.org/wiki/Ethnocentrism//07

http://www.farmington.ac.uk/documents/old_docs/Valentine.htm/01

http://www.farmington.ac.uk/documents/olddoc/Valentine.htm/01

http://www.gwu.nsarchiv/NSAEBB/NSEBB53/Index htm/, /10/97.

http://www.International Alert in Rwanda: Justice and reconciliation – the Gacaca process//06

http://www.irinnews.org/report.asp?ReportID=56408&Select Region=Great_Lakes/07.

http://www.jha.ac/greatlakes/b001.htm

http://www.Jhuccp.org.puhs/sp/19/English/19.pdf/07

http://www.Kigali memorial centre.org/doccentre/gacaca.php/03.

http://www.mdx.ac.uk/http://www/study/sshbib.htmhttp://www.international–alert/07 review/metaelements/journals/bciclr/262/09TXT.htm/07

http://www.news.bbc.co.uk/1/hi/world/africa/3557565.stm/06

http://wwww.news.bbc.co.uk/1/hi/world/africa/3573229.stm/06

http://www.oecd.org/dataoecd/47/36/3851593.pdf/04/11/08

http://www.org/ourwork/regional/greatlakes/gacacaprocess. phprentcryprusvillas.com/cyprus/pop ulation.htm/07

http://www.robertbellah.com/articles_2.htm/8/00

http://www.rudyfoto.com/cgi/contentt/full/324/7333/342".// "B4#B4/08"

http://www.rudyfoto.com/Rwanda Bibliography Page.html/07

http://www.rwandagateway.org/mot.php3?id_mot=20/9/07

http://www.sedos.org/english/liden2.htm/03

http://www.sopova Jasamina, "In the shade of the palaver tree" UNESCO Courier Journalist /06.

http://www.survivors;fund.org.uk/history/statsrwan.htm/01

http://www.survivorsfund.org.uk/pdf/briefingfromsurvivors.pdf/04

http://www.theol.uibk.ac.at/cover/bulletin/xtexte/bulletin157.html/08

http://www.unesco. Org/courier/1999/05/ur/singness/tx12.htm. 11/7/00.

http://www.unesco.org.courier/200001/uk/dires/txtl.htm

http://www.weblog.leidenuiv.nl/users/havemarch/archieves/2006/03/25/agacacacourtsession.htm 1/04

http://www.worldbank.org/development/02

http://www.wsu.edu/~dee/GREECE/ARIST.HTM/21/9/07

Appendix: 1

Section One: Introducing the Questionnaires to Anglican Church Leaders.

Prior to carrying out follow up interviews with selected individuals in each diocese an agreement was reached with bishops that access would be granted to interviewees.

Dear Colleague,

Following my ministerial study, I am undertaking research 'Reconciliation and the role of the Anglican Church'. Would you please help me by answering ANONYMOUSLY and posting this questionnaire as soon as possible in the enclosed prepaid envelope. Thank you very much, in anticipation, for taking part in this important piece of research, which I believe, will be of significance to the Anglican Church.

Faithfully yours,
Revd Henry Settimba.
(See enclosed questionnaire sample).

Appendix: II

A Questionnaire for Interviews:

Please comment on the question of differential in Rwanda, is it natural hatred or ideology?

What are the main social and religious problems in this area?

Do you think that it is wise for the Anglican Church to get involved solving social problems dealt with by the government?

If yes, on what level? As a pressure group?

How far has your Anglican Church, fellowship or organisation addressed problems like that of:

Why did the economy fail in Rwanda?

Why is it that after independence there was no development?

Was the conflict related to economy?

Has your Anglican Church in the past been involved in social action?

If yes, how is your Project or Organisation financed?

With all these problems, do you see any sign of hope for the country?

From your point of view, do you see people still regarding the traditional Christian values as essential?

If yes, in which way?

Would you live next to those killed or tortured your relatives?

Do you agree with those who say, 'Revenge is justice'?

Do you trust Anglican Church leaders?

Do you trust politicians?

Is the Bible teaching still relevant to life today?

Do you have anything else you would like to comment on?

Appendix: III

Comments for Interviews

Please, feel free to comment on any thoughts and feelings about reconciliation and the role of the Anglican Church in the questionnaires or to describe your experience how you survived genocide more fully. Please continue over leaf.

Name:
……………………………………………………………..

Address……………………………………………………………

………………………………………………………………

Telephone Number:
………………………………………………………...…

Thank you very much for filling in this questionnaire. Please return it in the free post envelope provided.

Appendix: IV– Rwandan Documentary

www.ingramcontent.com/pod-product-compliance
Lightning Source LLC
Chambersburg PA
CBHW050120170426
43197CB00011B/1655